AR4
CT
J2

WORKS ON
PAPER

WORKS ON PAPER

The Craft of Biography and Autobiography

Michael Holroyd

LITTLE, BROWN AND COMPANY

A *Little, Brown* Book

First published in Great Britain in 2002
by Little, Brown and Company

A CIP catalogue record for this book
is available from the British Library.

ISBN 0 316 85678 9

Typeset in Minion by M Rules
Printed and bound in Great Britain by Clays Ltd, St Ives plc

Little, Brown and Company (UK)
Brettenham House
Lancaster Place
London WC2E 7EN

Praise for *Basil Street Blues*

'An original, unforgettable book' – Victoria Glendinning

'A classic of English autobiography' – *TLS*

'The great biographer's small masterpiece' – *The Sunday Times*

'A perfect book: finely produced, full of humour and pathos' – *Mail on Sunday*

'A beautifully written, very affectionate story' – *The Times*

'Succeeds, perhaps uniquely, as both biography and gripping detective story' – *Northern Echo*

'A minor masterpiece' – Jeremy Lewis

'Fascinating' – Blake Morrison

'As arresting and honest as J.R. Ackerley's *My Father and Myself*' – Emma Tennant

'The funniest and saddest book he has written: a social comedy of manners touching on painful, universal truths' – Anne Chisholm

'A family that might have been created by Evelyn Waugh' – *Scotsman*

'A wonderful, searching, very personal book' – Julian Mitchell, *Spectator*

'A story as odd and unexpected, as poignant and moving, as any he has ever told' – *Independent*

'Freshly entertaining' – *The Irish Times*

CONTENTS

Autobiography, Diaries and Some Letters

From the Life

Introductory Note

I began my writing career reviewing fiction anonymously for *The Times Literary Supplement*, and non-fiction occasionally for various now-defunct periodicals such as *The Twentieth Century* and *Books and Bookmen*. Then, after the publication of my first two biographies, *Hugh Kingsmill* in 1964 and *Lytton Strachey* between 1967 and 1968, I went on reviewing more assiduously all over the place and in 1973 published a selection of the contributions I had made to British and American journals, called *Unreceived Opinions*. Gradually, over the next ten years or so, I switched from reviewing to lecturing – often abroad for the British Council, whose benevolent presence seemed to act as a universal alibi: 'I was with the British Council, my lord.'

This is a selection of these occasional writings from the last twenty-five years. I have included nothing that appeared in *Unreceived Opinions*. The emphasis is on biography and biographers, together with the related genres of autobiography and diaries. There are several short reviews, intended here, like pieces of a mosaic, to give detail to a general picture of contemporary non-fiction. If it sometimes appears sunny, even optimistic, this may be due to my having been sent better-than-average books by literary editors. I have also included a number of essays and articles that, arising from my own biographies, can be seen as satellites of those books. In the penultimate section, I have added a number of personal adventures at home and abroad, some polemical essays, others celebratory, a few perhaps satirical. Finally, as the beginning of the end, I take leave of readers in hospital.

Michael Holroyd, January 2002

ACKNOWLEDGEMENTS

These essays and reviews have appeared in the following journals and magazines: *Artes, The Author, Books and Company, Franco-British Studies,* the *Guardian, London Review of Books, New York Magazine, The New York Times Book Review,* the *Observer, The Sunday Times, Tatler, Threepenny Review, The Times, The Times Literary Supplement.* Others have been printed in books and catalogues published by: Anthony d'Offay, National Museums and Galleries of Wales, Chatto & Windus, The Eighteen Nineties Society, The Folio Society, New York Review Books, Holt, Rinehart & Winston, Methuen, Penguin Books, Phoenix Press, the Registrar of Public Lending Right, Secker & Warburg, Vintage.

'Introducing Mr Crisp' appeared as a preface to the American edition of *The Naked Civil Servant* (Holt, Rinehart & Winston, 1977); 'A Romance in E Flat Minor' was published in Susan Hill's anthology *People* (Chatto & Windus, 1983) and 'All Wrong on the Night' in Ronald Harwood's *A Night at the Theatre* (Methuen, 1982); *Peterley Harvest* was reissued with my introduction by Secker & Warburg in 1985 and reprinted as a Penguin Modern Classic in 1987; *The Whispering Gallery* was reissued with my introduction by

Phoenix Press in 2000. The preface to *A Passage to India* appeared in the Folio Edition (1983); to *The Polyglots* in the Secker & Warburg edition (1983); and to J.L. Carr's *A Month in the Country* in the New York Books edition (2000).

I am grateful to Philippa Harrison, Caroline North and Kate Truman for policing my text. They have allowed me to contradict myself, but never to repeat my contradictions.

'Let those who may complain that it was all on paper remember that only on paper has humanity yet achieved glory, beauty, truth, knowledge, virtue, and abiding love.'

Bernard Shaw
Preface to *Ellen Terry and Bernard Shaw: A Correspondence*

Biographies and Biographers

THE CASE AGAINST
BIOGRAPHY

To play devil's advocate, to act as spokesman for the opposition, surely this will be refreshing? I shall put myself in charge of the enemy for a day. I shall reassemble on the battlefield some of those assaults I have seen and experienced during my career as a biographer – as many as I can command. And I shall do it with relish. The experiment must be authentic.

Recently I read an attack by John Updike in the *New York Review of Books*. Compared with some others, the criticism was polite enough. Even the best biographies were too long, he suggested, and what was the point of them anyway? They didn't usually sell. And they weren't really needed. All that literary biographies could do was to send readers back to the subjects' own books. In short: they were reminders – and remainders.

That last sentence is mine, not John Updike's. For such was his good nature, and such had been his enjoyment of, for example, George Painter's Life of Proust, that his attack turned into an affectionate single cheer for biography – rather in the manner of E.M. Forster's two cheers for democracy.

But I believe I can do better than that: I believe I can quench that single cheer, because I can attack biography from the inside. The truth is that biographers flatter themselves – after all, who else will? They regard themselves as saints, apparently, because they are always thinking of other people. And yet they are not greatly loved. 'Every great man has his disciples,' Oscar Wilde famously said, 'and it is always Judas who writes the biography.' Thackeray told his daughters: 'When I drop there is to be no life written of me, mind this.' And J.M. Barrie set his curse on any would-be biographer by praying: 'May God blast anyone who writes a biography of me.' George Eliot, too, declared that 'biographers are generally a disease of English literature' – and this despite the fact that she lived happily with Goethe's biographer, G.H. Lewes. She was speaking collectively, not about her single exception. Nevertheless all biographers believe they are that single exception.

More recently Germaine Greer, describing biographies as 'predigested carrion', called on biographers to take up an honourable trade. She was echoing Rebecca West, who had offered a striking picture of twentieth-century biographers profitably picnicking round the tombstones of the newly dead, sucking the bones clean and flinging them over their shoulders – to be pounced upon, I might add, by those dogs, the reviewers of biographies.

All this invective, these insults, are perversely worn by biographers as if they were battle honours. Yet it is a battle they have not won. For this artillery of abuse has multiplied and magnified during the twentieth century and looks like being a good growth area for the verbal armaments industry of the twenty-first. But what provokes this barrage of hostility?

In rough-and-ready terms there are, I believe, three categories of biographer. First comes the biographer who writes about the very famous, among either the living or the warm dead. This class of biographer keeps company with film stars, murderers and the royal family. What people chiefly hate about them is that they make a lot of money. For surely they make it in a highly dubious way? They trade on other people's miseries, dine out on their tragedies, and make the trivial perpetually portentous.

Also they exploit our own weaknesses, our prurience, our snobbery. They are our worst selves. They encourage us to behave badly;

indeed they count on it. They are the virtual receivers, these biographers, of stolen money. They do not make money, they take money. And it is tainted money. We pay them for our addictions: they are our suppliers.

Nor are they proper writers, but simply jumped-up journalists – the illegitimate descendants of Boswell, that keeper of a great diary. They used to be called 'Grub Street biographers': creatures that inhabited the slum end of Fleet Street, and who, in the words of Joseph Addison (contributor to the *Spectator* magazine in the early eighteenth century), 'watch for the death of a great man, like so many undertakers, on purpose to make a penny of him'. It was impossible, he added, to reflect on this sort of writer 'without indignation as well as contempt'.

So not much has changed. These biographers still sway to the music of fashion, bringing down the mighty from their high places when it is safe and popular to do so; but allowing us to rise into a world of pretentiousness and vanity when it best serves their advantage. And always they take the easy way: purveying the simple story of romantic rumour and scandalous speculation pepped up, whenever the plot sags, by decorative invention. They thrive in an infantile climate where the cult of youth perpetually roams unmocked, unchecked. For they are writing fairy stories for adults who never grow up. These are the most newsworthy biographers of our own day and perhaps the easiest to attack. Fat sitting ducks.

But what of contemporary historical biographers, the political biographers of some last-but-one-prime minister? They are easily recognised hybrids with one foot in a university, the other in Downing Street or on television. This is the second category of biographer. The ambitious professor. Is he, is she, any better? Are they not trying to get the sales of the Grub Street merchants without their street vulgarity – the one jumped-up, the other dumbed-down?

Certainly these almost-instant political biographers are not greatly esteemed by their peers. They are looked down on by other historians who write for their academic selves, and they attract little interest from the self-employed professional biographers who write for almost no one. They are at the shallow end of history, steering close to what is called the Cleopatra's Nose school of history (the notion, masquerading as an ideology, that had Cleopatra's nose been a fraction longer, as long as say Pinocchio's became, or as long as Cyrano de Bergerac's was, then the course of history would have been dramatically changed). Can you get much more superficial than that? Even with a host of reference notes? It is the sort of history that film-makers love, the media history served up with music and a grave-voiced narrator.

There is something curiously obsequious too about these all-but-instant historians. They appear to be promising presidents and prime ministers a good end-of-term report, a favourable verdict, in return for a few invitations, a few decorations. But they are really history's butlers, continually absorbed by their duty of rating the events they announce in the order of conventional importance, always busy solemnly ushering in the facts, for ever replete with their ceremonial duties, and eternally guarding their self-esteem, like Admirable Crichtons, by reminding themselves of their intellectual superiority from their socially inferior position when they return to their isles of Academe. What a crew! A pox on the lot of them!

Finally there is the third category, the literary or artistic biographer. Surely they are better. Do they not go back to Dr Johnson? Are they not part of our literature? It is true that, like the poor, they seem to have always been with us. But the answer as to whether they are part of our contemporary literature is a resounding no. Ask any novelist, poet or playwright what she thinks about such biographers and you will not have to wait long for a heartfelt answer. Biographers are parasites. They are Fifth Column agents within the ranks of literature, intent on reducing all that is imaginative, all that is creative in literature, to pedestrian autobiography. They are the slaves of their absurd and meagre theories. They feed off literature: they attempt to replace it.

They also rob us of enchantment – they are continually trying to explain how the rabbit got into the hat before the novelist or poet produces her magic. And they pervert the poet's creative imagination by representing it as a mere conjuring trick. They overlook Marlowe's mighty line, and tell us with immense 'scholarship' – that is at vastly tedious length – what Byron had for breakfast. They are at best superfluous, these literary biographers with their relentless, their talentless, dust-jacket smiles. For the essential truth is simple: Flaubert was born, Flaubert wrote his novel, Flaubert died. It is his work, which is unique, that matters, not the ordinary experience he shared with so many others. That may be a branch of sociology which is itself a jigsaw with a thousand pieces of biography to it.

'A shilling life will give you all the facts,' wrote W.H. Auden in his poem 'Who's Who'. But it is the literary biographer, with his occasional obscene advance on royalties, who tips the poet sixpence on his death, after 'Telling what you did/When the sheets stared blankly back.' I could go on, but it is too painful.

Is it any wonder, then, that so many writers took the trouble to destroy their papers; or that many more, realising that they could not destroy the letters they had sent other people, drafted warnings to their executors against biographers? T.S. Eliot, Somerset Maugham, George Orwell, Jean Rhys, Philip Larkin all did this, or approximately this, in their wills – and much good it did them. For literary biographers have no conscience about such matters. They sniff money near the rotting corpse. They trample anywhere, digging, laying waste.

But what is it that those arsonists and will-makers so greatly fear? They fear for nothing less than their literary immortality. They fear that some inflated biography, some dead lump of a book with only the reflected light of some quotations in it, will eclipse their own work, blot it out, extinguish it. That is what, at their worst, literary biographies can do. And how often, how very often, they are at their worst! They fill up our bookshops, they crowd the shelves of our libraries leaving librarians with little money to buy genuine works of the imagination.

And there is worse than that. For these biographies are not even valued by literary critics who have been driven by all this awful gravedigging to insist that the author is finally dead, and that her text belongs now to the reader – guided of course by the critic himself. In short: biography, as even the French know, is a substitute for genuine criticism, a substitute for thought, and the very enemy of literature. This is surely why George Gissing described biography as 'a farce'.

Over the hundred years since Gissing made that comment, there has been a struggle between fiction and non-fiction writers as to who shall tell the story of our days, who shall open our eyes to their significance. Traditionally, of course, this has been the job of the historian. But something went wrong with history. Historians became like deaf people, Tolstoy observed, who went on answering questions no one had asked. Their heads were full of irrelevant pomp and the erotic pull of power. Centuries of such chroniclers, as Karl Popper remarked, had elevated the squabbles of political power into the history of the world. No wonder, then, that the novelist, the poet and the dramatist stepped forward to speak for us.

As the rift between history and literature widened so historians amended their agenda and developed their case against these story-tellers. And what they said was that life is not novel-shaped. It is not generally poetic. It is regrettably *in*artistic. Though literature may have all sorts of magical charms and rhymes and stories to enchant or chasten us, we hoodwinked ourselves if we believed we could learn, for example, more about the French Revolution from Dickens's *A Tale of Two Cities* than from reading Carlyle. Even if poets, novelists, playwrights could use their imaginations as divining rods in the search for underground wells of truth, the search was fundamentally flawed when they employed facts in the guise of fiction. For in supplying a story by invention we too easily admit what Defoe called 'a sort of lying that makes a great hole in the heart at which, by degrees, the *habit* of lying enters in'. In other words, we write what we want to happen rather than what actually happens. We write sophisticated autobiography, as all biographers of Shakespeare do.

Between history and the novel stands biography, their unwanted offspring, which has brought a great embarrassment to them both. In the historian's view biography is a kind of frogspawn – it takes ten thousand biographies to make one small history. To the novelist we are simply what Nabokov called 'psycho-plagiarists'. Yet biographers claim to have thrived on their outcast state. While so much history has been respectably academicised, and even the novel fenced off behind academic theory, the biographer is still free to roam wherever his instinct takes him. A vital literature needs cross-border trading. But what I have pointed to is cross-border hostilities seen from the enemy side. From such a perspective, biographers appear to have greatly exaggerated their power and significance. You have only to look at Public Lending Right figures to judge how little they are actually read. They comprise little more than guerrilla bands, with some small successes perhaps, but no chance of matching the major branches of writing. Who can claim more for them?

I believe I have found answers to these questions. But what I really want to find out is how my fellow biographers would defend themselves, what claims for biography they would make, and in what style they might launch their counter-attack.

1999

SMOKE WITH FIRE
On the Ethics of Biography

Towards the end of the 1970s, I was asked by the writer John Stewart Collis, then in his eightieth year and recently remarried, to visit him at his new home somewhere in the vastness of Surrey. It was a tortuous route and it was to lead me into a tangled situation. Collis had decided to make a new will and he wished to appoint me as his literary executor. We discussed his work, and he remarked that as soon as he was dead I had better race down and gather up his unpublished papers. We laughed and left it at that.

When Collis died on 2 March 1984, I was abroad. Later that month, I drove down to see his widow. It was a beautiful day, but I still found my way through that suburban Surrey jungle to the Collis plantation somewhat impenetrable – it was the last couple of miles that particularly mystified me. Peering through the window of my car for some sign, I saw rising into the clear sky a white current of smoke, about two miles off. I knew instinctively what it was and headed for it.

There was an incinerator in the garden, and Mrs Collis, as she reverently flung the last of Collis's correspondence with his first wife on to the flames, commented on how efficiently it still worked after all these years. I stood there, full of polite agreement, yet with one fistful of unconsumed letters hidden from her, the very embodiment of that baffled and besieged tragi-comic figure: the twentieth-century literary executor.

Standing there, as if at a second death, and driving back afterwards with that small packet of correspondence in the trunk of my car, I let my thoughts trail back over some earlier conflagrations of manuscripts. Most surprisingly, at first sight, Samuel Johnson had burned some papers relating to his life. Dickens made two big bonfires of his papers at Gad's Hill, including correspondence from Tennyson, Thackeray and Wilkie Collins, and wished to God that 'every letter I had ever written was on that pile'. 'I have not been doing much,' wrote the eighty-year-old Thomas Hardy, '– mainly destroying papers of the last thirty years & they raise ghosts.' Henry James welcomed these ghosts that flickered among the flames and smoke. It seemed to him that they were the guardians of a precious mystery out of which creativity issued. 'I made a gigantic bonfire and have been easier in mind since,' he wrote to Annie Fields in 1909. Half-a-dozen years later he was at it again, burning manuscripts, incoming letters and notebooks going back forty years in the garden of Lamb House. But of all the arsonists perhaps the most persistent was Sigmund Freud, who made the first of several bonfires of his papers at the age of twenty-nine. 'As for biographers,' he remarked, 'let them worry . . . I am already looking forward to seeing them go astray.'

The immediate feeling of many people on hearing that diaries, letters and other papers have been burned is that there has been something disgraceful in the life and it is the evidence of this disgrace that is being destroyed. Inevitably there will be some degree of truth in this assumption. All of us have griefs and fears, have stupidities, humiliations and regrets we would be rid of. We do not want them preserved in university archives, cooked up and served with a smile to the next generation. All this is acknowledged.

Of the various bonfires that passed through my mind on leaving Mrs Collis, the ones made by Dickens are perhaps most easily understood in this context. His popularity depended upon a peculiar lovableness, the regaining of a love he felt had been taken away from him when young. He wanted a good deal that was not so lovable to be destroyed, and much that was questionable to remain unquestioned. Critics often write of Dickens as if he, and not Carlyle, were the social historian of the nineteenth century, so we may legitimately ask whether it was ethical for a social historian to burn papers of social-historical value.

Yet we have a lasting gratitude to Dickens for giving us such exciting and romantic parts in the melodrama of his novels – those novels which take their inspiration more from the theatre than from adult life. For the fact is that most readers prefer theatre, prefer melodrama and romance, to a laborious reconstruction of actual life. Our need for myths and marvels is stronger even than our literal curiosity. Most of us love stories. Children are sometimes told not to tell 'stories' – by which adults mean lies. But when we grow up we go on telling stories, hoping that they are metaphors which will show our lives as having significant patterns, some moral foundation, and even a purpose. The question remains, however, as to whether, by wrapping up life in make-believe and supplying narrative by invention, we are not inevitably depicting ourselves in a false light.

There are, of course, reasons other than the ones I have attributed to Dickens for wanting, towards the end of our lives, to erase everything. When I was a child, my grandmother often cried out that she wished she were dead. I remember her tearing up and throwing away quite innocent things – early photographs, for instance – which she had kept for fifty or sixty years. It was done, I think, in the bitterness of dying after her long disappointment of living. 'Old age should burn and rave at close of day.' For some people, at least, it should; it does. Of course we do have some choice in how much of us survives. The surprise lies in how little we sometimes wish to survive. Perhaps the thought of people idly and ignorantly picking through the debris of our lives when we are dead; turning over the once-precious, now-useless objects; failing to recognise the strangely dressed figures in photographs, or the emotions invested in these figures – perhaps all this is the last straw. Better to burn these things and give others as little cause for trouble as possible. Something of this, I remember thinking, may have been in my grandmother's mind as she went about the business of destruction.

But few people destroy, or give instructions to destroy, possessions that had once been of value to them without some momentary regret, or some rising in them of contradictory feelings. When, a fortnight before his death, Samuel Johnson burned his mother's letters, he burst into tears, thrusting his hand into the ashes to see if any words were still legible. As a child he had loved his mother, but he had been unable to form a friendship with her after he grew up. 'You have been the best mother,' his last note to her began, 'and I believe the best woman in the world.' But when she died at the age of ninety, he had not seen her for twenty years. If she were to live again, 'surely I should behave better to her', he wrote. But that better-again world does not easily show up in a biographer's chronology. In Johnson's actual world, the woman he came to love most was Hester Thrale, and he burned her letters in quite another spirit – in anguish and in anger. He felt excluded from the happiness she had come to represent. 'I drive her quite from my mind,' he said after she had married Gabriel Piozzi and gone to live in Italy. 'If I meet with one of her letters I burn it instantly. I have burnt all I can find . . . I drive her . . . quite from my mind.' But of course he could not drive her from his mind, and over a hundred of her letters to him survive. With the infirmities of his body and mind, who can wonder that, though he loved biography above all other kinds of literature, Johnson should have burned the pages of his own life, where so much had been endured, so little enjoyed.

Though we may regret the burning of Johnson's papers, I imagine that we can all sympathise with his reasons for putting them to the flames. But what of Henry James? What of Thomas Hardy? Their reasons seem peculiarly literary and less obviously sympathetic.

Henry James's motive was to pre-empt a biography of himself. 'My sole wish is to frustrate as utterly as possible the postmortem exploiter,' he wrote to the nephew whom he appointed his literary executor. He wanted to protect his elaborate recreation of himself from what, in *The Aspern Papers*, he described as 'the most fatal of human passions, our not knowing where to stop'.

But did *he* know where to stop? He was obsessed, during the last decade of his life, with obliterating the poor accidents, stylistic flaws, of the past. He rearranged the meagre autobiographical material that survived in a series of prefaces, and enhanced it through the luxurious revision of his texts. It was, as he exultantly called it, a process of 'beautification': beautification from the flames and mystification from the smoke. He could never trust others to do what he had done for his own family in *Notes of a Son and Brother* – that is, to alter the transcriptions of their letters, omitting sentences and rewriting paragraphs whenever he judged them 'susceptible of a better turn'. Here we can truly see the fiction writer at work. As he worked, extravagantly adjusting the text, he imagined he saw the ghost of his dead brother at his elbow, urging him on with these improvements to their common youth. It was like his short story called 'The Real Right Thing', where the ghost of the recently dead writer strains forward from the darkness of the study in which his friend and biographer George Withermore is working and 'makes dim signs out of his horror', persuading Withermore to abandon the biography.

What was James's own peculiar horror? He feared, I think, a destabilising of his texts. In the permanence of those texts lay his aesthetic immortality and his power to regain access to life through new generations of readers. He believed he was protecting creativity itself. But does creativity need such exorbitant protection? Is it that frail? I sometimes feel I am being led by James along an infinitely circuitous route, up the garden path, and that when I reach the end, when I finally get there, I shall find nobody – just the rumour of a murder and no body.

But in Thomas Hardy's world, there does seem to be a dead body or two. Indeed Hardy rather preferred the dead to the living – he got on better with them. When dead himself, of course, his heart was removed from his corpse like the apotheosis of his separated work and life. Hardy came to terms with his past through the haunting and encoded memories of his poems. So, on his behalf, we may ask: are not biographers smothering the creative spirit by digging up these dead facts and depositing them on the living imagination of a poet? Certainly I can remember that when Robert Gittings's life of Hardy came out many readers were dismayed by the unpleasantness of Hardy's character, especially in relation to his first wife. Some said they would think less of Hardy as a novelist in future, or feel their enjoyment when reading him clouded. Yet surely this is a very sentimental way of reading literature, a very naïve view of the creative process? Nevertheless, perhaps this is what Hardy himself foresaw and attempted to forestall when he came up with the extraordinarily devious scheme of ghosting his own life for posthumous publication by composing his autobiography as if it were a biography written by his widow, Florence Hardy. It was good fun imagining himself as dead and it had the bonus of making an independent biography impossible for years. But eventually Hardy's smokescreen was no more effective against the persistently advancing horde of firefighting biographers than all the barbed wire of legal instructions in wills and appeals to executors which have become such familiar modern entanglements.

Many will have posted up warnings that trespassing biographers will be prosecuted. But still they come, showing how vain it is for the dead to seek control over the living world. How vain, how understandable, how misconceived. For those who fear biography have sometimes been the very people who made it fearful. 'One can discredit & dishonour such enterprises even if one can't prevent them,' wrote Henry James. So he cannot reasonably complain at discreditable and dishonourable biographies, since he has so ingeniously invested in them.

What do the long line of bonfires illuminate, what do they obscure? They have been raised, as in a Wagnerian opera, against two terrifying figures: the figure of Death himself, with his hourglass and his scythe, and of his still more awful companion, with his filing cards and word-processor, the 'biografiend', as James Joyce called us. This ghastly creature 'adds a new terror to death', because while claiming to have magic powers of resurrection he actually feeds off other people's hopes of immortality. It is this that Sigmund Freud must have feared when he made his bonfires. He wanted psychoanalysis to have the authority of a modern science, but his early correspondence reveals how much psychoanalytical theory depended upon emotional experience rather than expert observation. Freud believed his work was his immortality. He wanted to control it, and eventually he lays down his life for it.

What novelists and poets so dislike about literary biographers can best be seen from how biographers are portrayed in contemporary novels and poems. Novels these days are crowded with biographers. They creep through the pages of William Cooper, A.N. Wilson, Penelope Lively, Susan Hill, Alison Lurie, A.S. Byatt, Kingsley Amis, Saul Bellow, and are generally a naïve and calculating band of outcasts and impossibilists, careerists, murderers and grave-robbers – the unspeakable, to paraphrase Oscar Wilde, perpetually outfoxed. Let me give you some examples. In *Dubin's Lives*, Bernard Malamud presents the fifty-six-year-old William B. Dubin – a disciplined bulge to his belly, author of four bulging, disciplined biographies – who knows much about his subjects and little about himself. What sort of scholar is Dubin? He is presented as little more than a replica of his subjects, a caricature – loving nature while writing on Thoreau; becoming the rather unconvincing lover of a young girl when at work on D.H. Lawrence. This is a borrowed life, life without a centre. And since the past exudes legend, Bernard Malamud concludes, 'All biography is ultimately fiction.' But biography, he implies, is impoverished fiction – a simple game of draughts in comparison with the elaborate chess game played by the novelist.

A stronger condemnation appears in Muriel Spark's novel *Loitering With Intent*. Here, the vulgar frankness of non-fiction is seen as diminishing the mystery of life. It is the novelist in the story, with her vital language games, who has the talent for recreating life. Non-fiction is simply non-art, a deadening process.

Then there is William Golding's novel *The Paper Men*, in the opening chapter of which the tedious biographer Professor Rick L. Tucker is discovered at dawn with his eager prospector's face in a dustbin. 'What would he turn up, dull and indefatigable, treading through my past life with his huge feet, shoving his nose down to that old, cold trail?' the main character, a novelist, later wonders. 'A really modern biography without the subject's consent . . . How worthy was I of being dug around? Worth it to Rick, evidently . . . He would have access to more mechanisms than Boswell, not just paper, not just tapes, videos, discs, crystals with their hideous, merciless memories, but others, sniffers, squinters, reconstitutors, mechanisms doubtless that listened in a room and heard echoes of every word, saw shadows of every image that were trapped on the walls . . .'

Golding's Rick L. Tucker is a more technological version of Philip Larkin's Jake Balokowsky, the dire American academic, in his poem 'Posterity'. In Britain, I hasten to add, biographers are not generally academics. We are freelance writers. We write biography, amid much complaining, for the love of the thing – and there is no tenure in love. From James Boswell to Lytton Strachey, British biographers have traded in gossip and bad taste – which is simply to say we are fascinated by human nature.

But though we may avoid some of the satire in Larkin's poem, we cannot so neatly dodge the rancour of other poets. Auden, in his poem 'Who's Who', mocks the naïveté of biographers who are surprised by the ordinariness of their researched lives of extraordinary subjects. Robert Graves, in his poem 'To Bring the Dead to Life', suggests that biography is a branch of character-acting in which the subject is diminished by the biographer's limited acting skills. Graves looks forward eagerly to the death of the biographer when 'You in his spotted garments/Shall yourself lie wrapped.'

In her recent poem 'The Biographer', Carol Ann Duffy presents an envious, guilty, well-paid creature with absolutely no redeeming qualities. D.J. Enright in his poem 'Biography', reserves all his sympathy for the biographical victim who has been financially exploited.

> *Much easier than your works*
> *To sell your quirks*
> *So burn your letters, hers & his –*
> *Better no life at all than this.*

These poets and novelists do not acknowledge the literary biographer as a fellow writer. Has the hostility to biography increased

because things have got worse? To some extent. They have got better
and worse – and not for the first time. Johnson and Boswell are the
two father figures of modern biography: the one a poet and moral-
ist; the other an adventurer and the keeper of a wonderful journal.
The age which produced Johnson's *Life of Mr Richard Savage*, depicting the literary underground of Grub Street, also produced the Grub
Street biographers led by the notorious Jacob Tonson. According to
Professor Walter Raleigh, Tonson 'had learned the wisdom of the
grave-digger in *Hamlet*, and knew that there are many rotten corpses
nowadays, that will scarce hold laying in. So he seized on them
before they were cold, and commemorated them in batches.' The
fact is that a climate that nourishes biography as a humane and
artistic branch of literature also assists the scurrilous biographical
body-snatcher. We work in an unweeded garden.

But I believe we should not worry about posterity. It's not our
business. The future, like the past, is a foreign country, since from
the point of view of the future we are the past. Our posthumous
selves very likely have different priorities from our living selves. So I
do not support the deliberate destruction of papers. With the protection of posthumous copyright and the ability to place embargos
on papers in public collections, bonfires are an unnecessary vanity.
And they cause real loss. In Tom Stoppard's play *Arcadia*, Thomasina
Coverley grieves over the burning of the great library at Alexandria.
'All the last plays of the Athenians?' she laments to her tutor,
Septimus Hodge. 'Two hundred at least by Aeschylus, Sophocles,
Euripides – thousands of poems – Aristotle's own library . . .' But
Septimus Hodge tells her we must make do with what we have. 'We
shed as we pick up,' he replies, 'like travellers who must carry everything in their arms, and what we let fall will be picked up by those
behind.' At the end of the play, the twenty-two-year-old tutor and his
thirteen-year-old pupil dance in the Coverley family's large country
house, and he warns her: 'Be careful of that flame.' But the audience
realises there will be, and indeed there has been, a fire. For the play
proceeds in this same room along two parallel time sequences, one
in the early nineteenth century and the other in the late twentieth
century. And, as a result of the fire, Thomasina and Septimus do not

let fall enough for their successors to pick up. So all sorts of comic scholarly misunderstandings proliferate. Thomasina has learned that heat is lost through time, and we learn that time is wasted by fire. Which is why, in the ocean of ashes, islands of order are so small.

No serious biographer working this century will have failed to lay down some ethical foundations for his craft. I believe that the literary biographer can stretch out a hand to his subject and invite him, invite her, to write one more work, posthumously and in collaboration. Their chief business does not really lie in sensationalism but in attempting to chart illuminating connections between past and present, life and work – that is the biographer's aesthetic, that is his or her recreative process. Though it still has its uses as a reference work, biography is no longer a mere inventory of facts suspended between a chronology and some sources. We know the value of dreams and fantasies, the shadow of the life that isn't lived but lingers within people, and that the lies we tell are part of the truth we live.

This is our subtext, affecting the tone and giving dramatic tension to a biography. Miscellaneous scraps of paper – journals, notebooks, letters – are faint score sheets scripted by the dead from which the biographer tries to conjure sounds, rekindle life. 'The dead call to us out of the past,' Richard Holmes has written. 'They ask to be heard, remembered, understood.' Biographers are their messengers, charged with responsibilities that need imagination as well as accuracy – which was why Desmond MacCarthy described the ideal biographer as 'an artist upon oath'.

1998

WHAT JUSTIFIES BIOGRAPHY?

In the family of literature, biography is still very young and not yet very popular, despite what people say. The only true biographies, the novelist George Gissing complained, 'are to be found in novels'. Biographers, for their part, are sometimes tempted to believe that the only true history is to be found in their work. For in the family of literature, biography seems to be the product of a strange coupling between old-fashioned history and the traditional novel – though many suspect the real father to have been journalism.

Fifty years ago, in the 1920s and 1930s, the great debate was about whether biography was an art. Potentially, theoretically, it was: yet of all the multitude of Lives written, how few survived. 'Biography is one of the most restricted of all the arts,' wrote Virginia Woolf. 'The novelist is free. The biographer is tied.' And this is true. The novelist is free of all those bibliographies, indexes, reference notes and so on that bear as much relation to a living art as does a telephone directory (which nevertheless does have its uses in putting people in contact with one another). No wonder the biographer looks with awe at the fiction writer. He sees that the novelist is God, the sole creator of her world, able to utter the unspoken thoughts and feelings of her characters, explore memories, employ flashbacks – use all those devices usually denied the pedestrian biographer: devices to escape, for example, the prison of chronology. And when the modern novelist interrupts her narrative and disclaims omniscience, surely that is merely a device for giving her an extra dimension of authority.

And then what a lot of sexual activity she is allowed – on the page! If a modest biographer attempted to introduce half as much emotional exchange into his book as do the most distinguished grey-haired novelists, he would surely be thought outrageous. And yet it has been through the research made by biographers in recent times to find some of this freedom of theme, language and technique that, in the words of Shelley's and Coleridge's biographer, Richard Holmes, 'we have in fact witnessed something very rare: the rise – the rise to power – of a new literary genre'.

Only comparatively recently, I believe, has our craft shown signs of maturity as (in the description by Edmund Gosse) 'a faithful portrait of a soul in its adventures through life'. For a long time, biography was regarded as the poor relation of history – which, to put it tactfully, was unfair to both disciplines. The over-simple case that biographers have brought against traditional historians is that their discipline has been all kings and dates and battles. G.M. Trevelyan, the British social historian, died the death of an historian in that sense. The day before he died he had Macaulay read aloud to him. His last words were 'Peterloo'. 'What about Peterloo, master?' the nurse eagerly asked. '1819,' he breathed – and shortly after that he died. Dates and battles. And where history becomes the retrospective charting of economic and political weather, what is sometimes missing, biographers believe, is the individual on whom that weather rains and shines. For without him, without her, history is a remote thing. 'The general and rapid narratives of history,' wrote Dr Johnson in *The Rambler*, 'which involve a thousand fortunes in the business of a day . . . afford few lessons applicable to private life.' In other words, biography can humanise our history – that is one of its justifications. The social historian concentrates on what is common to all men and women in certain categories at particular times; the biographer is concerned with what differentiates one man, or woman, from another. One gives the overall, the other the eye-level view of what has happened.

Now the history based on statistical facts is never to be despised. But it is a great naïveté to believe that facts alone constitute the truth. 'I had long learnt that history was not an account of what actually happened,' wrote Queen Victoria, 'but of what people generally thought had happened.' This was particularly true of biography in the days when it existed under the shadow of history. It was Dr Johnson who first removed biography from this shadow and established it as an independent branch of literature. With his *Lives of the Poets* biography came of age.

What had been wrong before was that biography took as its motto that sentence from Ecclesiasticus: 'Let us now praise famous men.' Praise and men. The Lives of rulers or saints were meant to instil in us, the readers, the spirit of admiration and the habit of imitation. In other words, biography was used as a guide to good conduct, to model citizenship, an endorsement of the status quo, and an intellectual reinforcement of law and order.

Samuel Johnson changed all that. The biographer's first business, he advised, was not to dwell on 'those performances and incidents, which produce vulgar greatness', but to 'lead the thoughts into domestic privacies, and to display the minute details of daily life' – more, you might think, in the feminine than the masculine tradition. And indeed biography these days is used in the armoury of feminists like Claire Tomalin who have made an art of rediscovering the female experience lost in a male-dominated culture, as well as in the armoury of those who, like Hilary Spurling, cross the gender line, and cross geographical lines too. Johnson once boasted that he could write the Life of a Broomstick. 'I have often thought,' he wrote, 'that there rarely passes a life of which a judicious and faithful narrative would not be useful.' In other words, biography is not confined to the great and the good. It has some sociological justification. Though devoted to the notion of piety, Johnson was preoccupied with human nature. It was fitting that Boswell, leaving the piety aside, should have taken his precepts to heart and, in his *Life of Johnson*, brought them so wonderfully alive for us – in particular whenever he himself appears on the page. For in essence Boswell was the writer of a 'very pretty journal' – hence the original connection between biographers and journalists.

Boswell, it must be admitted, was an atrocious gossip. He had the virtue, in a biographer, of bad taste – which is to say he was not imposed upon by the polite fashions of his day. In fact he was a considerable menace, going round taking down actual conversations at dinner parties and in his club. No wonder he was eventually avoided by smart society. He was, as I say, a menace, but he was also a man of courage. He put aside popularity and, driven by his fascination with life, reported what he saw and heard. It is this fascination that gives us, almost two hundred years later, that feeling expressed by the King in *Hamlet* on hearing that his stepson had murdered Polonius: 'It had been so with us had we been there.'

After Johnson's *Lives of the Poets* appeared, Boswell tells us, 'a feeble, though shrill outcry' was raised against him. This was on account of his severity to Gray, Milton, Swift and some of his other subjects. But to suppress part of the truth deliberately, Johnson believed, however elevated the motives, is to produce a sentimentality – a substitution of a part for the whole. 'If we owe regard to the memory of the dead,' Johnson declared, 'there is yet more respect to be paid to knowledge, to virtue and to truth.' That was the principle, and practice strove to match it.

But then, in the nineteenth century, came earnestness. Biography was crucially infected by the blight of Victorianism. It was an intellectual, religious, sexual and social blight that turned people's energies from private into public life. Private life was hidden under a prim camouflage. In her fantasy-biography *Orlando*, Virginia Woolf parodied the traditional Victorian Life that clung to the respectable inessentials of everything.

> Directly we glance at eyes and foreheads we have to admit a thousand disagreeables which it is the aim of every good biographer to ignore. . . . Sights disturbed him, like that of his mother, a beautiful lady in green walking out to feed the peacocks . . . sights exalted him . . . the birds and the trees . . . the

evening sky, the homing rooks . . . all these sights, and the
garden sounds too, the hammer beating and the wood chop-
ping, began that riot and confusion of the passions and
emotions which every good biographer detests.

There was an exception to this Victorian formula, Froude's
Carlyle, but the general parade of biography was again one of uniform praise. Even Mrs Gaskell succumbed somewhat in her rather
sentimental Life of Charlotte Brontë. 'How delicate, decent is English
biography, bless its mealy mouth!' protested Carlyle.

A Damocles sword of *Respectability* hangs for ever over the
poor English Life-writer (as it does over poor English life in
general), and reduces him to the verge of paralysis . . . The
English biographer has long felt that if in writing his biography
he wrote down anything that could by possibility offend any
man, he had written wrong. The plain consequence was that,
properly speaking, no biography whatever could be produced.

But Carlyle had considerable difficulty when it came to applying
these principles to his own life. Practice and principle were out of
step. It was, he once remarked, as difficult to write a good Life as to
lead one. 'This was Carlyle's special gift,' wrote Froude (and this is
what all biographers would dream of having written about them):

to bring dead things and dead people actually back to life; to
make the past once more the present, and to show us men and
women playing their parts on the mortal stage as real flesh-
and-blood human creatures, with every feature which he
ascribes to them authenticated, not the most telling incident
invented, and yet as a result with figures as completely alive as
Shakespeare's own.

Shakespeare, in the Victorian age, was emasculated, and the art
of biography was embalmed with the fluids of piety. Some thirty-
five years before Lytton Strachey published his Life of Queen

Victoria, Bernard Shaw was calling for a new sort of Life writing –
the young Bernard Shaw, that is, who had no fear of biographers.
'Fifty years even of a bad queen's reign would make a longish
chronicle,' he admitted,

> and the history of a good Queen, such as ours, needs still more
> careful handling. The truth is that queens, like other people, can
> be too good for the sympathies of their finite fellow creatures. A
> few faults are indispensable to a really popular monarch . . . We
> know that she has been of all wives the best, of all mothers the
> fondest, of all widows the most faithful. We have often seen her,
> despite her lofty station, moved by famines, colliery explosions,
> shipwrecks, and railway accidents: thereby teaching us that a heart
> beats in her Royal breast as in the humblest of her subjects . . . We
> all remember how she . . . invented the steam locomotive, and . . .
> laid the Atlantic cable; how she . . . regenerated art by the Pre-
> Raphaelite movement . . . became Empress of India, and, in short,
> went through such a programme as no previous potentate ever
> dreamed of. What we need now is a book entitled 'Queen
> Victoria: By a Personal Acquaintance Who Dislikes Her'.

And yet such a book could never have found a publisher in the
1880s because of the thick atmosphere of superstitious loyalty that
engulfed the country. 'What is more *banal* than a pair of boots?'
demanded Shaw.

> What more uninteresting than an umbrella? But the Queen's
> boots! Are they *banal*? The Queen's umbrella! What would you
> not give for the reversion of it? When a tornado devastates an
> American province it is chronicled in a quarter of a column.
> Yet were a gust of wind to blow off our Sovereign's head-gear
> tomorrow, 'The Queen's Bonnet' would crowd Bulgaria out of
> the papers.

It was to clear away this dense climate of sentimentality that Lytton
Strachey launched his attack in *Eminent Victorians*. This book was

an attack on parents, an ironic sifting of those values of the previous generation which had laid a powder trail, Strachey believed, to the explosion of the First World War.

Strachey's preface to *Eminent Victorians* (which paid tribute to the writings of Fontenelle and Condorcet) has acted as a powerful manifesto for twentieth-century biographers. 'Human beings are too important to be treated as mere symptoms of the past,' he wrote. 'They have a value which is independent of any temporal process – which is eternal, and must be felt for its own sake.' Since then, the boundaries of biography have been enlarged, until its subject matter is pretty well now the whole range of human experience, insofar as it can be recovered. It is a matter not only of the legitimacy of subject matter, a new balance sheet containing the investment of income as well as sexual expenditure, but also of the variety of narrative modes. We do not imitate Strachey, but it was he who liberated the form for all of us. He was the *enfant terrible*. We are beginning to grow up.

Biographers have learned a good deal from novelists – even from the writers of detective stories and thrillers. Though the biographer may not invent dialogue, he may use short quotations from letters and diaries, poetry and prose, which have the immediacy of dialogue. So biography is beginning to have as many forms as fiction: it exists as detective work, as melodrama, as crime reconstruction, as pastiche, as physical and metaphysical travel, as interrelated non-fiction stories. By taking on these sympathetic forms, literary biography can supply parallel narratives to those of novels. 'Never trust the author,' warned D.H. Lawrence. 'Trust the text.' But by converting the author into a related text we do not break Lawrence's rule, but create a reading principle, with possibilities of illumination and enrichment, that should feature in any Poetics of Biography.

'While there's death, there's hope,' remarked one biographer. But the truthful biographer, is has been alleged, adds a fresh horror to death. What he has actually done, I would suggest, is to give our friends the dead an opportunity of contributing to the living world, of keeping them in employment during a very useful immortality.

It is understandable and right that people should seek to protect themselves and others whom they love during their lives. We all need our prevarications and evasions, our sentimentalities, silences, lies. We all have a need of privacy – it is out of our privacy that we write. 'There is no true creation without secrecy,' Camus said. But can there be a creative secrecy, a secret communication, between the living and the dead? During the posthumous turbulence over Sylvia Plath, Ted Hughes described the atrophy of moral imagination as being an inability to 'feel the difference between the living and the dead'. But I do make a moral distinction between the living and the dead. For if we have only these necessary evasions of the living, their prevarications, sentimentalities, silences, lies, as our knowledge of how people actually lived, as our guide to conduct, we will constantly mislead ourselves and produce unnecessary unhappiness by imposing impossible standards on ourselves and on others. Allowing the truth to be posthumously given, insofar as it can be recreated and understood, may be as useful to posterity in its way as donating kidneys and corneas. And yet it is so objectionable to think of ourselves as dead that some of us have a fastidious repugnance to the whole process.

And is it all worthwhile? The charge against the biographer is that the man is nothing, his work everything. But the man or woman *is* the biographer's work. 'Only the poems matter,' wrote Martin Amis of Philip Larkin. But he was responding not so much to Andrew Motion's biography of Larkin as to other people's reactions to and reviews of the book, with the result that he ended up, very untypically, with an antiquated cliché. Besides, 'to dismiss the poet and concern oneself only with the poetry' has, according to Hugh Kingsmill, 'a specious air of dignity and superiority to personal gossip. But in practice the separation of poetry from the poet obscures the most important truth about literature, that no man can ever put more virtue into his words than he practises in his life.' Of course we know that, as Olivier Todd, at the beginning of his recent biography, quotes Camus as saying, 'a man's works often describe his longings and temptations, and almost never his true story'. But we are not so literal-minded. We use more imaginative methods of testing the truth. We also test for promiscuous opinions-without-facts – which is a definition of prejudice. We test ideology, we put a judgement on fashion, we present boulders of facts that sometimes get in the way of the free passage of critical theory and practice. In short, we are a damn nuisance.

I have already presented an impressive list of witnesses against biography. It is, I think, worth examining this hostility, and the fear from which it springs. Robert Graves suggests that the art of biography is shaped and distorted by the biographer's need to identify with his subjects. He writes:

> *Subdue your pen to his handwriting*
> *Until it prove as natural*
> *To sign his name as yours.*
>
> *Limp as he limped,*
> *Swear by the oaths he swore;*
> *If he wore black, affect the same;*
> *If he had gouty fingers,*
> *Be yours gouty too.*

In another passage from this poem Graves utters a sombre warning to a biographer such as myself. The literary biographer, it seems to me, lives partly with the dead and his job is, in a sense, to defy the critic and resurrect the author. But then, the dead may be very happy where they are. For many writers, their work, which may live on, becomes more vital than their lives, which must come to an end. Besides, some writers fear that a knowledge of their lives actually hinders an understanding of their work, because the biographer reduces everything to personal motives.

Probably the most famously awful biographer created by a poet is 'Jake Balokowsky, my biographer', from Philip Larkin's poem 'Posterity'. British literary biographers have been able to dodge this attack by virtue of the fact that they are British and not American. American biographers are academics; in Britain, with the shining exceptions of Hermione Lee and Roy Foster, they are a maverick crew of self-employed amateurs. But they may not so easily dodge the rancour of other poets, such as D.J. Enright who, in his poem 'Biography', comes to the rescue of the biographical victim:

> *Rest in one piece, old fellow.*
> *May no one make his money*
> *Out of your odd poverty.*

What these poets fear is the eclipse in the reader's mind of all their illuminating work by all that drab experience. The moon is a dead body, having nothing but reflected light: but it can blot out the sun. So it is, they fear, with life and work. Whenever a writer, artist, musician, any man or woman of imagination, is made the subject of a biography, his or her light may be extinguished. Many novelists as well as poets have shared this superstition. But those who fear biography so much are the very people who have made it additionally fearful by putting in the way obstacles which impoverish the quality of the Life without preventing its publication. The caveat issued by T.S. Eliot against any biography did not prevent the sympathetically initialled T.S. Matthews and the scandalous Robert Sencourt from publishing Lives of the sort Eliot would most have disliked. It did prevent one of the great modern biographers, Richard Ellmann, who restricted his biography of Eliot to a masterly entry in the *Dictionary of National Biography*. And how ingenious we have to be to do justice to these reluctant subjects. Carole Angier triumphed over Jean Rhys's strictures against biography by taking the line that the dead Jean Rhys, who is still with us, may well think differently from the living Jean Rhys, who has passed away. It was then left to Peter Ackroyd to reveal how some benefit may be conjured from these legal disadvantages by showing us, in his *T.S. Eliot*, a biography without quotations, how the rest of us had been relying too much on long quotes. Ackroyd's *Dickens*, with its celebrated fictional conversations, is just one more example of how biographers are constantly testing the frontiers of the genre to see how they may legitimately extend their territory. Yet it may prove in the end that his quieter *T.S. Eliot* was the more influential work.

The last forty years have been full of such experiment and may be seen as a golden age of biography – a second golden age. The first was inaugurated by Johnson's *Life of Savage*, and in our age, it may well have reached its apex with Richard Holmes's Stevensonian *Dr Johnson and Mr Savage*. Biography will continue to change, will become more personal, more idiosyncratic, imaginative, experimental, more hybrid, and will move further from the comprehensive 'Life and Letters' structure.

Biographies of writers, W.H. Auden claimed, were always superfluous, usually in bad taste and they never threw light on the work. But he added: 'I do believe, however, that, more often than people realise, the works may throw light upon the life.' In another context, it is Auden who gives the real justification for biography when he writes: 'A work of art is not about this or that kind of life: it has life.' Biography, therefore, is not promotion or propaganda. It can give us, not just an inventory of facts, but the fertile fact, not trivia but the significance of the trivial in all our lives.

'A secret, at least tacit life,' Richard Ellmann wrote, 'underlies the one we are thought to live.' The biographer, like an archaeologist, attempts to bring this hidden life into view. Between the lines of the text lie the invisible lives of the writers. An examination of those blank streams across the page may disturb the text in a surprising way. To see only the written text and be blind to the unprinted part of the page is as restrictive to the reader as ignorance of the unconscious mind would be to a psychoanalyst. This is the Theory of *Re*construction. For the life of the writer is part of the text of his work, unsuspected sometimes by himself, as the unconscious processes themselves are unsuspected. Biography began as a reinforcement of the existing order. By re-examining the past and pointing it in a new direction, it may now be used to question our understanding of the present, and affect our vision of the future. That is what biographers such as Antonia Fraser, Victoria Glendinning and Philip Ziegler – the aristocrats of our profession – have been doing. By recreating the past we are calling on the same magic as our forebears did with stories of their ancestors round the fires under the night skies. The need to do this, to keep death in its place, lies deep in human nature, and the art of biography arises from that need. This is its justification.

1998

LE GRAND SHERLOCK

Earlier this summer, during two and a half days of sun, I was persuaded to join a Wordsworth and Coleridge pilgrimage in Somerset. One of the chief attractions was a rumour that Richard Holmes, currently working on a Life of Coleridge, would appear. For a day and a half there was much talk of Mr Holmes. How would he appear? Over what hill? Across what pond? From time to time messages would arrive which we carefully decoded. Then suddenly a man in a field called threateningly to us: were we looking for Mr Sherlock Holmes? We hesitantly agreed that we were. He pointed onwards and we increased our pace, stumbling like a group of Dr Watsons, in pursuit of this now legendary figure – whom we eventually caught up with innocently poised near a cream tea.

It was no surprise, then, to learn from his book* that in France this solitary and enigmatic traveller was also known as 'Le Grand Sherlock'. He has the magical sleuthing abilities of his namesake: but for every new biographical clue which is gained, something of himself seems vulnerable to loss, like an old skin shed, until the biographer himself grows insubstantial, almost invisible.

*Footsteps: Adventures of a Romantic Biographer (1985).

Mr Holmes picked up the biographical trail early. After ten years of English boarding schools, where he was brought up by Roman Catholic monks, he slipped the leash and set off in search of freedom and a new identity. It was 1964 and he was eighteen. 'Free thought, free travel, free love was what I wanted,' he writes. He was travelling in the footsteps of R.L. Stevenson – 'Monsieur Steamson', as the French called him – who, almost ninety years earlier, had journeyed down the Cevennes with his donkey. Mr Holmes's pursuit is a humorous and charming adventure in which his insights into Stevenson's character, particularly his relationship with Fanny Osbourne, whom he was later to marry, run parallel to a process of self-discovery.

Though he wanted to be a poet – and he has written poetry – Richard Holmes is inescapably a biographer: oblique, vicarious, elusive, passionately suspended between two lives as he gathers material for an autobiographical narrative through the biographical evidence of others – those he has chosen rather than been given through the facts of birth and upbringing. Already in his first chapter he is no longer Richard Holmes from Downside and Churchill College, Cambridge. He has taken on the temperament of 'Le Brun', a remarkable hat which is always being doffed to pretty girls and which leads him uncomplainingly into all sorts of odd encounters. What we are seeing here, and in his subsequent dreams, *promenades*, *souvenirs*, pursuits, is the making of a biographer and the development of a biographical philosophy.

The second chapter catches him up in Paris in 1968. It is the time of the student uprisings which, by suspending history, he identifies with the French Revolution as seen by the English Romantics. Seeking some mirror of the present in the past, he begins by looking at the revolution through the eyes of Wordsworth, but, needing the decisive experience of a first-hand witness, he soon becomes absorbed in the life of Mary Wollstonecraft. Once again he follows literally and imaginatively where the biographical materials lead, discovering 'a wholly different world-view of what a revolution required of its participants'. In particular he moves away from a boyish urge for bloody and dramatic action to the revolution of sensibility which Mary Wollstonecraft underwent. The tension of his narrative comes from the balance he constructs between romanticism and realism, between an historical and a biographical perspective where public events are matched against emotional development. It is the revolution of the heart that most engages him. There is great sympathy and even-handedness in the account he gives of Mary Wollstonecraft's love affair with the American Gilbert Imlay, and great tenderness in his description of their daughter Fanny. This is a specially fine and sensitive achievement because, as he is slowly finding out, the life of intimacy and day-to-day events is particularly difficult for a biographer to recapture. After all, much domestic life goes unrecorded in letters or even journals. The literary biographer may sometimes have a device for penetrating this silence: he uses the autobiographical subtext of his subject's books. Richard Holmes gives a perfect illustration of how this may legitimately and convincingly be done through Mary Wollstonecraft's little-known *Letters for Children*.

The third chapter, entitled 'Exiles', is a natural progression from what has come before. It takes the author to Italy four years later, and in particular to the Apennines and Tuscany, where he follows Mary Wollstonecraft's second daughter, Mary, now married to Shelley and living in a mysterious peripatetic *ménage à trois* with Claire Clairmont. This section may be read as a postscript to Mr Holmes's Life of Shelley, revealing some of his second thoughts on that triangular relationship which he now thinks he may have partially distorted to the disadvantage of Mary Shelley through having himself fallen in love with Claire Clairmont – another heady risk of writing biography.

This chapter gives a fascinating description of a biographer at work. Mr Holmes was possessed by Shelley – to the extent of dating one of his cheques 1772 instead of 1972. He speaks eloquently of his need to go to places as well as to papers, to balance outdoor with indoor research; of how he concentrated his mind by looking at pictures, statues, buildings and where possible the landscapes and seascapes Shelley himself looked at, finding in them clues to the sources of literary creation and giving himself the opportunity of reinterpreting Shelley's life from the inside.

There are dangers in craving such intimacy with the dead and sensing the past rather than the present as a living influence. Part of what lies behind this process is a lack of self-esteem which may cause the biographer to 'disappear' – and then reappear by mixing his identity with that of the biographee. This is one of the cardinal sins of biography, the aim of which is to resurrect the dead and not be absorbed into a dead world oneself. During his researches Richard Holmes kept a diary recording his own experiences on one side of the page and Shelley's on the other. Before long Shelley's narrative greatly exceeded his own. *Footsteps* is the product of this intertextuality and the imaginary conversations scored over those contrapuntal pages. Though he wears his learning with the lightness of a helium balloon, Mr Holmes is a considerable scholar whose command of facts and chronology saved him from the wrong sort of involvement with his subject. He achieved intimacy, but not *subjective* intimacy: the objective thread in the biographical pattern is preserved. He can look in at Shelley's life as well as look out from it – literally so from the houses where Shelley lived, using one of the biographer's technological aids to research: the camera.

Like many of our best modern biographers, Mr Holmes has sometimes dreamed of writing in one of the more venerable, not to say shorter, genres of literature. Once he had wished to be a poet; then he wanted to write novels. 'I would follow no one's footsteps but my own,' he declared. But by 1976, once more in Paris, his imagination is alerted, and that part of the past which lies dormant in us all is awakened in him by a remarkable photograph of Gérard de Nerval – and he is off again in someone else's footsteps.

This is the most dangerous journal of all. Nerval had been a solitary traveller accompanied only by his schizophrenic other self. He was also a labyrinthine dreamer whose physical and metaphysical rovings could not be fitted into the logical structures of biography that Mr Holmes had so painstakingly acquired since his Stevenson days. There were too many hallucinations and not enough facts. Besides, the romance that Nerval embodied, and Mr Holmes seeks, was extinguished by the modern industrialised society, with its railways and banks and materialistic values, then emerging in France.

'The spirit of Romanticism was being overcome by Realism,' he writes, 'like a candle being carried into a room fitted with electric light. One is tempted to say that, had Nerval been born earlier, he would have been saved by religion; had he been born later, he would have been saved by psychoanalysis.'

As it was, he could not be saved. When the solid ground started to slip away, 'my own position as biographer began to be shaken with doubts', Mr Holmes records. Nerval was a manic depressive whose mental alienation seemed to call for a psychoanalytical study beyond the limits of biography. In addition, there were dangers in being trapped in the mind and memory of someone who had spent periods in an asylum and eventually hanged himself. To these dangers Mr Holmes was alerted by an alarming accident, in which he fell through a skylight at the top of a building where, astrologer-like, he was searching for his phantom quarry in the skies. He was rescued by a *femme inspiratrice* – another vital element in the male biographer's career – who glimmers romantically through the pages of this book as a guiding spirit, first appearing at the end of his Stevenson journey, then summoning him to Paris during the students' revolt, taking him at the end of his Nerval misadventures to a late-night showing of *Les Enfants du Paradis*, and finally returning him, in the last sentence of the book, '*chez toi*'.

Mr Holmes's dream-biography of Gérard de Nerval, opening with his death and ending with his birth, was never published. Instead he channelled the material into a radio play and has now translated his experiences and some of his research into this moving and exhilarating dream-essay which charts the frontiers of biography. The cumulative effect of the travels, revolutions, exiles and dreams that form this book is to widen those frontiers.

Some fifty years ago Virginia Woolf likened the biographer to the miner's canary 'testing the atmosphere, detecting falsity, unreality, and the presence of obsolete conventions'. Compared with fiction and poetry, biography had only recently begun its career, but such experiments as Lytton Strachey's *Elizabeth and Essex* or A.J.A. Symons's *The Quest for Corvo* pointed the way to further discoveries. Richard Holmes's *Footsteps* is another such experiment, and an enterprising example of biography-in-action that may be read at several levels of literary and psychological detection. It is also a work of originality that offers a solution to the main problem of biography identified by Virginia Woolf. The biographer wants the best of both worlds – the artistic freedom to invent and the reliance on authenticated fact – to make a book 'that was not only a biography but also a work of art', she wrote. But 'fact and fiction refused to mix' because biography, needing facts provided by people other than the writer, imposed conditions in which they destroyed each other.

Richard Holmes has overcome this obstacle by imposing different conditions. He selects those facts from other people's lives that have been signposts on his own journeys. But he also maps his occasional misreadings of these signposts and his wanderings from the authenticated route when enticed by visions, speculations, fantasies and other inventions which are nevertheless the facts of his travels. These facts and fictions do not destroy one another, but achieve that 'amalgamation of dream and reality' Virginia Woolf looked forward to, 'that perpetual marriage of granite and rainbow'.

1985

THE WHISPERING GALLERY

The Whispering Gallery is a curiosity. It purports to be some frank, often indiscreet, occasionally sensational pages from the diary of a highly distinguished, retired diplomat who, at the time of the book's brief publication at the end of 1926, was apparently determined to conceal his identity behind an anonymous title page. 'My life has been almost wholly passed in the midst of big events and among the leading actors, the controlling agents, of those events,' he writes with a pleasing *double entendre* that went unrecognised by early readers of the book. For *The Whispering Gallery* was actually an audacious, satirical work of make-believe composed by Hesketh Pearson, an actor then in his late thirties, who had indeed passed most of his career among leading actors in the midst of big events on stage, and also with the 'controlling agents' of those events, the playwrights. Pearson was eventually to become better known as a biographer than an actor, being poised in the late 1920s between these two careers. But *The Whispering Gallery* could hardly have been a more ill-starred curtain-raiser to his writing life. Why, then, had he done it? The answer appears to form part of a pattern in his life. For this was not the first time he had risked his reputation and courted bankruptcy.

He had been born in 1887 at Hawford, near Worcester, one of the four children of a gentleman farmer, churchwarden and keen amateur sportsman, and his second wife, the daughter of a clergyman. In his autobiography, Pearson described his father, nicknamed 'Pompous Pearson', as being 'invariably friendly but rather remote and awe-inspiring', while his mother who, he suspected, never wanted children, he calls 'wonderfully forbearing' – adding quickly that he 'never lacked her love'. But though his childhood at home was not unhappy, he increasingly felt a need to distance himself from this 'rather matter-of-fact and undemonstrative' family. He never shared his father's solemn passion for sport, while 'religion made no impression on me whatever'. In his biographies he tended to belittle the influence of parents on children, preferring to believe that 'one inherits more from a few million ancestors than from two people immediately responsible for one's birth'.

The unhappiest years of Hesketh Pearson's life were undoubtedly those he spent at school. He went first to Orkney House, a 'place of torment' run by a sadistic headmaster devoted to the flogging of young boys. But however ferociously he was punished, 'I simply could not keep out of mischief'. He seemed fated to do everything of which adults disapproved. He was incurably adventurous and almost unteachable, blessed with a happy nature, yet vulnerable to violent spasms of temper, suddenly aroused and quickly forgotten, that would recur over most of his adult life. 'I cannot explain the cause of my tempers,' he wrote in his autobiography, *Hesketh Pearson by Himself*, though he thought they might have been 'exacerbated by my hatred of compulsion, and school was one compulsion. I was a born rebel, and I rebelled against a discipline that seemed to me futile.'

After five years at Orkney House School, he went to Bedford Grammar School where, though he learned little, he was happier. He had initially been placed in the civil and military section of the school from where it was hoped he would go on to Sandhurst, but when this plan collapsed, and after his father had failed to persuade him to read the classics with a view to becoming a clergyman, he was transferred to the mercantile class, where he languished amiably enough. Much of the literature he was taught, from Shakespeare to Scott, which he later came to love, he loathed at school because of the impersonal way it was presented. Instead, he found his own authors, beginning with the detective stories and historical romances of Conan Doyle and Stanley Weyman, then Victor Hugo's *Les Misérables*, and the novels of Dumas and Balzac, which he read in French, having picked up the language not at school but during some holidays in France.

Pearson emerged from his formal education as a man without qualifications. He drifted into a city shipping office from which, after two and a half years, at the age of twenty-one, he was liberated by a legacy of a thousand pounds from an aunt. This he spent travelling in South America, the United States and Canada, returning in 1908 to manage a car showroom in Brighton belonging to one of his brothers. By 1910, having helped this business into liquidation, he was penniless and obliged to live again with his parents.

But these had not been wasted years. He had enjoyed several happy educative affaires, and also provided himself with an artistic education by reading widely, listening to music, and becoming increasingly responsive to the English landscape. He was particularly influenced by the work of Oscar Wilde and Bernard Shaw, and the Shakespearian productions of Beerbohm Tree. Wilde, Shakespeare, Tree and Shaw, all of them to be subjects of his biographies, were the four authors of what he called his 'revelations', leading him to maturity.

In 1911, regardless of his father's opposition and despite his own lack of training, Pearson joined Beerbohm Tree's theatre company at His Majesty's, later acting in Harley Granville Barker's productions at St James's and also working with Sir George Alexander, whom he often understudied. In one of his first speaking parts, a minor character in Alfred Sutro's *The Builder of Bridges*, he met and fell in love with a tall, dark actress, Gladys Gardner, with whom, as 'a prudent preliminary' to marriage, he had an affaire. The play was touring the country, and late one night, sitting on the sands at Scarborough, he asked her to marry him. She accepted, which was just as well because as a result of Pearson's prudence she was already pregnant. They were married in the summer of 1912 and their son Henry was born 'prematurely' seven months later.

His stage career was halted by the war, but in 1915 he was invalided out of the infantry suffering from tuberculosis. The army, he felt, reimposed many of the senseless disciplines of school, and he proved to be a mutinous soldier. Nevertheless, he volunteered the following year for the Army Service Corps. For three years he served in Mesopotamia and Persia, rising from private soldier to captain, being cited for 'gallant and distinguished service in the field' and being awarded the Military Cross (something he omitted to enter in *Who's Who* and did not allude to in his autobiography). What he did describe was his near-death from a combination of dysentery, malaria, septic sores and a serious head wound. He attributed his miraculous recovery to reciting (even under the anaesthetic) the plays of Shakespeare, several of which he knew by heart.

After the war he returned to the stage. But though he was slowly gaining a fair reputation as an actor, it was erratic work and he found difficulty making enough regular income for his family. Fortunately he was also writing. During the war, as his biographer Ian Hunter writes, 'he had been sending dispatches and feature articles back to the *Star* and the *Manchester Guardian* . . . on topics as varied as Egyptian archaeology and an Oriental version of *Hamlet* performed in Baghdad'. Afterwards he went on to publish two books arising from his wartime experiences.

A Persian Critic is a series of colloquies, some of which had previously appeared in *The Times*, between a host and guest which, we are asked to believe, take place after the author, caught stealing mulberries from a garden in Hermanshah, is invited by the owner of the tree into his house to discourse on English and French literature.

The second book, *Iron Rations*, which Pearson dedicated to his batman, is a mixture of fiction and non-fiction, a dozen short stories followed by nine essays, which he wanted to preface with a variation of the customary disclaimer: 'When I say that the characters and episodes in this book are imaginary and have no relation whatever to real people and actual happenings, it will of course be understood that both characters and episodes are straight from life and are strictly true in every detail.' The publisher, however, objected, and readers of the book are simply warned that 'the characters are imaginary' and that the author 'has selected their names at random'.

Both books, which were politely and even favourably reviewed, had been preceded in 1912 by a far more controversial volume. *Modern Men and Mummers*, which largely derived from Pearson's pre-war years on the stage, may be regarded as a forerunner of *The Whispering Gallery*. On the front of the jacket, the publisher, Allen and Unwin, declared that though most of the subjects of his essays were used to the limelight, the author 'throws it where it is least expected, turns it on humorously, maliciously, with Puck-like ingenuity'. The tone varies between the fulsomely eulogistic (on Frank Harris and Bernard Shaw, who 'corrected' the essay on himself as he would later 'correct' Pearson's famous biography of him) to the impertinent and opinionated. There is an amusing interview with Lytton Strachey whose influence on Pearson, together with that of Frank Harris, is partly responsible for both *Modern Men and Mummers* and *The Whispering Gallery*. These writers, Pearson believed, had released non-fiction from the obsequious routine of hagiography and transformed biography itself into an art that could be as imaginative and free as the novel.

The best essays in *Modern Men and Mummers* are those about the actor-managers and playwright-producers whom Pearson had had an opportunity to observe closely. Though they are on the whole affectionate, they also contain passages of criticism the harshness of which was then unusual. Even his hero Beerbohm Tree is described as a 'big baby' whose whimsicality was 'unbearable' during the rehearsals of tragedies, and who had been responsible for many 'atrociously bad plays'. George Alexander is depicted as an artistically immature snob who traded in 'the drama of the genteel', catering to London Society in its theatre-going 'as the manager of the Savoy Hotel catered to the taste and foibles of that Society in its restaurant-going'. We are also shown the popular actor-manager Frank Benson, who had been responsible for spreading Shakespeare through the country and training many fine Shakespearian actors, as being impossible to understand on stage, not so much because he

bellowed incoherently but because he misquoted every other line –
and he always took the chief parts.

Pearson seems to have been indifferent to public opinion and, as
he later admitted, 'was lucky to keep out of the law courts'. There
was, as one reviewer wrote admiringly, a libel on every page. After
publication he did receive a threat of legal proceedings from the
financier and politician Horatio Bottomley which would almost
certainly have landed him in court if Bottomley himself hadn't
shortly afterwards landed in prison. By an odd stroke of irony, the
book led to an offer from the magazine *John Bull*, which Bottomley
had founded in 1906, for Pearson to write pen portraits of famous
people each week for the next three years.

The famous people, or 'modern men' in *Modern Men and
Mummers*, had attracted Pearson's most aggressive writing. Lloyd
George is shown as a fountain of rhetorical evasiveness; the famous
dean of St Paul's, Dean Inge, is reduced to 'a class-prejudiced clergyman'; and as for that jack-in-the-box of political careerism,
Winston Churchill, Pearson predicted that 'nothing short of death
will prevent Winston from becoming Prime Minister of the country
for which he has so nobly sacrificed all his principles'. In an age
of acerbic new journalism, Pearson was encouraged to come up
with more of these aggressive opinions, and congratulated by
W.A. Darlington in the *Daily Telegraph* on having 'mixed with his
ink a touch of vitriol'.

And there was another temptation. Some reviewers of *Modern
Men and Mummers*, while praising Pearson as a good reporter of
other men's words, added that he possessed no good words of his
own. Here was a challenge he had to answer. He did so by inventing
an amusing conversation between G.K. Chesterton and Bernard
Shaw. This was published in Middleton Murry's *The Adelphi* in
1923, and Pearson was gratified to see it taken up by several
American and British journals as if it were a verbatim account and
not a parody – it was even translated into Polish and printed in full
by a leading Warsaw newspaper. The joke could hardly have worked
better or gone further. Twenty-five years later it was to appear in
Louis Biancolli's *The Book of Great Conversations* and, more recently

still, treated as important source material in a scholarly volume by a hapless American academic. Pearson was encouraged in his belief that the biographer and historian are justified in using invention whenever it can 'improve on fact'. He had been sailing between fiction and non-fiction for several years. With *The Whispering Gallery* he set a bolder course.

One reason for writing this book was the need to make money. *Modern Men and Mummers* had put his stage career in jeopardy, and after his contract with *John Bull* came to an end, he looked desperately for a new source of income. John Lane at the Bodley Head was to offer him an advance on royalties of £250 – equivalent to about £7,000 at the end of the century.

But there were other motives too. *The Whispering Gallery* is a counter-attack on those figures of authority – his rather bullying father, sadistic schoolmasters, numbskull army officers – who had made his life intermittently wretched and exacerbated his fits of temper. These moments of temper are reflected in what his friend Hugh Kingsmill was to call his 'sunstroke style'. Pearson himself seems to have recognised something of this. Though careful not to mention *The Whispering Gallery* by name in his reminiscences *Thinking it Over* (it never appeared among his publications listed in *Who's Who*), he suggests that 'a good deal of irritation I experienced in the war' seeped into the book.

But there was a good deal of fun too. It was irresistible to be able to call Asquith, the ex-prime minister, 'an old woman in trousers' and to attribute the phrase to Lord Northcliffe, or to write of Margot Asquith that 'she must be in the swim, even at the risk of being out of her depths'. He had the freedom to invent conversations that read as if they were scenes from plays, to try out all sorts of juvenile epigrams and paradoxes – and if they didn't work, then the failure was apparently other people's. It was almost worth failing, and giving them the bluntest language. He also had the freedom to use rumour and speculation as if it were fact. We learn that Lord Randolph Churchill had tertiary syphilis, and that the Prince of Wales (later Edward VIII) was embittered by falling in love with someone he couldn't marry. 'I wonder what they [the newspapers] would say if I were to take their advice and marry according to my own inclination?' the heir to the throne is made to say – a percipient speculation almost six years before his meeting with Wallis Simpson. Other pages have the merit of taking on the popular press – for example Pearson's extraordinarily vitriolic pen portrait of the assassinated Tsar Nicholas II ('if any man deserved his fate, he certainly did') contrasted with the reasonable description of Lenin ('an impersonal kindness, a concrete coldness but an abstract warmth') which was written when the *Daily Mail* and other newspapers were campaigning virulently against Russian communism. His opinion that Germany was responsible for the Great War, stated at a time when liberal thinkers were arguing that she was the victim of the Versailles Treaty, could gain no credence until it was argued in the work of revisionist German historians forty years later. Pearson was like a boy with a hammer, hitting all over the place, sometimes with accuracy, sometimes with unnecessary abandon. He did not mean to hurt people's feelings, he later explained, so much as to relieve his own, and he came to see the book as part of his education at the public expense.

The publication of *The Whispering Gallery* was an extraordinary event. John Lane and his fellow directors at the Bodley Head quickly realised the promotional advantage of bringing out the book anonymously, but stipulated that Pearson, who had presented himself as an agent for the anonymous author, reveal his identity to one of the company directors. The person chosen was Allen Lane, later to become celebrated as the founder of Penguin Books. The name Pearson gave him in strict confidence was that of a senior diplomat called Rennell Rodd.

Sir James Rennell Rodd PC, GCB, GCMG, GCVO, KCMG, CB, soon to be created Lord Rennell of Rodd, was the sort of English establishment figure Pearson particularly disliked. He was a classical scholar, occasional poet, and a professional diplomat who had served in Berlin, Athens and Cairo, been Britain's envoy extraordinary and minister plenipotentiary to Sweden, and ambassador to the court of Italy. At the age of sixty-eight he was preparing to enter Parliament as the Conservative member for St Marylebone. At first sight his career, studded with foreign decorations, may have appeared sufficiently various and far-flung for him to have been to all the places and known all the monarchs, emperors, presidents, crown princes and prime ministers who, in the pages of *The Whispering Gallery*, press their confidences upon the anonymous author. Certainly Allen Lane seems to have believed that Rodd was the secret diarist. And yet even Inspector Clouseau could have spotted that this was impossible. The author reveals that, like Lord Kitchener, he had not been to Oxford; Rodd had gone to Balliol College, Oxford. The diarist lists his recreations as: 'heraldry, wild birds and squash rackets'; Rodd's recreation was fencing. Rodd had never been posted to Washington where Woodrow Wilson unburdens himself to our diarist, or to St Petersburg and Moscow, where he observes the frailties of Tsar Nicholas II. The whole reckless, radical and indeed republican tone of *The Whispering Gallery* is quite different from the decorous three volumes of *Social and Diplomatic Memories* which Rodd himself had published between 1922 and 1925. But the Bodley Head directors believed the book would be a bestseller. In his book *God's Apology*, an account of the friendship between Pearson, Kingsmill and Malcolm Muggeridge, Richard Ingrams tells us that review copies were sent out in November 1926 with accompanying slips stating that *The Whispering Gallery* would be in the publisher's view 'one of the most talked-of books of the season'. Lane added: 'We can vouch for the authenticity of the volume as we know the diarist personally.'

The opening chapter of the book is what the *New Statesman* was to call a brilliant and truthful description of the late Lord Northcliffe, founder of the *Daily Mail*, who is shown attempting to bribe our anonymous diarist for secret information. This led immediately to a dramatic attack on the book by the *Daily Mail*. Under a series of outraged headlines – 'A SCANDALOUS FAKE EXPOSED – MONSTROUS ATTACKS ON PUBLIC MEN – REPUDIATIONS BY FIVE CABINET MINISTERS', the paper denounced the book as a reckless invention which imputed 'conscienceless egotism and disgraceful levity' to many honourable British statesmen. It then launched into an editorial exposé. Bosphorus was spelled Bosphorous; General Townshend was robbed of his middle 'h', and the author repeatedly misused the auxiliaries 'will' and 'would', when reporting the words of Joseph Chamberlain. The *Daily Mail* commented: 'Those who know Mr Chamberlain and have documents written by him in their possession know that he spoke the King's English.' Elsewhere Lord Robert Cecil was quoted as saying: 'At no time in my life has Lord Balfour ever called me "Robert", nor have I ever smoked a cigar,' while Asquith complained that he had never called Lloyd George 'David' or been addressed by him as 'Asquith'. The political conversations were condemned by Winston Churchill as 'puerile in their ignorance'.

The publishers were delighted by this fuss, which quickly spread to other newspapers. In an *Observer* leader headed 'Ghouls and Garbage', its editor, J.L. Garvin, described the author as 'an imposter and a cad' and the book as 'an unscrupulous farrago'. Three editions of *The Whispering Gallery* quickly sold out and John Lane retaliated: 'The book seems to us to ring true . . . There is no question of it being withdrawn.'

All this suddenly changed when the *Daily Mail* switched its attack, accusing the 'Disreputable Publisher', John Lane The Bodley Head, of being party to a disgusting fraud, and refusing to take advertisements from them for any of their books. What then happened has been described by Richard Ingrams.

> The directors of John Lane were by now rattled. They decided that if anyone was going to carry the can it would have to be Hesketh Pearson . . . [They] went down to the *Daily Mail* and denounced Hesketh Pearson as the villain of the piece . . . and acknowledged that they had been the victims of 'a most ingenious hoax' . . .
>
> The next day all Hell was let loose on the wretched Pearson. Under the heading 'A case for the Public Prosecutor', the *Daily Mail* thundered: 'Messrs John Lane have been victims of one of the most impudent literary forgeries on record . . . The next step in this sordid affair lies with the public prosecutor.'

A former lord chancellor, Lord Birkenhead, joined in the fray, praising the *Daily Mail* for having performed 'a real and lasting service to the community', and Sir Rennell Rodd himself, whom Allen Lane, breaking his vow of strict confidence, had gone to see, called for 'some action to be taken for the protection of the public'.

The action taken was by John Lane The Bodley Head which, anxious to avoid prosecution itself, withdrew the book from publication and swore an affidavit charging Pearson with attempting to obtain money by false pretences. Pearson himself, who in a paralysis of panic had continued to maintain that Rodd was the author, believing that by doing so he was protecting Allen Lane, had actually repaid the £250 to the publishers before the criminal charge was laid and could therefore logically be accused only of an attempted fraud. His biographer, Ian Hunter, records that on 25 November he returned to London from an acting engagement in Cardiff pursued all the way by photographers and reporters, who continued over the weeks to besiege him.

A warrant had been issued for his arrest and he surrendered himself into custody at Marlborough Street Police Court. His brother-in-law, Colonel Dane Hamlett, arranged bail of £1,000 and took charge of the defence. The case was set down for hearing at London sessions. Sir Patrick Hastings, a man devoted to the theatre and the ablest barrister of his day, was briefed for the defence.

Friends and colleagues from the stage and literary communities, from Noël Coward to Frederick Lonsdale, rallied to Pearson's side, and many unknown people sent sympathetic messages. But everyone advised him to plead guilty. Bernard Shaw wrote that his choice was 'between the heaviest sentence the court can give him and a lenient one. If he puts up a defence he will get the heavy sentence . . . but if he pleads guilty and throws himself on the mercy of the court, apologising to Sir R.R. and the Lane Firm . . . he may get off lightly.' Pearson's family suggested he should plead for mitigation on the grounds of insanity brought on by his head wound in Mesopotamia, and only Frank Harris, the pornographic author of *My Life and Loves*, writing from the south of France, advised him to claim that memoirs are a well-known form of fiction: 'Say that a widely-known literary man told you this. It will make the court laugh.'

On the evening before the trial, at the London Sessions on 26 January 1927, Patrick Hastings called Pearson to his Temple chambers and advised him to plead guilty. If he did so he was likely to be bound over, whereas if he was found guilty by the jury he would get up to six months' imprisonment. But Pearson was determined not to capitulate to what he considered an unfounded accusation. He had been guilty of folly, but was not a criminal. Had he really wanted to fool the publishers, he would have chosen a dead diplomat as the secret author. He refused to apologise to people who were attempting to get to shore by pushing him off the raft. Patrick Hastings promised to do all he could to obtain a verdict in his favour, and the following morning went on the attack in court, asking Allen Lane to compare *The Whispering Gallery*, which contained nothing lubricious, with other books on their list. Allen Lane refused to read out passages from Ovid's *Art of Love* and Apuleius's *Golden Ass*, though at the same time denying they were obscene books. The erotic illustrations to these and other books (the Bodley Head had also published a modern anonymous novel purporting to be 'letters from a lady to the captain of a ship') were passed round the gentlemen, but not the two ladies, of the jury, and regarded by the judge through the fingers of a hand with which, in horror, he covered his face.

When Pearson was called to the witness box, the prosecuting counsel, Sir Henry Curtis-Bennett, asked him why he had chosen Rodd's name. 'I think it was because I couldn't think of anyone less likely to have written the book,' he replied.

'So you started the lie taking the most unlikely person in your view?' he was asked.

'Yes, to show that it was a lie.'

'Do you realise what you are saying?'

Pearson repeated that he had admitted lying and would save the prosecutor's breath by confessing to double the number of lies with which he was being taxed – at which point, Pearson having confessed that he had been 'mad', the prosecuting counsel sat down.

The jury was out for less than half an hour before returning a verdict of not guilty. At the celebration in a pub nearby, several members of the jury told Pearson that his engaging candour had won them over. He himself later attributed the avalanche of publicity that had engulfed the book and himself to one of those outbreaks of mania due

> not to their ostensible cause, but to the annoyance with life felt by the majority of people, whose accumulated disappointments generate resentment, the expression of which is held in check by conventions and circumstances until released by the creation of a public scapegoat, on whom they can vent their baffled fury and join in the hue and cry without forfeiting their social respectability. I had read of these epidemics in the cases of Byron, Oscar Wilde, Parnell and Dreyfus . . . I naturally warm towards scapegoats. But it is not pleasant to be one, and I did not think it funny at the time.

The epidemic ended as quickly as it began. The publishers, realising they had not behaved well, handed over his royalties from the book, which, together with his American royalties, enabled him to reimburse those who had paid for his defence. But he had not escaped without damage. No British publisher would look at his work for more than three years, and the next book 'by the author of The Whispering Gallery', a series of biographical discourses called Ventilations, which argues the case for introducing fiction into biography to reach an 'essential truth', was only published in the United States. Until 1931, Pearson earned most of his income from the stage, one of his most successful roles being the villain in a melodrama called The Acquittal.

Pearson was to rebuild his career in the 1930s, beginning with a Life of his forebear, the physician Erasmus Darwin, which was proclaimed in a leading article in The Times Literary Supplement as 'one of the models of sensible ancestor-worship'. By this time he had changed his mind on biographical methodology. 'It is only after one has experienced the labour and anxiety of searching for the truth that one knows how to value it.'

The Whispering Gallery is a curiosity, not simply on account of its short dramatic history, but also because it may now be seen as a primitive experiment to extend the frontiers of biography. This is not a one-book cul-de-sac, but part of a long, intermittent and uncertain road continually being explored by biographers. It has led to several celebrated experiments, from the conversations staged by Peter Ackroyd in his *Dickens* to the passages of nineteenth-century pastiche inserted by Andrew Motion into *Wainwright the Poisoner*, for which Hesketh Pearson's book stands as a distant, weatherbeaten signpost.

2000

THE CASE OF THE
BLOOD RELATIVE

In *God's Apology: A Chronicle of Three Friends* (1977), Richard Ingrams describes Hugh Kingsmill as a great teacher who found it easier to bring out the best in others than in himself. For both Malcolm Muggeridge and Hesketh Pearson he was a catalyst to happiness and achievement, while in terms of royalties and literary reputation appearing to achieve little on his own behalf. 'The truth is there is some voodoo on the whole of your relations with the publishing trade,' Rupert Hart-Davis told him. 'No matter how good your books are, some publisher always seems to lose money on them.' He had a naturally sunny temperament, was a stimulating, shrewd and sometimes hilarious conversationalist, though his personality was too ebullient for some people. His friends Malcolm Muggeridge and Hesketh Pearson wrestled against his influence at first: then embraced it happily.

Both of them fell into the role of Boswell to his Dr Johnson. Kingsmill used the example of Johnson as a corrective first to the adulation felt by Pearson for Frank Harris, Bernard Shaw and Lytton Strachey; and then to the unhappy effect produced by D.H. Lawrence's phallic mysticism on Malcolm Muggeridge. Muggeridge went some way to accepting Kingsmill's detached perspective on

the political world. Humour began to replace the despair of his earlier writings, and some of his best pages, radiant and spontaneous,
appear in his letters to Pearson in their book *About Kingsmill*.

Optimistic and opinionated, Pearson was seething with contradictory impulses and enthusiasms when Kingsmill first met him in
1921. The effect of Kingsmill's 'teaching' was to resolve many of
these contradictions and give his friend a sense of direction. Pearson
threw up his career on the stage and, with what Richard Ingrams
describes as his 'gallery of English wits and mischief-makers', became
one of the most prolific and popular biographers of the 1930s and
1940s. The description 'popular biographer' used to make him smile.
He was over fifty by the time he could afford to live from writing
alone. But he had a very good public library readership. It was not
until after his death in 1964 that I realised how many readers of my
generation, and rather older, had been brought up on his biographies – several of which (his Lives of Erasmus Darwin, Sydney
Smith, Shakespeare, Gilbert and Sullivan and others appeared as
early blue-covered Penguin Books). There was some falling-off in his
last books, though his *Dickens* (1949) and *Walter Scott* (1954) are
good.

Pearson was wary of biographical theories. 'No one should
attempt to combine practice and theory,' he asserted during a lecture
at the Royal Society of Literature. He had himself published a
volume of biographical criticism called *Ventilations* in the United
States. But that was in 1930 when 'having no practical experience, I
knew everything about it', he explained. 'Now, after writing the lives
of seventeen people, I find I know nothing about it.' My own theory
is that his biographical technique was derived from his stage career.
He *acted* his subjects. On the stage his performances had been
remarkably erratic: very good when the subject suited (that is,
resembled) him, and extraordinarily wooden when it didn't. In principle, the same is true of his biographical performances – only now,
under Kingsmill's influence, his instinct sharpened and he chose
skilfully whom he acted on the page. To some extent he 'pearsoni-
fied' his subjects, who tended to express themselves in explosive
Pearsonese. His pen portraits were done in primary colours. As John

Rothenstein observed, it is only when you examine the underlying draftsmanship that you can see how solid it is.

Readers knew where they were with Pearson. As he understudies each congenial subject, he is joyfully partisan. He was read primarily for enjoyment. By the end of his biographies, readers could feel that they knew Hazlitt, Labouchère, Oscar Wilde, Tom Paine, as they knew someone in the same street. His treatment was informal and impressionistic, depending on anecdotes and the dextrous building up of incidents to achieve its effect. He didn't bother with dreary documentation, but his use of quotations is extremely deft. Much of his scholarship, or rather knowledge, is concealed in the interests of making something vivid. He is cheering – and sometimes infuriating – to read, for he often wrote as if he had to catch the next post.

'I could not go through the travail of writing a biography,' Pearson once said, 'unless I were inspired by a feeling of affection and admiration.' He turned down a lucrative invitation to write a Life of J.M. Barrie and another to write on Montagu Norman, governor of the Bank of England, because he did not like them; and from *The Last Actor-Managers* he eliminated Gerald Du Maurier for much the same reason.

For someone so sympathetic to his subjects, it is surprising to find in what hot water his books sometimes landed him. Though he mellowed in later life, he had been extraordinarily impetuous when young. Liking people who blew respectability to pieces, he did not hesitate, more than once, to demolish his own. His first book, *Modern Men and Mummers* (1921), containing frank pen portraits of several actor-managers, helped to wreck his stage career; while his notorious *The Whispering Gallery* (1926), which purported to be 'Leaves from the Diary of an ex-diplomat' almost landed him in prison. Having lived down that scandal over the next dozen years, Pearson's reputation again came under siege after the publication of his *Conan Doyle*.

Doyle was a boyhood hero of Pearson's. The Sherlock Holmes stories had been his fairy tales. 'Sherlock was the genie, the wizard, the Fairy Godfather of my childhood,' he wrote. 'He was my Andersen, my Grimm, my Swiss Family Robinson, my Robinson

Crusoe, my Gulliver, my Jack-the-Giant-killer, my Henty, my every-thing that other boys liked and I didn't.'

It must have seemed a harmless step when, in 1941, he wrote to Adrian Conan Doyle asking for help in writing his father's life. Their meeting at the Savage Club in London was a success. Pearson exam-ined the family papers and their correspondence continued amiably and intermittently for more than two years. In 1942, Doyle wrote: 'I know you will write the book as you yourself see the facts, unswayed by any but your own powers of perception, and I neither expect nor desire anything more fair than that.'

Biographers rely on the families of their subjects in much the same way as portrait painters rely on their sitters. Both are grate-ful for essential help, but they cannot let this gratitude interfere with what they see. Since Pearson, as a matter of principle, wrote of people he liked, there seemed no danger. Adrian Conan Doyle's undemanding attitude appeared imaginative: and in a sense it was.

On 21 September 1943 Pearson sent him the completed book with a covering letter. 'You will not agree with some of my opinions,' he urged, 'but I think you will find my portrait of your father as sympathetic as I can assure you it is sincere . . . I have done my best to produce a book that will provoke an *intelligent* interest in his work; and I have been careful, in my note of Acknowledgement, to dissociate you and your brother from the views I have expressed.'

Adrian Conan Doyle liked the book – or so it seemed. Three days later he is writing to Pearson: 'May the book prosper as it deserves. Already I have dipped extensively and am now settling down to the contents with great interest.' The first cloud was very small. On page 187 he took exception to Pearson's statement that his father was impressed by titles. The book was 'so excellent', he hoped this 'little error', as he called it, would be removed in a second edition.

A week later Adrian Conan Doyle went into hospital for an oper-ation. He took the book with him and was soon writing from his bed to say that he looked forward to a really good press. The first review he'd seen – by G.W. Stonier in the *New Statesman* – happened to be a tediously written dissertation insufficiently appreciative of his great father, and he'd written to Stonier rather strongly to point this out to him.

One of Pearson's arguments had been that Doyle was, emotionally and intellectually, 'the man in the street' (Doyle's own description of himself). But, unlike the man in the street, he was articulate, and so destined to be the medium through which ordinary Englishmen at the end of the nineteenth century expressed the longing for action and excitement which had been gathering through decades of peace. Adrian Conan Doyle suddenly saw the danger of this argument in the hands of critics such as Stonier. There was a great difference between being able to reach the man in the street and being the man in the street. To Pearson he wrote: 'Because your biography is so extraordinarily good in so many other aspects, I am not hesitating to point out to you that it seems to have missed that definition.'

Reviewing the book in the *Spectator*, Graham Greene had written: 'Mr Pearson as a biographer has some of the qualities of Dr Johnson – a plainness, an honesty, a sense of ordinary life going on all the time . . . in this biography it is Mr Pearson who plays Watson to the odd enigmatic product of a Jesuit education, the Sherlock-hearted Doyle . . . it is one of Mr Pearson's virtues that he drives us to champion the subject against the biographer.'

Unfortunately Adrian Conan Doyle could not see it in this light. What he saw was publicity being given to his father's Watsonish characteristics. In a letter to *The Times* written from the Berkeley Hotel, he announced under the heading 'SHERLOCK HOLMES'S IDENTITY' that it was high time the truth be placed on record: his father was no Watson but, to the life, Sherlock Holmes. 'What a libel!' commented Bernard Shaw. 'Sherlock was a drug addict without a single amiable trait, and Watson was a decent fellow.' In his reply to *The Times*, Pearson tried to smooth things over. But the storm erupted suddenly next year. On 20 February 1944, Adrian Conan Doyle sent Pearson an extraordinary letter. It complained of his having received a glut of correspondence, often from complete strangers, protesting about the book and blaming Adrian for this travesty. Because of his illness he had not been allowed by his doctors to read it in full before now.

He had done so that month. 'I was so dumbfounded,' he wrote, 'that I read it again and then for a third time.'

The basis of his complaint was much the same as before, though his reaction was now extreme. Doyle, as depicted by Pearson, was a slow-minded Watsonish son of the people who in no way resembled 'the blood-proud man who was my father'. The letter ended with a whiff of lawyers. 'You will appreciate that in view of the fact that our father was both a public man and the scion of an ancient House, the family have no intention whatever of allowing the matter to stand in its present disguise.'

This letter came as a shock to Pearson, who sat down to answer it vigorously point by point. The reasonableness of his arguments was here and there interrupted by outbursts of indignation. Luckily he sent the draft to various friends, including Bernard Shaw. 'Let nothing persuade you to argue with this man,' Shaw replied. 'It could do no good and be an expensive and very wearing waste of time.' The letter which Pearson finally sent was in fact drafted by Shaw. It read:

> Dear Adrian Doyle,
> I am very sorry to hear that you have changed your first friendly opinion of my book; but what can I do? The book is out, and two editions are in the hands of the public. I could not withdraw nor suppress it even had I changed my opinion of it, which I have not. You must not forget that it would be a miracle if a professional biographer's opinion were an echo of a son's opinion; and I have cleared you and your brother of all responsibility for my judgements in the note of Acknowledgement.
> There is nothing for me to discuss. But if you can throw a new light on your father, do so in print by all means; nobody will be more interested than
> Yours sincerely
> Hesketh Pearson

Since there had been no libel, no breach of agreement or of copyright, there was nothing the Doyle family could do but mount a retrospective campaign against the book. The danger of this was that it might stand as an excellent advertisement for yet another edition. Adrian Conan Doyle took this risk, and towards the end of 1945 published a pamphlet called *The True Conan Doyle*. It is something of a literary curiosity and an interesting footnote to what it calls Pearson's 'alleged' biography. The tone is one of filial piety, with patches of vast rage. Reviewing it in the *Manchester Evening News*, George Orwell explained: 'It is an "answer" to the recent biography by Hesketh Pearson, and it has the air of pained indignation that such writings are apt to have. One would gather from it that Conan Doyle came nearer to perfection than it has been given ordinary mortals to do.' There is also an engaging lack of humour to the pamphlet, the author placing his father's name as the title of the memoir and then adding as his qualification for writing it the three-guinea-a-year Fellowship of the Zoological Society. A preface had been supplied by General Sir Herbert Gough, a cavalry officer with decorations for gallantry, and reference was made to the author's service in the navy. It concluded with compliments: 'Conan Doyle was the perfect pattern of a gentleman'; 'there can never have been a more honourable man than Conan Doyle', and so on. These compliments had been culled from a late minister to the tsar, an admiral in the German Imperial Navy and, rather curiously, the author of *Peter Pan*. Among the Pearson camp confronting this force was Winnie-the-Pooh's A.A. Milne.

'BOOK CAUSES STORM' one newspaper headline stated. Reviewers were wary. Some stayed silent, others hedged – but James Agate came out fighting: 'No, Sir, you must make a stronger case before you enlist my aid.'

In 1947 Pearson's book went into paperback and, helped perhaps by family opposition, sold out in a month. Adrian Conan Doyle had telephoned the publisher to say that he intended taking action against Pearson in the criminal court – adding that John Dickson Carr was writing the authorised biography with a preface by Winston Churchill and his own full co-operation. When this book appeared (without the Churchill preface), Pearson reviewed it in the *Listener* as blatant hagiography. 'But what are the shades in the picture,' he asked, 'the faults and shortcomings that would help us to accept the virtues and save us from the despair of witnessing perfection in another man? Alas, they are but virtues in disguise.'

For another twenty years the running battle ran on, breaking out at one moment in France with the publication of Pierre Nordon's biography, and again in Britain in 1959, the centenary of Conan Doyle's birth. To celebrate this centenary, Pearson had suggested giving a short radio talk based partly on a number of letters he had received with new information following the publication of his biography. The BBC liked his script and scheduled it for broadcasting in May. Suddenly the air was thick with solicitor's letters – warning Pearson and the BBC against 'falsehoods and disparagements' and threatening legal action.

Conan Doyle's published writings were still in copyright in Britain. Adrian Conan Doyle could prevent the BBC using almost any Sherlock Holmes or Brigadier Gerard stories, as well as historical novels, for twenty-one years: and this he promised to do if the Pearson talk went out. The BBC had no sensible course in such extraordinary circumstances but to appeal to Pearson for permission to surrender – which he gave. Pearson was paid for his talk but it was never heard.

Now that the protagonists are dead, the dust of battle subsided, posthumous copyright abated and Pearson's biography reissued, one can only marvel that such a modest and generous work should have been made so controversial. Pearson had written a tribute to a man who, by converting dreams into brilliant entertainment, had given him many happy hours early in life. It is a nostalgic book. The man he celebrates is a writer whose fairy tales were detective stories and historical romances, and who wrote of himself:

> *I have wrought my simple plan*
> *If I give one hour of joy*
> *To the boy who's half a man*
> *And the man who's half a boy.*

1978

KATHERINE MANSFIELD'S CAMPING GROUND

On 7 August 1922, in a letter for her husband John Middleton Murry, to be opened after her death, Katherine Mansfield wrote:

> All my manuscripts I leave entirely to you to do what you like with. Go through them one day, dear love, and destroy all you do not use. Please destroy all letters you do not wish to keep and all papers. You know my love of tidiness. Have a clean sweep, Bogey, and leave all fair – will you?

The next week, when writing her will, she made her wishes still more sweepingly plain. 'All manuscripts note books papers letters I leave to John M. Murry likewise I should like him to publish as little as possible. He will understand that I desire to leave as few traces of my camping ground as possible.'

Five months later, in January 1923, Katherine died at Gurdjieff's Institute for the Harmonious Development of Man, near Fontainebleau. She had been inhaling the breath of cows and, following an uncontrollable paroxysm of coughing, gasped: 'I believe . . . I am going to die.' Then the blood came plunging from her mouth, oozed through her fingers and the towel she pushed against her lips. Two doctors hurried Murry from her room. She stared at the door: but he was not called back until after she was dead.

Over the next quarter of a century, Murry took possession of her. Unfortunately, he had a genuinely dreadful memory. He forgot, for example, to pay the bill for her funeral, so that (until her father put things right some years later) she was buried in the paupers' part of the cemetery at Avon. He also forgot the reality of their life together. 'Now the only thing that matters to me,' he told Ottoline Morrell, 'is that she should have her rightful place as the most wonderful writer and the most beautiful spirit of our time.'

The materials for this spiritual cosmetic were at hand among the papers she had hoped he would destroy. During her life she had published only three volumes of short stories: *In a German Pension* (1911), *Bliss* (1920) and *The Garden Party* (1922). But posthumously, under Murry's supervision, she grew miraculously prolific. He brought out two more volumes, *The Dove's Nest* (1923) and *Something Childish* (1924), which included unfinished fiction and brought her collected oeuvre to eighty-eight stories. He made a book from her verses; he made another book of her reviews; and, having paraded them through the columns of his magazine the *Adelphi*, he made several books out of her journals and letters. According to C.K. Stead, 'Murry published something like 700,000 words of those papers he was instructed to tidy and leave fair.'

Professor Stead (who produced an unindexed edition of the letters and journals in 1977) and the other academics who have been circling round the Mansfield papers in New Zealand are in the uneasy position of being accessories after the fact. For if Murry had not disobeyed Katherine's wishes, there would be little enough material for them to edit, comment upon and add footnotes to: their occupation would be gone. Professor Ian A. Gordon, in his introduction to *The Urewera Notebook*, comments rather severely upon Murry for having 'discarded, suppressed, edited, and manipulated' her journals in order to raise up his pious memorial to a dead wife. But the plucking out of harsh views on friends and fellow writers (as with Leonard Woolf's and James Strachey's edition of Virginia Woolf's correspondence with Lytton Strachey) was inevitable. The truth is that Murry added nothing to Katherine's writing that was not already there, that he made her popular, and that he kept her work continually in print and handed on all the material intact so that, to his own disadvantage, she could subsequently be 'rediscovered' by us.

Katherine Mansfield's camping ground having been thrown open to the public, those who swarmed in, guided by Murry, found that they had set foot on holy ground. Katherine had become a myth, Murry having, as Antony Alpers writes, 'sealed her in porcelain'. Though his idealised picture of her as 'a princess manifest, a child withouten stain' created a sentimental cult that swept through France, it shocked many of those who had known her in England: 'Why that foul-mouthed, virulent, brazen-faced broomstick of a creature should have got herself up as a pad of rose-scented cotton wool is beyond me,' remarked Lytton Strachey after reading Murry's edition of her journal in 1927.

It is fashionable to upbraid Murry for this prim embalming. As Antony Alpers modestly acknowledges, he became 'one of the most unpopular men to be found in the world of English letters'.* Even the *Dictionary of National Biography* reports him as being 'the best-hated man-of-letters in the country'. People who could agree on nothing else were united in their enthusiastic disgust over his bad taste. It is unusual, for instance, to find Wyndham Lewis (for whom Murry was merely a 'crafty gushbag') so overtaken in the matter of invective. Virginia Woolf, who saw in Murry a posturing little man with bad teeth and a profoundly perverted nature, wrote: 'He has been rolling in dung, and smells impure.' For Carrington, he was a 'great decaying mushroom'; to D.H. Lawrence, an 'incorrigible worm'; though Aldous Huxley thought him more of a 'slug' who (with regard to Lawrence) had invented a new literary genre, the 'vindictive hagiography, malice expressed in terms of worship'.

*Antony Alpers, *The Life of Katherine Mansfield* (1980).

So the comedy of abuse rattled on, losing something of its humour as it was taken up by writers who never knew Murry. He lies 'supine' in Brigid Brophy's psychoanalytical pages and crawls, a monster of 'appalling egoism', through the last-but-one biography of Katherine Mansfield, by Jeffrey Meyers. But in correcting Murry's emphasis it is easy to fall into another form of sentimentality which attributes all Katherine's embarrassing mannerisms to his influence. Meyers describes only as 'exaggeration' the complete fabrication of D.H. Lawrence's vindictive gossip: 'I hear Katherine's letters sell largely, yet Murry whines about poverty and I hear he *inserts* the most poignant passages himself. Ottoline [Morrell] declares that in the letters to her, large pieces are inserted, most movingly.'

This is a trap into which Antony Alpers does not fall, having met and corresponded with Murry while writing an earlier biography of Katherine Mansfield which was published in 1953, and which helped to remove some of Murry's saintly cosmetics. 'Murry himself had not known of many things of which he first read in my first biography,' Mr Alpers has explained, 'for KM had used concealment – deception too – with him.' That is undoubtedly true. But Katherine always knew she was concealing the truth ('If she tells lies,' Frieda Lawrence wrote of her, 'she also knows more about truth than other people,') whereas Murry's frankness was often a kind of falsity arising from his deep self-deception. It was the shining earnestness of this self-deception that initially appealed to people. He radiated 'a kind of religious enthusiasm', Huxley remarked. 'At first, people tended to catch fire from this enthusiasm. But after a while they began to discover that the flame was only a stage effect.' He attached himself to others, but since he could not cope with real people, he changed them into literary concepts, wrapping them up with high-flown intellectual notions, then whirling round them in a violent ritualistic dance until he could celebrate Frank Harris as another Shakespeare, James Stephens as greater than Milton, Dostoyevsky and D.H. Lawrence as of the same order as Christ: and only a little above the lot of them, in 'her rightful place', Katherine Mansfield. There he could love her.

Antony Alpers's new Life, as he explains in his preface, is not a revised edition of his earlier book but 'a distinct and different biography'. He has placed himself in the almost ideal position of beginning his research while Katherine Mansfield's friends were still alive and producing the final results of this research after they are all dead – a programme which, with intervals for books on dolphins and legends of the South Seas, has taken up almost thirty-five years. His book, which is reinforced by an excellent chronology, is the most reliable guide to the facts of Katherine Mansfield's life, to what is hesitantly known and to what (sometimes more resoundingly) remains unknown. But it does not greatly alter our view of her since she emerged from the mists of Murry's highmindedness.

She 'craved for experience and a name', wrote Hugh Kingsmill in 1938. She had been born Kathleen Mansfield Beauchamp, the third daughter of a prosperous New Zealand businessman who had wanted a son. Unloved by her mother, who 'didn't handle babies' (her parents left her several months in England when Kathleen was one), she grew up insecure, chubby and invaded by terrors. Influenced probably by the talk about her father's first cousin, the author of *Elizabeth and her German Garden*, she announced at the age of nine that she was 'going to be a writer'. Antony Alpers notices a death wish in her very early work. 'I shall end of course by killing myself,' she wrote, aged eighteen, in a notebook. It was as if she wanted to murder the unloved Kathleen Beauchamp, find a new name and become another person through her writings. 'Life here is impossible,' she complained from Wellington. But in London, through her imagination, she could recreate her adolescence in New Zealand, rewrite the personalities of her parents, be in command of it all.

'Would you not like to try *all* sorts of lives?' she asked a friend. For Katherine the pen was a magic wand. She stepped into her stories and impersonated the lives of her characters. Her own life was organised like a series of rehearsals for these stories; and the bewildering number of names she gave herself and those near her (most famously changing Ida Baker into 'Lesley Moore') was an indication of how she used her experiences as experiments to be made real through fiction. Her engagement to a musician, her strange one-day marriage to

George Bowden, her subsequent pregnancy by the musician's brother, her lesbian escapades, her selection of Ida Baker as remorse-lessly self-effacing lifelong friend – a sort of understudy, dresser and sweetly poisonous competitor to other friends – all have the feel of unreality, of farce or melodrama, unless treated as the pressing of raw material, the forming of memories, to be distilled in her work.

Murry (whom Lawrence was to use for Gerald in *Women in Love* and Aldous Huxley, more convincingly, as Burlap in *Point Counter Point*) must have seemed wonderfully fruitful material to her. You could do with him what you liked. His 'stage effects' provided end-less possibilities for acting. Like her, he was attractive to both sexes (to Lawrence and to Frieda, for example), his dejected expression and crumpled posture stirring protective feelings among women and adding fresh complications to the marriage. From Katherine he received little protection. Her smouldering fires seemed faintly to kindle him, and, Hugh Kingsmill observed, 'when he was about to deliver an opinion he used to look across at her and then, straight-ening himself, gaze past one at an unseen audience', his voice ringing out like an auctioneer's as he quantified the value of one writer versus another.

This biography is far more substantial than its predecessor, yet there is a sense of something missing. An early review by Fleur Adcock in *Quarto* notes the book as having 512 pages, though, in fact, it only reaches page 466. It is as if there had been extra pages full of excellent matter that Mr Alpers, feeling it to be too well-known, at the last moment obliterated. He is so aware of all that has been written about Katherine Mansfield that he tends to impoverish his book by undervaluing some accounts simply because they have already been published elsewhere. When he gets hold of an unpub-lished item, he puffs out an announcement of it: 'The story of this catastrophe . . . has not been told before'; or, 'The reason for this extract's remaining unpublished until now will emerge in Chapter XI'; and he chucks in a poem called 'October' because it 'didn't get into the collected *Poems*', and so, he adds, 'here it is'.

All this is symptomatic of something that has happened to Mr Alpers since the publication of his first biography. In an article in

The Times Literary Supplement of 28 March 1980, he tells how, 'partly on the strength of the book, I was invited in 1966 by Dr George Whalley to join the Department of English at Queen's University in Kingston, Ontario'. Here he received 'research funds and sabbatical leave' to work on this new biography, which he dedicated to George Whalley. Unhappily, the engaging open-air Antony Alpers, South Seas and dolphin man, is constantly being interrupted by the sabbatical Professor Alpers, teacher of English and American Literature at Queen's University. These two characters (assisted by the American but never the British editor) appear to have written the book in awkward collaboration, sometimes using the first person plural, and often occupying a good deal of the page in hurling at each other furious examination questions that neither one is able to answer: 'What was she referring to? . . . What had really led to this event? . . . How does one discover what Kathleen did in Wörishofen? . . . Was she simply short of money? . . . Did Virginia dislike perfume altogether? Is there any in her novels? . . . Was Katherine simply mistaken in thinking she was pregnant by Francis Heinemann? Did she knowingly mislead LM? Or was she – against all medical probability – in fact with child? . . . How does someone who has no religious faith and is only thirty-one "accept" the imminence of death? How does anyone do that at thirty-one? How does a woman possessed of a talent which is just on the point of turning into something more – something very much more – accept the fact that this may never be? And if there was once, when young, a romantic wish to die, and a courting of death, what then? Will there be guilt, and a dark attempt to shift the blame?'

These are not real questions. Long before we can dial through to Ontario and press our own special insights on the author, the narrative lunges on, leaving us redundant. Nor are these questions used to echo Katherine's own feelings and help put us in her place. They are merely shadows thrown by the problems of research. This might be appropriate had Alpers constructed his biography as a search, like A.J.A. Symons's *The Quest for Corvo* or J.R. Ackerley's *My Father and Myself*. But since this is not his method, the screen of rhetoric becomes an irritating intrusion between his subject and the reader.

'But this is biography,' protests the professor on page 203 of his book. He has certain ideas about biography. Though the book is described on the jacket by the publisher as the 'definitive biography' of Katherine Mansfield, the author himself has sensibly written: 'Such a thing as the "definitive biography" does not exist.' He has set about constructing an almost inflexible chronological account. It can't strictly be done, of course, but his attempt is brave. The narrative is like a horse that he is constantly having to urge forward, then rein up short, to keep it abreast of actual time. It makes for a bumpy ride, like that of a rocking-horse going backwards and forwards and getting nowhere. For example: '. . . of which we saw an opening scene in the previous chapter . . . As the reader will discover . . . The point is of some importance, but will have to be left aside for the moment . . . The subject of Kennedy's relationship with Katherine will return in the next chapter . . . already cited in Chapter VI . . . it calls for a chapter to itself . . . but it belongs to a later chapter . . . will be heard of in due course . . . has been given in Chapter XIV . . .'

Another of Professor Alpers's biographical notions is to revive the panoramic method last fully employed by Philip Guedalla in his *Palmerston* of 1926 – that is, making a mosaic of contemporary happenings. This kind of kaleidoscope, which has long been thought obsolete, is full of nostalgia:

The war being three years past, she was soon to write *The Fly*. Around the corner, as it were, downstream at Lausanne, was T.S. Eliot, granted sick leave by his bank to recover from a breakdown caused by his marriage. He had brought with him a long poem . . . A mile or so upstream from Sierre, at Muzot, was Rainer Maria Rilke, whose *Duino Elegies*, held in suspension throughout the war, would soon miraculously complete themselves within a space of eight days. In Paris James Joyce awaited the publication of his Odyssey composed from the fragments of a single day in Dublin in 1904, while at 44 Rue Hamelin, racked by asthma and all the ills of a youth whose mother had unmanned him with her kisses, lay Marcel Proust, completing his own great work about time present and time past. At

Hogarth House, Richmond, on 4 November, Virginia Woolf, who had been ill again during the summer, wrote the last pages of *Jacob's Room*, an experimental novel which declared that for one human being to know another is not possible. Lawrence, down in Sicily, was about to spit on Europe for the last time and depart. Living next to Basil Blackwell's bookshop in Oxford, in the best of psychic health, was W.B. Yeats, whose latest volume . . .

There's scholarship for you!

Antony Alpers has a nice sense of irony, and a sense of adventure too. He sometimes begins a sentence dramatically only to have it snatched from him by the sabbatical professor from Ontario: 'This hectic letter . . . which is quoted in Sylvia Berkman's critical study of her work . . .' The result is that Antony Alpers's humour and shrewdness are too often checked, and his common sense set aside, by the professor's pseudo-profundities – the most striking example being his replacement of Chekhov by the XVth Idyll of Theocritus as the most important influence on Katherine Mansfield's writing. This reads like a parody of professorship.

'Literary biography,' he has written, 'is an exercise in cutting up the artist to find out how he works.' But if that is the case, you will be presented with the bits and pieces of a dead artist, not the recreation of a living one. Antony Alpers is a painstaking and accurate worker: his book will be indispensable as a work of reference. But because he has decided to impersonate a professor, we are never allowed to forget that we are in a book. All too seldom does he allow Katherine to rip through adventures which, though she believed them to come from the novels of Dostoyevsky, belong more to the world of Stephen Leacock. Nor does he seek to borrow that chameleon quality of Katherine's which, in Keats's words, 'is constantly informing and filling another body', and which is the ideal attribute for a biographer. Instead, whenever Professor Alpers gets in full control, he gives us a variation of Murry's book-imprisoned writing – which 'though drawn from a live emotion was written in a dead language'.

1980

THREE LIVES
Joe Orton, Rudyard Kipling,
E.M. Forster

The most famous thing about Joe Orton is his death. Nothing, in terms of publicity, became him so well. On the first page of his Life, we find his death – in bed, with his 'head cratered like a burnt candle', while his friend and murderer, Kenneth Halliwell, lies naked in the centre of the room, plastered with the playwright's blood, and various policemen peer politely at the 'evidence'.

Halliwell and Orton were homosexual, had met at the Royal Academy of Dramatic Art in London, and lived together. An aggressively timid man, Halliwell, who had some money, was initially the father of the relationship, affecting a sinister superiority over his 'pussycat' Orton. What they shared was anger, anger against society and a need for revenge that was exercised by six months in jail for 'damaging' library books.

It was most loving damage. On the cover of a manual on etiquette by Lady Lewisham they conjured up a provocative female nude. Another volume was improved with an illustration of Edith Cavell locked in a prison cell with a set of mammoth genitalia. 'During the Second World War,' the caption reads, 'I was working from dawn to dusk to serve the many thousands of sailors, soldiers, and airmen. American GIs came in shoals to my surgery and some had very peculiar orders for me.'

Orton and Halliwell could survive everything together except success – that was the one calamity they had not bargained for. By the mid-sixties, *Entertaining Mr Sloane* and *Loot* had established Orton, in the words of the critic Irving Wardle, as 'one of the sharpest stylists of British new wave . . . a consummate dialogue artist and a natural anarch'. He was spoken of along with Firbank and Pinter – but no one spoke of Halliwell except Halliwell, who was fond of using the royal we: 'a genius like us'. Halliwell's humour was unconscious, and he had no talent. He had given up writing, acting, and painting – an ambitious list; he had spent most of his inherited money, and he was altogether diminished by Orton's celebrity. Desperately anxious to save his friendship with Orton, he felt increasingly impotent. He could not even express his anger convincingly – until the end.

John Lahr's understanding of Orton's work is deeply felt and intellectually sophisticated. His book* has many insights, but its structure is confused. There are so many good sentences apparently set down in the wrong order, yet it is well worth the reader's shuffling them like a pack of cards. Mr Lahr argues eloquently that Orton's plays give us 'a heritage of laughter created out of a lifetime's hunger for revenge'. His humour enabled him to triumph over his barren beginnings in Leicester and his isolation in London. It gave him detachment and a method of disarming his enemies. His salvation was laughter, 'which pierces so, that it assaults/Mercy itself, and frees all faults'.

Kipling would have known what to do with a specimen like Orton: a regular 'dose of cleanin'-rod' would have been the making of him. Though his own childhood had been cruel and miserable, Kipling was enthusiastic about corporal punishment: 'I have often been beaten,' he said, 'and I richly deserved it.' As for homosexuality, he nourished a deep hatred of the schoolmaster who had once suspected him of such 'impurity', and he dreamed of placing him in a

Prick Up Your Ears: The Biography of Joe Orton (1978).

novel where 'to finish the revenge I'll marry him to a woman who shall give him something else to think about'.

As with Orton, the inspiration for much of Kipling's work was revenge, and the creation of a cleansing boys' world in which he imagined himself performing all the military and athletic deeds that poor eyesight and health had denied him. 'There are times when I feel utterly lonely,' he confessed. 'But then I can watch the fire and weave tales and dream dreams.' In his life he was a timid man, shrinking from emotional intimacy with women and distracting himself with the contemplation of vivid outdoor excitements that could never bruise his feelings. His books turn the world inside out, making it a battlefield where the nameless enemy within is exposed and vanquished.

Kipling's animal wariness, his instinct for self-protection, made him morbidly frightened of biography, which he described as the 'Higher Cannibalism'. The story of the late Lord Birkenhead's book* is enough to chill the blood of any biographer. As the present Lord Birkenhead explains in his introduction, Kipling's daughter, who retained complete control of this book and who helped with its research, read the first draft in 1948 and refused the author permission to publish it. She gave no reasons, though Charles Carrington, author of a subsequent Life of Kipling, reveals that she disliked Lord Birkenhead and believed his book to be riddled with amateur psychoanalysis. Lord Birkenhead, who continued to revise and add to his book, died in 1975, and Kipling's daughter died the following year.

The biography contains no dreadful secrets and adds little to the facts made available in Carrington's book. Lord Birkenhead's attitude seems similar to that of the outstanding schoolmaster who taught Kipling English literature and who felt for him 'admiration coupled with dislike'. The narrative is readable and well balanced and gives an account of Kipling's life that neither hides nor exalts his flaws. Lord Birkenhead was prepared to criticise Kipling himself but liked to defend him against the criticisms of others. Though there is

*Rudyard Kipling (1978).

no psychoanalytical jargon, he is good at showing Kipling's odious conceit and bumptiousness as having been the means by which he survived the violent shock of his childhood in England away from his parents, a shock that killed his capacity for loving and replaced it with resentment.

'Kipling was one of the few people he deeply regretted not having known,' P.N. Furbank reveals in his biography of the novelist E.M. Forster.* Forster thought that 'most Indians, like most English people, are shits', but for him, no less than for Kipling, India had been a salvation. Yet their Indias were very different places. Kipling's India, which represented a happiness from which he had been unaccountably sundered when a child, was a world too remote and savage to seem real to Forster, who did not seek revenge but a country of forgetfulness to distance him from his confining past, allowing him to develop into someone else. He was a fine example of the feeble intellectual Kipling abominated – a spoiled darling in a fatherless, manless household who had retreated in tears from the jostling, athletics-ridden atmosphere of the public school to which Kipling retrospectively gave such snobbish allegiance. 'School was the unhappiest time of my life,' Forster wrote. He feared that the whole adult world would be like his school. In Greece and Italy, especially in India, and even in the Bloomsbury world of Cambridge, he found an atmosphere as unlike the barbaric climate of school as was possible. Forster was a deliberately unexciting figure. He reminded Lytton Strachey of a mole, drab-coloured and unobtrusive. His personality seemed tentative, his manner buttoned-up, his speech pedantic; he was given to wondering whether he might not be over-cautious – and failing, through caution, to reach a conclusion.

Forster had been rescued from what Mr Furbank describes as a life 'full of aunts and tea parties and little jokes and chocolate hares' by his friendship with a magnificent-looking Muslim called Masood who 'woke him up out of his suburban and academic life and showed him new horizons and a new civilisation'. He became more

*E.M. Forster: A Life (1978).

exploratory, broke through barriers of class and colour, and experienced a few homosexual affairs that, though tame enough by Joe
Orton's standards, made him feel 'a grown-up man'.

If Forster seems at times like (in Virginia Woolf's phrase) 'a
vaguely rambling butterfly', Mr Furbank is his sympathetic shadow.
He follows him closely as he flutters, glides, hovers over a surprisingly wide landscape, and spies out the novelist's ghostly voyeurist
role. He matches Forster's nimble, quiet wit with his own engagingly
wry humour. It is a most skilful performance, less an attempt to
recreate life upon the page than to create a narrative in which Forster
is the posthumous collaborator. I only wish his American publisher*
thought as highly of the book as I do and had gone to the trouble
and expense of paginating the pages. This is a piece of rotten publishing, for which the publisher has taken the American edition of
Quentin Bell's *Virginia Woolf* as a model, and it will be deplored by
anyone who cares about well-produced books.

1978

*Harcourt Brace Jovanovich.

EDITH SITWELL

At the end of 1946 a young American called on Edith Sitwell, then in her sixtieth year. He was writing a book on W.B. Yeats. 'His one interest,' Miss Sitwell complained to John Lehmann,

> ... is exactly what terms Mr Y was [on] with Mrs Maud Gonne and others. He says he is going to base the book on the effect this had on his poetry!!! oh, oh, oh! Is it not <u>awful</u> that every great man has got to be exhumed and nailed down at the crossroads with a stake through his heart? ... The young man was quite well-intentioned.

This young man turned out to be the biographer Richard Ellmann, whose book *The Man and the Masks* was published two years later.

At first sight Edith Sitwell's hostility to biography is surprising. After all, she had written some biographies herself. And did she not share the Sitwell genius for loitering in the limelight? 'She is liable to make herself a little conspicuous,' Evelyn Waugh ventured. Her frozen Plantagenet image, together with the Hanoverian profile of her brother Osbert and the baroque figure of her younger brother Sacheverell, was part of an eccentric triumvirate that became instantly recognisable to millions of people who never opened a book. 'The three Sitwells,' wrote Rebecca West, '. . . are among the few illuminants England possesses which are strong enough to light up post-war England. They are legatees of perhaps the most glorious group that English life has ever produced, the Whig aristocracy of the eighteenth century.'

Edith Sitwell felt she had been unpopular with her parents throughout her childhood. 'I was in disgrace,' she wrote, 'for being a female.' Taken from one grandiose and ornate house to another, she lacked affection and the sense of having a home. Lonely and sensitive, she found emotional nourishment in music and reading, and after the age of sixteen in the companionship of a governess.

To make up for this neglect, she wanted attention – but she did not relish investigation. It was through her strange remoteness that she arranged to become celebrated. Her publicity was a painted screen behind which she hid; and in commonplace terms she explained it as a method by which she sought to sell her books.

Though Edith Sitwell was a biographer, her subjects were either historical (Elizabeth I, Queen Victoria) or, if literary, never contemporary. They provided her with another means of self-fulfilling escape, enabling her to tell her own story secretly. Into the deformed figure of Alexander Pope, for instance, she projected some of her uncertainties about her own appearance, her inability to attract love and the validity of her hate, creating a vicarious method of self-revelation that gives the book its peculiar sympathy. Her gift was for gorgeous and elaborate camouflage; for making oblique use of what, if directly employed, would by her standards be vulgar or painful. She described as 'wonderful' how Shakespeare had kept his private life and all his sexual bitterness hidden from the prying eyes of Ben Jonson. But she knew very well the connection between literature and life. In a letter to the novelist Olivia Manning, she wrote: 'Most great poetry comes through the personal becoming universal . . . If one has no personal emotions, one isn't a poet – or a human being . . . to write great poetry, one must experience.'

About her poem 'The Death of the Giant', which reveals her obsession with death, she confided to John Lehmann: 'Incidentally – <u>only for God's sake don't say so</u> – were it a novel it might be called a roman à clef. I am the giant in question, although for poetic reasons I changed the sex of the giant.'

But in biography there could be no such poetic licence. The facts, put flat upon the page, added up to a plausible flat lie since the dimension of poetry was absent. For to Edith Sitwell, the transmutation of the personal into the universal was achieved through the simultaneous process of declaration and concealment. Biography merely stated and therefore, however scrupulously researched, stated wrong. As the genre grew more intimate so the subject was slowly stripped naked. It was the fashion of the times to mistake this nakedness for truth. Poetic truth, she believed, was to be found in her own life in the unique style of clothes and language she evolved, reflecting the person she had substituted for her parents' unloved child. It was a triumph of adaptability. Her odd physique, orchestrated so majestically with silver paint and oriental turban, with coral and jet bracelets, with huge lumps of topaz and sparkling turquoise on her attenuated gothic fingers, was a testament to her willpower: at once a diversion from her unhappy past and a declaration that she would meet the world on her own terms.

Investigative biography moved dangerously close when, towards the end of her life, Parker Tyler approached her for help over his Life of Pavel Tchelitchew, the painter who had been the focus of her one abiding unrequited love. 'I dislike discussing my personal life, and never do,' she wrote to him, 'and for that reason I never write about my personal friendships – I have had friendships with several great men.' And when Parker Tyler came to see her the following year, she begged him: 'Don't hand him [Tchelitchew] over to the wolves.'

Her fear of biography arose in part from a conviction that the world was crowded with wolves. But she also despised the craft because her own non-fiction work was produced out of the necessity to make money. Potboilers such as *Victoria of England* or *Fanfare for Elizabeth*, though they usually contain some marvellously impressionistic passages, were often diffuse and rather formless, heavily paraphrased from writers such as Lytton Strachey and included recycled paragraphs from her own previous books. They rested on secondary sources, extended and not always accurately transcribed quotations, and a cavalier attitude to chronology: 'What does it matter in two hundred years,' she questioned, 'if the clock has struck 1709 or 1739?' It was splendid, but it was not biography.

From her general denunciation of biography she could exclude the art of autobiography, which was part of the glittering armour you put on before issuing forth from your bright pavilion to do battle with the world. Her brother Osbert's five-volume autobiography, a monument to the mythology of Sitwellism, delighted her. Her own posthumous autobiography, *Taken Care Of*, is a highly partial and patchy job that retells her favourite jokes and acts as little more than an appendix to her brother's great work.

Edith Sitwell died at the end of 1964. Since then a number of books have been published that agreeably perpetuate the Sitwell legend – from John Lehmann's *A Nest of Tigers* to John Pearson's *Façades*. In his introduction to what he described as a personal interim assessment of 'the Sitwells and their Times', John Lehmann wrote in 1967 that the time had not yet come for a full survey of Edith Sitwell's work. 'Again, I do not think it is possible yet to write a full biography of Dame Edith,' he added, '. . . the material is not yet assembled, the perspective is not yet deep enough.'

Since then the dragon of biography has been circling nearer Dame Edith. In 1967 her secretary Elizabeth Salter published a brief memoir, *The Last Years of a Rebel*; three years later a volume of her *Selected Letters* appeared. And now, her manuscripts, drafts, personal papers, working notebooks and correspondence (except for her letters to Pavel Tchelitchew, which were walled up in Yale University for the rest of the century) having been assembled in the Humanities Research Center at the University of Austin in Texas, the dragon she so much feared is upon her.

It turns out to be a two-headed yet kindly beast. Mr Elborn's book,* which contains a useful bibliography, has received particular help from Sir Sacheverell Sitwell, at whose suggestion it came to be written. It is a straightforward account of her life and career, rather pedestrian in structure and admiring in tone. Dame Edith would have found

*Geoffrey Elborn, *Edith Sitwell: A Biography* (1981).

nothing here to make her blood boil. Mr Elborn sympathetically records the sagas of her literary skirmishes and squabbles, and the paranoiac pursuits of her old age. If they often seem childish, this was largely because they derived from her own difficult childhood.

Between Mr Elborn's book and Ms Glendinning's* there are no great differences as to fact. But where Mr Elborn writes out of respect, Ms Glendinning writes from love and has produced a more sophisticated and penetrating work. In her foreword, she confesses to 'a very protective feeling' that developed during the course of writing her book. This protective feeling helps to surround her work with the life-supporting atmosphere that all good biographers seek to create. Ms Glendinning orchestrates Edith Sitwell's notoriety, chronicles the rows, revenges and ripostes by which she came to afflict the public. She refers more than once to F.R. Leavis's famous dismissal of the three-in-one: 'The Sitwells belong to the history of publicity rather than of poetry.' But this, she argues, rests on a false dichotomy. Edith Sitwell 'does not belong to the history of publicity rather than of poetry, but to the history of poetry *and* the history of publicity'. It is a balance expertly kept throughout the book. Victoria Glendinning quotes a passage from *Alexander Pope* and tells us to substitute Edith for Pope:

> The naïveté and fundamental simplicity of Pope, his craving for romance, his warm heart, his genuine response to and understanding of the affections of others; these qualities are seen, side by side with a good deal of genuine silliness, a certain amount of artifice, and an intent and strained gaze fixed upon the verdict of posterity.

Though she was devoted to her brothers, Edith Sitwell objected to the three of them being treated as an 'aggregate Indian god, with three sets of legs and arms, but otherwise indivisible'. Victoria Glendinning is particularly successful at releasing her independent spirit from this corporate identity while keeping her two talented brothers in perspective.

*Victoria Glendinning, *Edith Sitwell: A Unicorn among Lions* (1981).

'I always was a little outside life,' Edith wrote in a poem dedicated to her brothers. Ms Glendinning places her back in the context of her early life. Her parents' marriage had been 'held together by propriety and property, and stimulated chiefly by animosity and misunderstanding'. There is a horrifying account of the orthopaedic contraption ('a sort of Bastille of steel') in which she was placed to correct her bent spine, her weak ankles, her crooked nose. It was not by such mediaeval engineering that she was to be refashioned, but by her creative imagination. She needed to be a 'genius' to recreate herself, to overcome pain and plainness by the picturesque and by the magic of her poetry. She superimposed pagoda country on the English landscape; she gave herself a new childhood, an invented place full of fun and colour and odd sounds, to which uncomprehending adults gave the name 'nonsense'.

> *Whirring, walking*
> *On the tree-top,*
> *Three poor witches*
> *Mow and mop.*
> *Three poor witches*
> *Fly on switches*
> *Of a broom,*
> *From their cottage room.*
> *Like goat's-beard rivers,*
> *Black and lean,*
> *Are Moll and Meg,*
> *And Myrrhaline.*

But when she tried to mix her fantasy with the actual world, difficulties erupted. Arnold Bennett decided that the Sitwells 'exult in a scrap'. But Edith only enjoyed winning battles. The hysterical unhappiness of her early years led to a hypersensitivity to criticism that, in Charles Osborne's words, 'encouraged extremes of sycophancy in some and enmity in others' and obscured her real merits. She saw enemies everywhere, took everything personally, and was made miserable by some critics' lack of generosity.

Her love for Pavel Tchelitchew, too, brought her much unhappiness. He was an aristocratic exile from Russia, a handsome artist over ten years younger than herself who, though a worshipper of the female muse, was homosexual. While he existed in her romantic imagination, and she in his, their charade of courtly love was a delight for both of them. At their best, Victoria Glendinning writes, they 'were magically clever children'. He did not want a real woman; she did not want real intimacy. But actuality could not be kept out for ever. He lusted after fame and fortune; she needed to imprison him in her lustrous fantasy. He rebelled; she felt rejected; and their garden of happiness was invaded by jealousy and envy. Like everyone who feels disliked by parents, Edith Sitwell had no confidence in being able to attract love from the adult world – though ironically it was the success she attained in this world that Pavel Tchelitchew felt he needed. 'The withdrawal of love,' Victoria Glendinning writes, 'was for Edith as for a small child the most dreadful, unforgivable, unforgettable crime.'

This is a sensitive, excellently structured biography. Victoria Glendinning weaves in all sorts of information from the sales of books, reactions to reviews, the developments and fashions in poetry, the ebb and flow of friendships in a most skilful way, always seeking new methods of moving the narrative forwards. She is adept at balancing internal terrors and anxieties against the outward show of gestures and gallantries.

The gaze so intently fixed on the verdict of posterity can now relax and smile. This sympathetic yet objective work transmutes the personal into the universal in a way that Edith Sitwell believed was only possible in poetry, because it conforms to Robert Gittings's definition of what the best biography should be: 'poetry with a conscience'.

1981

VITA

When editing the three volumes of his father Sir Harold Nicolson's diaries in the 1960s, Nigel Nicolson disclosed in the *Spectator* that 'my only cause for hesitation was whether to reveal my father's racial prejudices and my mother's extreme conservatism'. He revealed both: and five years later went on to reveal in *Portrait of a Marriage* the homosexuality of both his parents. 'Let not the reader condemn in ten minutes,' he wrote in his foreword, 'a decision which I have pondered for ten years.' This ten-year span, which included the time when he wrote 'A Problem of Discretion' for the *Spectator*, registered a considerable change in the climate of biography.

The new climate is one from which Victoria Glendinning has greatly benefited. Her life of Edith Sitwell was a richer and more imaginatively conceived book than could have been written before the post-Stracheyan revolution. But with new opportunities have come new challenges, and with Vita Sackville-West* it has been more difficult for her to form a rewarding collaboration.

In her preface, Ms Glendinning takes a rather defensive tone from which some of her difficulties may be inferred. Vita Sackville-West

---

*Victoria Glendinning, *Vita: The Life of V. Sackville-West* (1983).

will be 'an inspiration' to some, she writes, but to others she may seem 'unlikeable'. This biography, she adds, 'is less than comprehensive'. There is almost too much material documenting Vita's marriage to Harold Nicolson; there are almost too many books covering other aspects of this territory, from the prize-winning lives of Harold Nicolson by James Lees-Milne and of Virginia Woolf by Quentin Bell to the autobiography of Violet Trefusis. Since the ground to either side of her is already so well mapped, Ms Glendinning has decided that she must deviate as little as possible from a strict chronological route along Vita's personal story.

There is another problem and it is a serious one. *Vita*, she writes, 'is a biography and not a work of literary criticism'. Yet Vita was 'first and foremost a writer'. Glendinning does the best she can with the books. Her comments are shrewd and percipient, and she skilfully quarries out of Vita's writing what she can in the way of autobiographical interest to strengthen the connective tissue of her narrative. She describes Vita's most commercially successful novel, *The Edwardians*, as 'vulgar, vivid, problematic, false and fascinating as its subject matter, the wealthy upper classes of Edwardian England', but explains how Vita established her popular success 'by recreating the lavish, feudal, immoral *ancien régime* of her childhood'.

Vita Sackville-West is a tempting subject for a biographer. Her own posthumous chapter of autobiography, which her younger son found in a locked Gladstone bag and augmented into *Portrait of a Marriage*, was rightly regarded by many as a landmark in the progress of modern biographical writing – something unforeseen in Harold Nicolson's *The Development of English Biography* (1927). The structure of *Portrait of a Marriage* – two chapters by Vita Sackville-West alternating with three by Nigel Nicolson, interspersed with a chronology – was unusual, and the degree of frankness over sexual matters seemed sensational when it was first published in the early 1970s.

The advances made since the Second World War in freedom of biographical technique and subject matter had been so rapid that some critics were alerted to a literary awakening. A.O.J. Cockshut went so far as to claim that for 'nearly two centuries we have been living through a golden age of biographical writing' that we had been culpably slow to recognise. Others chronicled these improvements from such masterworks of the late 1950s as George Painter's *Proust* and Richard Ellmann's *James Joyce*, which had been transplanted from that amputated limb labelled 'Biography' in the mortuary of English Studies to the living body of contemporary literature. Shelley's biographer, Richard Holmes, one of the luminaries of this biographical resurrection, described biography as 'the most successful and intellectually stimulating form which has held a general readership in Britain since 1960'.

Discretion, Lytton Strachey said, is not the better part of biography. The dangers of indiscretion, however, had been well delineated by Nigel Nicolson in the *Spectator* in 1968. People likely to be the subjects of biography, he warned, would 'destroy their most intimate letters and be very careful what they wrote in their journals . . . So the private records of our times, perhaps the most articulate in history, will be paradoxically sparse, unless we impose on ourselves some sort of limitation on what is to be published and when.' As an example of a book that should not have been published in the revelatory form in which it appeared, Nigel Nicolson named Lord Moran's diary; as an example of something published prematurely he instanced *Chips: the Diary of Sir Henry Channon*. 'If I had been Paul Channon,' he wrote, 'I would have hesitated to be quite so frank so soon.'

Portrait of a Marriage was described by Nigel Nicolson as 'a panegyric of marriage'. Certainly it blurred the conventional ideals of marriage and widened the definition of a successful one. Victoria Glendinning's portrait of this marriage does not greatly conflict with Nigel Nicolson's, but her more detailed account shows that, though it began romantically and ended endearingly, there was much guilt and stress along the way. Nigel Nicolson's verdict now seems, understandably, a little sentimental. Virginia Woolf even questioned whether it was a marriage at all. Vita and Harold were playmates, friends, fellow actors in the melodrama of their relationship. 'Some men seem born to be lovers, others to be husbands; he belongs to the other category,' Vita observed some time before Harold contracted venereal disease. Not caring for domestic affections, she wanted life to be conducted 'as a series of *grandes passions*', he noted after they had been married for twenty years. 'Had I been a passionate man, I should have suffered tortures of jealousy on her behalf, have made endless scenes, and we should now have been separated.'

There were scenes, and they came near to separation. She longed for 'some apocalyptic happening that would fuse the separate parts of her life'. The best he could do was to surrender his diplomatic career, after which he was miserable. 'I feel that without it I should become not a cup of tea but a large jug of milk.' The excitement Vita sought in sexual elopements he derived from performing in the decorated spectacle of public life. He had dreamed of being viceroy of India; wanted to be a member of Parliament for almost any party; and set his heart on a peerage. But his parliamentary career was modest and he had to content himself with writing the Life of George V and receiving a knighthood. He took it like a reverse in love: 'Being assessed so low diminishes my prestige,' he confessed.

From their correspondence Ms Glendinning received 'the impression of theatricality and deliberateness'. Above all else, they were actors in a play that for much of the time bewildered them. They performed extremely well discussing marriage on the radio together and as participants on the American lecture circuit. But on more natural or spontaneous occasions they were often stagey. Victoria Glendinning quotes a passage from Nigel Nicolson describing a solemn scene that took place when he was seventeen.

> She paused one evening at the bottom step of her staircase, turned to me shyly and said: 'I have written a new poem, and I would like to dedicate it to you.'
>
> 'Oh, don't do that,' I replied unthinkingly. 'You know that I don't really understand poetry.' She went into the tower without a word, and when she came to dinner I saw that she had been crying.

Most of the novels, poetry and gardening books are dealt with honestly, in their almost clockwork chronological succession. But Victoria Glendinning takes a short passage from *All Passion Spent* out of its time-sequence and places it at the threshold of Vita's adulthood, heralding the ambiguous fantasies that were to shape her life. 'For the thoughts that ran behind this delicate and maidenly exterior were of an extravagance to do credit even to a wild young man. They were thoughts of nothing less than escape and disguise: a changed name, a travestied sex, and freedom in some foreign city.'

Vita Sackville-West was a divided and misplaced figure whose life can too easily take on the appearance, not of an 'adventure story' as her biographer wishes, but of scenes from some fantastical pantomime. She was enveloped in the mists and illusions of romance, and believed that she 'should have lived in an age when seriousness and noble thoughts found an echo'.

Knole, the great country house where she had been brought up, was a magical place. Its courtyards, deer park and gardens, its stone leopards along the roofline, the mermaids and dolphins of the ballroom frieze, its galleries and tapestries and silver furniture were the scenery of her imaginative life. But after her marriage to Harold Nicolson this Eden was 'denied to me for ever' since, as a woman, she could not inherit the place. 'There is some sort of umbilical cord that ties me to Knole,' she told her husband fifteen years after their marriage. All her life she dreamed of Knole – at night 'the deer galloping down the stable passage, their hooves rattling on the wooden boards'; and in the daytime too, writing: 'I want Knole . . . I've got an idea about it: shall we take it some day? . . . I've taken Dad's revolver. And the bullets.'

In fact the circumstances of her childhood had not been happy. From her parents, who had lovers and who eventually separated, she inherited incompatible qualities. Her father was a quiet, waistcoated, pipe-smoking man; her mother, whom Victoria Glendinning likens to Becky Sharp, a self-centred exotic who fascinated and enslaved her daughter. Vita grew up as a greedy and rather plain, spoiled but largely unloved child who protected herself by creating through her writing a private world of fantasy.

She loved her father: but her relationship with her mother was more like a turbulent affaire. Her life after marriage developed into a series of emotional escapades. Women continued to fall in love with her and she went, in one country after another, from one woman's arms to another's. 'Vita loved to be loved,' writes Victoria Glendinning. Love, which promised to fill her emotional vacuum, 'deludes us into thinking that life is worth living', Vita wrote. But she remained a lonely person, unable to simplify her life, unable to renounce anything because she felt something was already missing. 'So what was missing?' asks her biographer at one point. In one sense it was her ability to adapt to the world. She seems to have felt misconceived in life outside Knole, and none of her infatuations, even the most extreme of all, with Violet Trefusis, could make up for the loss.

In her writing too she tried to blend fantasy with the real world. But though several of her books sold well, her ambitions outran her talent. She wanted to be poet laureate. 'I *will* get myself into English Literature,' she wrote rather desperately. 'Somehow or other.' But English literature, as she envisaged it, was a mirage. She wrote, as Virginia Woolf bluntly commented, with a pen of brass. But like Lady Ottoline Morrell, she had the power to stimulate other writers. She influenced Geoffrey Scott's *The Portrait of Zélide*, entered Ronald Firbank's *The Flower Beneath the Foot* as Mrs Harold Chilleywater (who 'had developed a disconcerting taste for fiction') and enlivened passages of Roy Campbell's *The Georgiad*.

> *Her gruff moustaches dropping from her mouth*
> *One to the North, the other to the South,*
> *Seemed more the whiskers of some brine-wet seal*
> *Than of a priestess of the High Ideal.*

Her most extraordinary incarnation is in Virginia Woolf's *Orlando*. 'I was always sexually cowardly. My terror of real life has always kept me in a nunnery,' Virginia Woolf had written. What she wanted from Vita ('a real woman') was the illusion of reality – 'to make the world dance'. There was, as Quentin Bell put it, 'some caressing, some bedding together', and Virginia responded in *Orlando* with what Nigel Nicolson described as 'the longest and most charming love-letter in literature'. It was published shortly after Vita's father died and it gave her comfort. For, as Victoria Glendinning shows, the book restored Vita to Knole and restored Knole to Vita as her own books had never done. 'I feel, somehow, that Knole knows about *Orlando*, and is pleased,' she wrote to Harold, who replied that Virginia had written a novel 'in which you and Knole are identified for ever, a book that will perpetuate that identity into years when both you and I are dead'.

She was most natural in her garden. Victoria Glendinning ends her book in the garden at Sissinghurst, where Vita had done most to replace Knole and in writing about which she communicated most intimately with her readers. It is a just and sympathetic conclusion to a book that has many excellences. Victoria Glendinning is one of our most talented biographers, but she has not wholly succeeded in reconstructing Vita's succession of romances as a single adventure story. So many of the amorous episodes are similar that eventually 'love makes everyone a bore', as Virginia Woolf rather enviously remarked. The narrow chronological narrative, too, becomes constricting when it does not allow Victoria Glendinning to alter the focus of her story without trespassing on to other biographers' territory.

Though inviting, Vita turns out to be an awkward subject for biography. It is possible to see her life more as epic comedy than grand adventure. She had little sense of humour, but the spectre of unconscious humour was often present and instinctively picked up by her friends. Victoria Glendinning quotes appreciatively from the letters, journals and books of Denton Welch, Ethel Smyth, Virginia Woolf and Peter Quennell, but does not develop this vein herself. In *Some People* Harold Nicolson had used the incongruities of humour to create a small but genuine biographical innovation that, by implication, sets much of his life in a comic perspective. But twenty years later, in *The English Sense of Humour*, he reduced humour to a means of self-protection that often had debilitating effects on the character. In a famous essay on this book, Hugh Kingsmill retorted that it was 'lack of character which has a debilitating effect upon humour. As a diagnosis of the abuse of humour in the last one hundred and fifty years, Mr Nicolson's essay is excellent . . . But of humour on the level where it is impersonal and disinterested, an illumination of reality not a refuge from it, Mr Nicolson has nothing to say.' Perhaps the next step forward for biography is to accommodate this spirit of humour and reveal the conflict between illusion and reality.

1983

A SECRET LIFE
Harley Granville Barker

Harley Granville Barker is still a legendary figure of the theatre. His birth, like that of two other mythical characters of the time, Edward Gordon Craig and T.E. Lawrence, was enveloped in mystery. On the certificate his father's name appeared as Albert James Barker, whose occupation was given as 'Gentleman'. Elsewhere, though not with much conviction, he was spoken of as an architect. It was also said that he would sometimes expand with pride over his family connections, but as no one quite knew what these were, this did not signify much. Eventually he wandered off into France and died, it was rumoured, of consumption.

The dominating figure of Barker's upbringing (as with Gordon Craig and T.E. Lawrence) was his mother. She was a well-known elocutionist with approximately half the name of an Italian brigand, Bossi-Granville. As a boy, Barker used to perform precociously at her literary recitals; and all his adult life he kept in a silver locket a picture of her before her marriage. She did not risk sending him to school, but nurtured him in an atmosphere of good speech and drama where he picked up a wide knowledge of Dickens and Shakespeare.

As he grew up, Barker had difficulty in establishing his masculinity and with it a clear sense of his identity. According to Beatrice

Webb he was 'a most attractive person – young and good looking in a charming refined fashion – with a subtle intellectual expression'. But she added: 'I do not yet see a very definite whole.' It was this incompleteness that bewildered and fascinated people. He could be sensitive, charming; but he could also appear peculiarly intemperate and cold-blooded. Though successful at an early age as an actor he was plagued with depression. Like T.E. Lawrence he seemed all things to all men – a characteristic that may have special uses on the stage. With Bernard Shaw and his wife Charlotte, first Barker and then Lawrence established a special kinship: and at different times there was a good deal of gossip to the effect that each was the illegitimate son of GBS.

Eric Salmon, who has ostensibly aimed his book* at destroying what he calls 'the Barker Legend', is a bit of a romantic. He cannot resist fantastical speculation. His first chapter begins with a Mysterious Envelope said to contain 'secret and shocking' information about Barker that inexplicably disappeared when it was supposed to be opened on the centenary of Barker's birth. He then observes that 'Shaw treated Barker as if he were his son'. The two men, he adds, were 'remarkably close' at the Court Theatre. Sometimes they went on holiday together. What explanation could there be, he wonders, for the fact that Shaw lent Barker quite large sums of money and then 'unhesitatingly cancelled the debts on those occasions upon which the financial burden on Barker became too much'? Barker was, too, 'a constant visitor' at the Shaws' house, treating it at times as if it were 'his own home'. As a special exhibit, Professor Salmon produces a civilian suit of clothes that Barker kept there during part of the First World War.

There is more evidence too: a photograph, for example, of Shaw and Barker sitting together in which they look 'serious and intense'. Why was this? Salmon advises us to cover with a hand Barker's hairline and consider whether he doesn't resemble Shaw at a similar age – an operation made rather cumbersome by his failure to include an early picture of Shaw. And there are still more tricks up

*Granville Barker: A Secret Life (1983).

his sleeve. When Barker played Tanner in *Man and Superman* he was made up to look like GBS – and succeeded! Was this coincidental? 'And one last point,' Salmon notes. 'Both men had red hair.' That surely should clinch it – but not quite. For their hair was 'of different shades, apparently'. That comma followed by 'apparently' seems sinister, especially when you take into account that GBS was a music critic and Barker's mother was fond of imitating birdsong. In a doubly pregnant paragraph Salmon explains that Shaw had come to London almost eighteen months before Barker was born. He often appeared at local concerts and occasionally accompanied his sister's singing at the piano. She also, let it be noted, had red hair. It was not unlikely, then, that Shaw dropped in to listen to a little bird-mimicry and found himself overcome by the charms of 'Miss Granville', as Barker's mother innocently styled herself. Here are the methods of Dr Watson at his best. Salmon owns that he can provide few reference notes as support and urges us to remember that this does not amount to conclusive proof. Nevertheless: 'It does suggest a reasonable possibility to which later events tend to give an additional degree of credibility.'

There is less credibility in these pages than credulity – a credulity that in a less blatant manner pervades the whole book. Salmon's thesis is interesting. He believes that, contrary to what was popularly supposed, Barker never deserted the theatre in the middle of his career. He simply 'moved into a different department of it'. His *Prefaces to Shakespeare* and other critical writings, together with his last unperformed plays, *His Majesty* and *The Secret Life*, were 'tied absolutely' to the theatre: 'The theatre is in the very life-blood of them and he writes, with modesty but with complete assurance, as a man of the theatre.' The most that Salmon will allow is that in the final decade of his life Barker began to 'despair of a theatre which seems incapable of providing him with the right kind of audience or the right kind of actors or the right kind of organisation for new plays of a really challenging kind'. Barker's sense of frustration with the contemporary theatre, Salmon believes, came from his 'blazingly uncompromising idealism'. Though he almost never entered a theatre for over a quarter of a century, he remained 'a complete *homme de théâtre*' in the sense that he was 'trying to transform the theatre into another form of art altogether, a form so tenuous that it could not live in the rough air of public performance'.

Though ill-equipped to deal with the ironies and inconsequences of life, Salmon is in some ways an appropriate critic for Barker. He has studied his work in detail, cares about it passionately, and devotes to it the kind of criticism that Barker himself directed at Shakespeare. He does not connect the writings to the life, which he deliberately makes 'secret' by omitting facts, but to the machinery of the stage. But since he has less theatre experience than Barker his criticism is correspondingly less sophisticated. The book reads more like a succession of lectures (he uses the word 'say' instead of 'write') or contributions to scholarly journals rather than an integrated single work. He refers to a photograph 'opposite page 18' of C.B. Purdom's biography of Barker, evidently unaware that it has already appeared in his own book opposite page 8. He frequently instructs us to 'note' this or 'notice' that as if we were in a classroom. In an attempt to tie the chapters together he switches us rapidly backwards and forwards: 'as has already been noted above', 'see, for example, pages 107 and 117 of this present book', 'which has already been mentioned in Chapter 6', 'as was mentioned in Chapter 8', 'something further will be said in Chapter 11', 'as was suggested in Chapter 7' and so on.

Barker's career was divided into three sections. About his abilities as an actor there need be no dispute. The best drama critics of the day – William Archer, Max Beerbohm and Desmond MacCarthy – all agree that, though he had a tendency to underplay some parts, he was a subtle and poetic performer with the ability to lift a whole cast. But he did not much enjoy acting. 'I do believe my present loathing for the theatre is loathing for the audience,' he wrote in 1918. 'I have never loved them.'

His achievement as a producer (what we would now call director) was more original and controversial. He revolutionised stage production in England by introducing the repertory system, eliminating 'stars' in favour of teamwork, and replacing the old actor-manager with the new director – 'the one person whose only job,' Salmon writes, 'was to co-ordinate the functions of all the others, to give pattern and coherence to the whole play, to conceive an over-all interpretation of the piece which would faithfully reflect the author's intention.' Actors sometimes found his instructions alarming. 'I want you when you enter to give the impression of a man who is steeped in the poetry of Tennyson,' he is reported to have told Dennis Eadie. His psychological approach very reasonably suggests to Salmon a parallel with Stanislavsky. But it is unfortunate, when establishing Barker's 'absolute faithfulness to the text of the play and the discernible intention of the author', to compare him with the man who mutilated Chekhov by tacking on to the text all sorts of ludicrous events (such as candelabra falling off the ceiling while people are dancing in *The Cherry Orchard*).

As a playwright Barker has often been compared with Chekhov, and it is here that his reputation is most in contention. The general opinion among theatre people was that Helen Huntington, a rich American divorcee with literary and social pretensions, made him throw over the stage after their marriage in 1918. She provided him with a luxurious style of life into which he could retreat and where he could compose unfinished and unperformed plays and academic papers about the theatre he almost never went to.

This picture of him, which was established in the public mind by C.B. Purdom, is energetically disputed by Salmon. He unfolds long plot summaries and generous extracts, and though his approach is completely different from that of Margery Morgan, whose interesting book *A Drama of Political Man* invites us to see Barker's heroes as reaching 'the fulfilment of their moral being in the public realm', he joins with her in challenging the theatrical neglect these late plays have suffered. His persistence and earnestness are impressive enough to establish, if not a favourable verdict, at least a prima facie case that should be tested by the National Theatre or the Royal Shakespeare Company, both of which have recently produced early Barker plays.

Salmon argues that Barker's characters move 'in a secret world of their own which their souls struggle to find and, having found, then defend as best they may against the tyrannies of both communal and domestic living, against the depredations of both public and private life. And the best defence, Barker's work constantly says, is secrecy.' In other words he searched for his identity through his work, which was given dramatic tension by a personality that today might be described as manic-depressive. Salmon's extreme critical sympathy evokes a good subjective description of Barker's guiding principles as a dramatist. Almost all the plays, he writes, chart 'the commerce between secrecy and sex and between both of them and the outside world'. *The Secret Life*, for example, brings together the two main instincts of Barker's world: 'the necessity of living alone and in secret; and the mysteriousness of the force of sex on the patterns of civilised living'. But though it is true that *Waste* 'is a play about sex', the dominant imagery (as Salmon concedes) is barrenness.

The central question arising from these last plays is whether they are sterile: stillborn and beautifully embalmed creatures of Barker's fastidious mind, conceived for a Utopian theatre of his imagination. 'Feel deeply enough to do desperate things – whether they're silly or whether they're mad,' says one of the characters in his unfinished play *The Wicked Man*. 'We could alter the world by Wednesday week.' The suspicion surrounding Barker that Salmon fails to dispel is that, lacking spiritual vitality, he never felt deeply enough. He sought protection from life – through a number of childless women in whom he prompted a maternal instinct; through the theatre itself, where he sought asylum from the world outside; and eventually in the Jacobean mansion into which he retired from the vulgarity of the contemporary stage.

It is not surprising that Barker should also have stimulated a feeling of protectiveness in literary critics. As his hagiographer, Professor Salmon cannot admit too many facts into his narrative. But he is an honest as well as a sentimentally generous critic and he cannot wholly overlook the unnourishing climate of unreality in which Barker spent his last thirty years. Between 1915 and 1923 he notes 'an increasing atmosphere of unreality, as if the sense and meaning of any artistic work could be retained only by an effort of the conscious will'. And between the early 1920s and the start of his comfortable rootless life in France and America in the mid-1930s,

Barker inhabited 'a kind of dream world' in a 'fairy castle' waited on by a staff of fifteen servants, including liveried footmen. 'There was, no doubt, something a little unreal about it all.'

At the conclusion of an obituary letter about Barker to *The Times Literary Supplement*, Shaw quoted Swinburne: 'Marriage and death and division make barren our lives.' Barker, too, as his moods of depression deepened, seems to have felt that his talent had been buried alive. 'My life is useless,' he admitted. But his admirers will be encouraged by this book to hope that the plays of his artistic maturity, with all their skill, idealism and self-exploration, will soon emerge from their silence and create their own world of reality in the theatre.

1983

'008'

Peter Fleming was as legendary a personality in the 1930s as his younger brother Ian became in the 1950s. Yet despite his guns and his work for British Intelligence, the Peter Fleming legend was a very un-James-Bond-like affair: more fiasco than fantasy.

As Duff Hart-Davis's *Peter Fleming* (1974) shows, he was a restless, open-air character, a Bulldog Drummond with a touch of Bertie Wooster, who launched himself into the sort of far-flung adventures that Rider Haggard might have invented. In the disastrous decade of the 1930s he became a hero embodying escapism and romance, keeping the frivolity of the 1920s remorselessly alive. But, to the objective eye, his exploits seem rather pointless. So many of these wild goose chases ended up as chases, almost literally, after wild geese.

The interest of his travels lies less in their achievements than in the incentive behind them. He had been born into a solid, spacious world of big houses patrolled by servants. Much of his childhood was infected by a mysterious psychosomatic illness – a protest, perhaps, against the lack of love within this rich and powerful family. 'I suspect,' he wrote, 'that my childhood ailments, and the semi-convalescence that followed them, helped to make me rather a solitary person and to immunise me . . . against the devastating pangs of loneliness.'

His father was a hero: a man of unscalable virtue, 'gay and gallant', as Winston Churchill called him, who, with blatant modesty and courage, always did the proper thing. In 1917 he made a brave, impeccable death at the front line, and was awarded a posthumous DSO.

Peter, aged ten, became 'head of the family'. Initially he had given way to grief, but once the shock wore off he acquired the self-control that passes for maturity. His emotional growth seems to have been halted by this tragedy. The spectre of his paragon of a father haunted him. His image, Peter wrote:

> was preserved solid and upstanding in the minds of his sons by our mother's strong love for him, reinforced by a sense of duty . . . which impelled her to keep him always in our minds. Sometimes she invoked him *in absentia* as an agent of discipline . . . but mostly she invoked him as an example, as an ideal to live up to.

Eve Fleming, Peter's mother, was a startling figure, clothed in garish fancy dress, who struck fantastic attitudes on the edges of sofas and chairs, and filled the drawing-rooms of the polite world with her confused ebullience. A dreadful source of embarrassment to her sons, she exercised on their behalf a ruthless sense of ambition.

To fashion a life removed so far as possible from this embarrassment yet that did no dishonour to his father, became the *motif* of Peter's life – and, in a more perverse way, perhaps, of Ian's, too.

Both of them flourished at Eton, Peter as a scholar, Ian as an athlete: and both of them treated life afterwards as a schoolboy's romp. Peter kept melancholy at bay by violent peregrinations round the world – tours which he converted into best-selling tours de force: *Brazilian Adventure, News from Tartary.*

His repeated complaint during an intensely active career was that nothing ever happened to him. In the sense that almost nothing touched him deeply, this was true. His emotions were so repressed, he appeared to live a superficial life where little was real. This unreality was best conveyed by his humour, sometimes facetious, always self-deprecatory and peculiarly English, that celebrates the pomposities and absurdities of the adult world where he finds himself on holiday.

'A good joke' was his highest term of praise, and he described his marriage to the actress Celia Johnson as 'the best joke so far'.

The war provided him with further opportunities for shining. But by 1945 the time for jokes seemed to have run out. His wartime career in deception made him a natural candidate for high political office, but he retreated to his home in Oxfordshire to play 'the squire', publish Fourth Leaders in *The Times* and become 'Strix' in the *Spectator*.

He enjoyed a late-flowering success with his military-historical books in the 1950s, and his life continued to reverberate to a phenomenal amount of shooting. It was appropriate that he should fall down dead of a heart attack, gun in hand and 'in cracking form', ghillies and stalkers to the right and left of him, and a covey of grouse departing into the distance.

He emerges from Duff Hart-Davis's biography as a well-mannered, rather empty man who pursued adventure so as to distract himself from inner tedium. It was his humour, delightful at its best, that saved him from tiresomeness.

It would have been fun to have written his biography in something of Fleming's own style, and to have made his life an entertainment. Duff Hart-Davis has resisted this. He uses language plainly and without pretension. It is only three years since Peter Fleming died and this may have restricted the publishable material. But he has told the story simply and produced an amiable book that is part biography, part geography – full of chaps and maps.

1974

PORTRAITS IN MINIATURE
The Dictionary of
National Biography

The short essay has been an even greater casualty over the last forty years than the short story. The age of *belles lettres* has vanished, passing decorously away with the death of E.V. Lucas before the Second World War. Of Lucas, in a previous *Dictionary of National Biography* volume, E.V. Knox wrote: 'He undoubtedly broadened the horizon of culture for a great number of readers by the easy introduction which he gave them to books that they would not otherwise have read, and pictures that they would not have seen; at the same time he helped to liberate the language of the critic and essayist from undue pendantry and affectation.'

I doubt if anyone would write of Lucas so optimistically now. His books are out of print; the general reader for whom he wrote has almost disappeared; and the language of criticism, seldom more obfuscated with pedantry, has retreated within the fortifications of our universities. But this is one of the problems of writing about people within twenty years of their death. It is difficult, as Knox acknowledged with Lucas, 'to estimate the permanent worth of his work'. This difficulty accounts for the omission of such people as Gerard Manley Hopkins, Gwen John and Wilfred Owen.

Untopicality is otherwise no bad thing in the essay. What is needed is a bedrock of fact (rigorously checked by the editors and their assistants) on top of which the most extreme personal opinions can flourish. This is what the *Dictionary of National Biography* sometimes provides and what still makes it potentially one of the best anthologies of the short essay.

A fine example in the present volume* is Kingsley Amis's rather dashing entry on Ian Fleming. In an age 'less rigidly hierarchical in its attitudes to literature', he writes, Fleming's spy thriller *Casino Royale* would have been 'hailed as one of the most remarkable first novels to be published in England in the previous thirty years'.

Another perhaps more unconsciously inspired selection of author and subject is provided by Anthony Blunt's piece on the artist, art dealer and intelligence officer Thomas Harris. Writing from private information and personal knowledge, Blunt describes Harris as gradually having freed himself from his commitment as dealer, to exercise his 'extraordinary imaginative power' in organising 'the most successful double-cross operation of the war'. Such a tribute will long be cherished for its irony.

In a different vein the choice of George Greenfield, a literary agent, to write on Enid Blyton, who 'did not use the services of a literary agent', was equally felicitous. From his 10-per-cent view, he writes enthusiastically that 'ten thousand words a day was a good cruising speed and she was known to complete a full-length book for children between a Monday and a Friday of the same week. So vast was her output that her books were rumoured to be created by a team of ghost writers.'

She was checked momentarily by the paper shortage of the war, but by the 1950s had assembled forty British publishers and 'became a major public figure with the creation of Little Noddy', largely because manufacturers had rushed to produce 'Noddy toothpaste, Noddy pyjamas and Noddy drawings on cereal packets'.

*E.T. Williams and C.S. Nichols (eds.), *The Dictionary of National Biography 1961–1970* (1981).

A few amiable errors have slipped in. If Sir John Rothenstein loses his head over the number of Augustus John's children, who shall blame him? And it adds to the book's charm to see Lloyd George's second wife represented as a man. Equally endearing are a number of obiter dicta, among which my own favourite is E.M. Forster's 'I warmed both hands before the fire of life. And put it out.'

A shortcoming of the *DNB* is that it will never reflect, for example, what we may learn of Oscar Wilde from the forthcoming biography by Richard Ellmann. One strength, however, is that it can indicate what we have missed through Mr Ellmann not having written his book on T.S. Eliot. His essay on Eliot achieves a wonderful balance of elegance and precision. Eliot, he writes, 'described the creative process as an escape from personality'.

The personality cult that Eliot believed threatened the twentieth century with a cultural breakdown is well illustrated by the progress of the *DNB*. The 'Note on Facts and Figures' that accompanied the 1951–60 supplement showed to what degree the standard celebrities were beginning to outnumber those who embodied the creative process – more politicians, sportsmen and members of the armed services than painters, novelists, sculptors, philosophers.

And it is the performers and administrators who increasingly dominate the arts – producers rather than playwrights; conductors rather than composers; publishers rather than poets. This tendency seems to have grown rather more extreme in this latest volume. Churchill is given forty-five columns and Attlee twenty – too many, I suggest, when compared with, say, Sean O'Casey or Joe Orton's two-and-a-half.

In his introduction, Sir Edgar Williams points to a new feature. Contributors have been able to write with greater freedom than in the past on the intelligence service and on homosexuality. This is certainly an advantage. But there is another difference between this volume and its predecessors.

In place of the uniform biscuit-coloured dust-jackets with their simple scarlet and brown typography, Oxford University Press has substituted on a chocolate background a multicoloured jumble of pictures. There is the Wyndham Lewis portrait of Eliot rejected by the Royal Academy, an almost unrecognisable picture of Bertrand Russell by Roger Fry, and a portrait of Churchill by Frank Salisbury not listed in the editor's Churchill entry. Finally, as if to emphasise this new preference for the image over the word, the selection of names has been moved from the front of the jacket to the back, and the life of the mind in Britain retreats one more step.

1981

ELIZABETH LONGFORD:
A TRIBUTE

It comes as something of a shock to learn that Elizabeth Longford did not begin her career as a historical biographer until her mid-fifties. How is it possible that, beginning so late, she was able to achieve so much, especially in the light of her claim never to have been 'a quick worker or a quick reader'?

From her early years she was possessed by a strong sense of destiny – what at the age of twenty-one she called 'an overpowering but inexplicable conviction that something unalterable had been mapped out for the future'. That map soon became crowded with events and experiences that broadened her knowledge of both domestic and public life, and deepened very remarkably her natural sympathy: all of which came to enrich her writing.

It was not obvious in the early years that she would be a writer. She seemed confronted by a bewildering series of choices. She had been born Elizabeth Harman, the eldest child of doctors (her father was a Unitarian opthalmic surgeon) in a London street of doctors, on 30 August 1906. At school, drawing was considered her main talent, though she herself announced at the age of twelve that she was going to be an actress. Sometimes it appeared as if she were actually trying to escape her destiny. 'English has proved a wash-out,' she wrote to her mother soon after reaching Oxford. 'I am going to read greats.' English, she felt, was something for women: she wanted the challenge of a 'man's subject'. At the Workers' Educational Association, its atmosphere of optimism tempered with hardship acting as a good corrective to the magical world of Oxford, she witnessed poverty and developed her interest in left-wing politics; at the London School of Economics she studied monetary rather than literary subjects.

But her passion for literature, diverted this way and that by many varied interests, proceeded from a strong source. 'I had played with words as soon as I could talk,' she wrote in her memoirs, *The Pebbled Shore*. As a child she read adventures, romances, histories. By the time she reached adolescence, poetry was beginning to form her secret world. She was also making her first attempts as a writer. When she was thirteen she completed a gothic novel, *On the Stroke of Twelve*, filled with the most voluble characters. In her early twenties she began a play with the somewhat philosophical title *The Absolute and the Absolutely-not or The Egg and the Ego*. But she was not ready yet to be a writer. That she did not eventually become either a novelist or a playwright she would later attribute to her preference for people who actually existed over those who might have been – and also to having suffered no unhappy love affairs.

At Oxford she was surrounded by what *Isis* described as 'a multitude of discerning admirers'. According to Evelyn Waugh, the future leader of the Labour Party, Hugh Gaitskell, invited her to dinner in Paris hoping to propose marriage, but at the last second the words failed him. Back at Oxford the warden of Wadham College, Maurice Bowra, was bolder. But though Bowra appeared to her like 'Voltaire and the Sun King rolled into one', she did not accept him. Hugh Gaitskell and Maurice Bowra were her chief mentors at Oxford, one heralding her towards a political career, the other towards an aesthetic life. But her future, which would incorporate politics with aesthetics, lay with Frank Pakenham, whom she married in 1931 at the age of twenty-five.

Could any historical biographer-in-the-making have chosen better? The second son of an Irish peer, Frank Pakenham may be said to have had an intimate as well as an aristocratic connection with the lineaments of British history, being descended from, among others, Charles II's mistress Barbara Villiers and the mistress of the Prince Regent, Lady Jersey, whose eldest Jersey grandson was to marry a daughter of that most sober of prime ministers, Sir Robert Peel.

Frank Pakenham's later conversion to Catholicism was to lead to his wife's conversion after the Second World War. But in the early years of their marriage it was she who converted him – from a Conservative to a socialist. Frank Pakenham, who later succeeded as the seventh Earl of Longford, was to have a distinguished career in politics, serving as personal assistant to Sir William Beveridge while he was producing his crucial report on social insurance, and also as lord in waiting to the King, minister of civil aviation, first lord of the Admiralty and secretary of state for the colonies – all of which gave his wife a front seat from which to observe the processes of contemporary history. Meeting one of her future subjects, Winston Churchill, at Chartwell in 1938, she wrote: 'I already had something of the biographer's natural interest in people and their families, and the memory of this glimpse of a famous family at home was to lie at the back of all my future encounters with them.'

It was as a crusader, whether against pornography or unjust imprisonment, that Frank Longford was to display his special qualities of courage, persistence, sincerity and a heedlessness of ridicule or unpopularity that, together with his lack of interest in appearances, would eventually endear him to the public as a prince of eccentrics. The private source of these public attributes Elizabeth Longford herself touches on with great sensitivity and insight in her memoirs.

Between the wars, though she was to contest Cheltenham for the Labour Party and stand as a Labour candidate for the King's Norton division of Birmingham, domestic life was gradually to take priority over her political activities. This was hardly surprising because, between 1932 and 1946, she was to give birth to eight children (four daughters and four sons). With the coming of grandchildren, her literary destiny would reach beyond herself: her family would produce an extraordinary library of biographies, detective fiction, history, novels and poetry.

After the Second World War, though she contested Oxford for Labour, her political interests began to express themselves more in journalism and this led her inevitably towards the pleasure of writing for its own sake. Her first work of history, written under the name Elizabeth Pakenham, was a meticulous investigation of the Jameson Raid of 1895–6 which had involved her great-uncle Joseph Chamberlain. She had wanted to write a biography of Chamberlain, but the papers not yet being available, the career of Elizabeth Longford, the biographer, was postponed until 1964, the year her celebrated *Victoria RI* was published.

I take an almost proprietorial interest in Elizabeth Longford's career because I have come to believe that she has been influenced by two of my own biographical subjects. Her father had begun taking her to the plays of Bernard Shaw at an early age, and by her twenties she was lecturing on GBS for the University Extension Course. Just as Evelyn Waugh assisted both her husband's and her own conversion to Catholicism, so it was the writings of Bernard Shaw, opening her eyes to much humbug on the professional face of Britain, that made Elizabeth Longford a socialist. Even before she became a Labour candidate, she saw herself potentially as a Shavian political woman, 'perhaps a mixture of Saint Joan and Major Barbara'.

She was also much influenced by Lytton Strachey, whose *Queen Victoria* she had been given as a school prize. Strachey's books liberated biography from its lapse into nineteenth-century sentimentality, and Elizabeth Longford, though never catching Strachey's habit of caricature, took advantage of that liberation. 'Thanks to Strachey,' she wrote, 'I never had to demolish the mental image of Queen Victoria as a frumpish mistress of a royal "we" who was neither amused nor amusing.' Strachey's *Queen Victoria* was the one biography of the Queen that she read before starting research for *Victoria RI* among the royal archives in the Round Tower at Windsor Castle. What Strachey gave her was not a debunking or iconoclastic attitude, but an informality that enabled her to get closer to her subjects and hold a balance between the contrary pulls of private and public life.

Like her husband, who entitled one of his autobiographical volumes *Five Lives*, Elizabeth Longford seems to have lived several lives before becoming an historical biographer. All those previous lives have come together and contributed to her writing life. The young artist has gone on to create a gallery of vivid historical pen portraits; the aspiring actress has become a biographer who, as it were, puts on the clothes and speaks the lines of her subjects in an exercise of imaginative empathy grounded on scholarship; the Oxford student who turned her back on 'women's subjects' such as English literature was to cross the gender line and take on 'men's subjects' such as Wellington, Churchill, Byron and Wilfrid Scawen Blunt; the near-novelist has embraced a literary form that, in its recreation of individuals through the magic of narrative, aspires to the condition of the novel; and the public figure who spent much time on the hustings, in committees, and later on radio and television has used all her experience to communicate eloquently through the written word.

To historical biography Elizabeth Longford has brought the highest standards of research, a skill at blending analysis with narrative, much fun, excitement and responsibility, and an unquenchable curiosity about her fellow human beings. But her outstanding gift is one of sympathy that creates an atmosphere in which her characters can breathe and come to life on the page. 'I believe biography chose me,' she wrote ten years ago. It was a perfect choice.

1996

LOITERING WITH INTENT

If everyone has a book in him, presumably it is an autobiography. 'All men, whatever their condition, who have done anything of merit,' wrote Benvenuto Cellini, 'if so be they are men of truth and good repute, should write the tale of their life with their own hand.'

Such might have been the motto of Sir Quentin Oliver, who, in 1949, forms his curious Autobiographical Association. Its members, all very important people, have agreed to write their memoirs and lodge them safely with the association for seventy years – so that no living person will be offended – after which they will be invaluable to historians. The trouble is that Sir Quentin is a most awful snob who seems to believe that talent can be conferred by title or acquired by inherited rank. None of the members, despite their social distinction, has any literary talent. This gives Sir Quentin's new secretary, employed to help with syntax, local colour, punctuation, style and other trivialities, the opportunity to enliven her office hours by introducing into these dreary narratives some episodes of honest invention.

For Miss Fleur Talbot is a character of altogether different persuasion. She is that dangerous creature, a novelist, working in 1949 on her first novel, *Warrender Chase*. She is convinced that Sir

Quentin has given these autobiographers disastrous advice: he has told them to be utterly frank – as if frankness had anything to do with truth. What is truth? she muses, and stops to answer thus: 'I could have realised these people with my fun and games with their life stories, while Sir Quentin was destroying them with his needling after frankness. When people say that nothing happens in their lives I believe them. But you must understand that everything happens to an artist; time is always redeemed, nothing is lost and wonders never cease.'

But why should writers of autobiography be inartistic? Perhaps most people are artists *manqués*, or in any event, vicariously artistic. For these memoirists, when presented with the opening chapters of their refashioned life stories, do not rebel. This having been tested, Sir Quentin takes over the job of helping these memoirs along. What sort of racket is he up to? Can it be blackmail? The only way Fleur can solve this mystery is to work out a conclusion through her creative imagination. This process begins to shape the material of her novel and provides a plot for Muriel Spark.

The theme of Muriel Spark's *Loitering With Intent*, its tension and design, are made from the conflicting disciplines of fiction and non-fiction. Sir Quentin's and Miss Talbot's aims are different, yet intertwined. He wishes to set the Thames on fire with tales of immoral happenings and to reach out and influence the writing of history. She seeks power and immortality by other means. Life, as she loiters through it, is to be distilled into fiction: that is her intent – to turn events and transform experience so that actual happenings, ordinary people, seem unreal in comparison with her mythology.

For both of them, the Autobiographical Association is a bale of straw from which to make their bricks. Since lies and inventions are part of life, fiction and non-fiction cannot be separated and presented as the truth. Why else would Sir Quentin, who suspects Miss Talbot of using her novel (like a witch's wand) to influence the future of his association, steal the proofs of *Warrender Chase* to use in his case histories? Why else would Muriel Spark choose the form of Fleur Talbot's autobiography in which to write her novel? Partly it is to give herself an ingenious technical problem, for she (like

Fleur) finds these problems of structure absorbing and inspiring to solve.

Loitering With Intent is a very clear novel that defends itself against many hypothetical criticisms by making the characters themselves address these criticisms to Fleur (who, we are further warned, always hopes that 'readers of my novels are of good quality'). If this novel seems to you light, or harsh, or amoral, or over-detached, then this perhaps is how it should seem, since it is ostensibly written by someone who is herself called harsh, who thinks of herself as detached, and whose writing never goes in for psychological motives but treats a story 'with a light and heartless hand, as is my way when I have to give a perfectly serious account of things'.

The members of the Autobiographical Association are instructed to follow the example of Newman's *Apologia*, with its accent on 'exposure'. Fleur Talbot's autobiography does not go in for exposure in any frank confessional way, but attempts through patterns of words to convey ideas of truth and wonder. She congratulates herself in retrospect on having failed to remind Sir Quentin of Proust's fictional autobiography. And here, perhaps, is the planted clue to what her inventor, the novelist Muriel Spark, has done in her succinct and oblique style. In which case, somewhere or other, some complementary work of non-fiction may exist. It would be typical of a biographer to quarry out such a thing.

1981

THE ENEMY WITHIN
Rebecca West

At the age of five Rebecca West's ambition was to become a successful general in the British Army. Instead she grew up to be what Virginia Woolf called 'a buffeter & a battler' in the ranks of English literature – someone who could 'handle a pen as brilliantly as I ever could', wrote Bernard Shaw, 'and much more savagely'.

But as Victoria Glendinning makes clear,* she was fighting herself a lot of the time. For she became two people: Cicely Isabel Fairchild, the daughter of lonely and incompatible parents, who saw herself as friendless and vulnerable, and who, being highly conservative, longed to win emotional security for herself through wealth and social prestige; and Rebecca West, the instantly successful Ibsenite pseudonym she chose for the militant feminist with socialist sympathies whose 'splendid *disturbed* brain' seemed in thrall to the kingdom of darkness.

'Reverential postures did not come naturally to Rebecca West,' writes Victoria Glendinning. In other words she was bloody rude. She needed enemies to quell the warfare within. Almost anyone would do as a target. Vera Brittain was 'a trumpeting ass'; W.B. Yeats

*Victoria Glendinning, *Rebecca West* (1987).

'an old fraud'; Strindberg 'could not write'; Ibsen 'cried out for ideas for the same reason that men call out for water, because he has not got any'; Tolstoy was 'a lonely zestless boring egotist who wanted to write a big book'. Yet she could be devastated by an unsympathetic review of herself. 'The literary world,' she exclaimed in astonishment, 'gets fuller and fuller of bitterness.'

Men provided the most welcome army of opponents. 'There is something so desperately unloveable, even unlikeable, about the male sex,' she wrote. Her first love affair was with H.G. Wells, 'the Old Maid among novelists', with whom she remained tempestuously involved for ten years. Her marriage in 1930 to Henry Maxwell Andrews, a merchant banker and winter sportsman who 'gave me a certain sense of security', was very much Cicely's choice and somewhat derided by Rebecca, who found him dull and slow. Perhaps it was merciful that he was also rather deaf. After almost forty years of marriage Cicely gave him 'a quite gorgeous funeral' but Rebecca confessed that she had 'never known anything as near happiness as the relief I felt when he died'.

Fortunately she took care that they had no children. Her one child was 'H.G.'s brat' Anthony, who had been brought up to call her 'Auntie Panther'. As an adult his feeling of persecution fed off hers, and their 'tragic rows', Victoria Glendinning writes, 'were to punctuate and poison the rest of their lives'. It was as destructive a way of passing these years, Rebecca acknowledged, 'as my worst enemy could have devised'. But the tragedy was that her worst enemy had been herself.

In a surprising passage Victoria Glendinning appears to admit that Anthony 'effectively demolished the reputation of his mother both as a writer and a human being'. What she has been able to resurrect is her reputation as an inspired, investigative journalist. Her attacks on Germany ('If only we had put every man woman and child of that abominable nation to the sword in 1919') and on communism united the respectable Cicely and the rebarbative Rebecca, giving the one money and the other exposure. She combined the gifts of a thriller writer and a popular preacher, and from feeling herself outside ordinary humanity came to be at the centre of events.

At the age of eighty-seven she is outside the Iranian Embassy in London counting the 'swaddled corpses' as they are lowered from the burned-out building.

Victoria Glendinning's achievement in this scrupulous and sympathetic book is to present Rebecca West as 'an agent for change and a victim of change' and to make the reader feel a tremor of admiration for the old dragon.

1987

H.G. WELLS

In his 'Experiment in Autobiography', H.G. Wells revealed that two years before he was born his mother had lost a favourite child, her daughter Frances. From this date, he thought, she had grown embittered, venting her suppressed resentment on him and opening an unhappy fissure in his character, one part of which was generous and sympathetic, the other nervously irritable.

From Norman and Jeanne MacKenzie's well-researched biography* a rather different explanation emerges. Sarah Wells, the daughter of an innkeeper, had developed a puritanical passion for religion. She was seldom happy outside church. Snobbish, full of anxiety and care, she had subsided, by the time Wells was born in 1866, into a depressing household drudge 'shod in old slippers and wearing a stuff dress with a sacking apron'. Her husband Joe was then a small shopkeeper in Bromley, presiding incompetently over a miscellaneous collection of old crockery – odd jam-pots and table-glass – and allowing the family finances to drift towards bankruptcy.

By temperament Joe was a romantic, restless and impractical, given to grandiose whims that were never put into action. He had

* *The Time Traveller: The Life of H.G. Wells* (1973).

been trained as a gardener, his wife as a hairdresser; but both had been miscast in their lives and were deeply at odds. The more dishevelled their marriage grew, the more voluminous was her criticism of his ineptitude; but the greater her criticism the more he lost confidence and the more his confidence faded the more anxious she became.

It was this perpetual conflict between his parents that was faithfully translated into Wells's nature. His early years were passed largely in the basement kitchen of their house with his mother and two brothers, while Joe Wells dashed desperately out to cricket matches. 'What a life this cricket making me a slave,' Sarah complained. It was a low, useless game 'merely for amusement'. In her own personality there was room for little amusement. Even her children were mainly a source of worry to her. As the youngest – petulant, physically small and never strong – Bertie was pampered by this anxious, unhappy woman, made to feel the need to 'get on', to assume in the house the role his father refused to play.

The death of her daughter Frances had become the focus of Sarah Wells's depression; it was not the cause. Of more significance was her decision in the summer of 1880 to leave Bromley and become housekeeper at Up Park, a grand house in Sussex. This supplied the upholstered sense of security that all her assiduous churchgoing had somehow failed to provide. But to Bertie it was a rejection that he bitterly resented. Sarah had needed to escape from what she called the 'miserable half living' at Bromley; but so had her thirteen-year-old son. It was not long before, contrary to her plans, he joined her at Up Park and became acquainted with all that fine foliage of pretences that makes up the structure of English society.

These were not happy years, but they were to prove useful to Wells as a novelist. His mother was determined to turn him into a chemist or a draper; drapery, in her scheme of things, was next to godliness. Driven to defend himself against her rigid assertion of authority, Wells developed a 'queer little mood of obduracy' that seemed essential to his survival. He read, absorbed knowledge prodigiously, passed examinations, made himself precariously free and self-supporting. But it was as if he needed his mother's opposing will to steady him, give him stamina. At the Normal School of Science in South Kensington, he came under the ideological influence of the biologist T.H. Huxley, but when Huxley retired due to ill health, Wells squandered his chances, becoming inattentive and undisciplined – and his dream of making a career as a scientist was shattered.

He thrived on bad fortune, could not adjust himself later on to the good times; they made him curiously uneasy. He had been caught by the magic of books during a series of illnesses when he would read everything within reach – travel, natural history, the adventures of explorers and generals. Much given to daydreaming, he would imagine how, were he another Cromwell or Napoleon, he would remake the world, spinning fantasies of victory over imaginary enemies. 'In fact Adolf Hitler,' he wrote many years later, 'is nothing more than one of my thirteen-year-old reveries come true.' It was when he tried to translate these fantasies into practice down among the Fabians that the trouble began. Like his parents, he had seriously miscast himself.

Norman and Jeanne MacKenzie's biography charts Wells's life with great exactitude. It is a sober, sensible account, full of insights, thoughtfully presented, well-structured, readable; a thoroughly good biography. The authors understand Wells; from good *New Statesman* stock, they understand too the junket of British politics. But they do not, I believe, understand literature so well and it is here that the only shortcoming of their book lies. What separates the journeyman from the creative writer, the MacKenzies explain, is symbolism. It was the 'symbolic power' of Wells's stories that enabled him to take 'literary London by storm'. What he was looking for in literature, his biographers insist, was 'a means of relating his own special experience to the norms of society'.

Encumbered with this belief in literature as a superstitious therapy, it is not surprising that the MacKenzies can find little room in their book for Wells's most imaginative work. They do not overrate his fidgeting on the periphery of politics, but because politics excites them it occupies an inordinate number of their pages. They examine too the utopias, encyclopaedias, the fantasies and fables, the scientific romances, the desperate repeated appeals for salvation that continued to pour from Wells year after year. But *Kipps* and *The History of Mr Polly* get a relatively poor showing. It is not that the MacKenzies fail to appreciate these books, but that they have not been able to fit them into their study of Wells as a 'time-traveller'. 'His gift for anticipating the future was indisputable,' they write. 'So was his capacity for cataloguing the ills of the world in passionate invective.' The combination of these two talents was the source of his influence. Wells and Bernard Shaw were rated as the most influential writers in the first thirty years of the twentieth century. But the core of Wells's influence lay in his inherited sense of insecurity, his anxiety, and the need he felt to escape from present-day reality – all of which found a sure echo in a country moving from solid Victorian traditions to the complex uncharted territory of the modern world. For Wells the enemy was always the present; the future was hope. He still saw himself as a frustrated man of action who would somehow change the world. He was applauded by others as a great prophet, foretelling the future; but his poetic genius was that of a great dramatic humorist in the Dickensian vein whose source of inspiration was his own past.

For all this 'time-travelling' Wells never escaped this past, though escape was at the centre of his politics and his romances. By intense activity he seems to have hoped to move out of earshot of the disharmony in his nature. For he externalised his difficulties, and in doing so spread havoc. As the MacKenzies show, his love affairs were usually disastrous because he could not enter other people's lives without looking for the exit, or without treating each loved one as a door leading out of someone else's world. The claustrophobia of marriage was only endurable for him after he set up an alternative household with some mistress; and between these two homes, linked with infidelities, he would violently oscillate. But always the disharmony grew louder as more and more voices joined the orchestra; for it was an extravaganza they were playing.

Wells was cut off from religion, which he saw simply as Church of England, by a reaction against his mother's depressing puritanical beliefs. And he was divorced by class prejudices from art and culture, believing them to be the academic pursuits of an Oxford and Cambridge élite. The rest was science. But all the money and fame it brought him, all the visions it suggested, could not obliterate the pain and distress of life. At the end, public affairs only irritated and disgusted him. There was no organisation of which he felt himself a part. 'This world is at the end of its tether . . . the end of everything we call life is close at hand and cannot be evaded.' Echoes of his own divided nature seemed to fill the world of his old age, and there was nowhere he could take refuge. For what he had done with his own internal contradictions was to broadcast them so that they multiplied; and what he had done with time, despite all his ability and charm, was finally to waste it. That, at least, was how it felt in ultimate despair.

1973

Autobiography, Diaries and Some Letters

BOUND UPON A COURSE
John Stewart Collis

'From the hour of my birth she hated me,' John Stewart Collis wrote of his mother. 'Ours was not a united family ... Beautiful as were the garden and surroundings at Kilmore, there was no peace or happiness to be observed or felt.'

Jack, as he was called, had been born at this house on the border of County Dublin and County Wicklow in 1900. His father was a Dublin solicitor, physically fearless but unadventurous in mind and spirit. 'My father did not get on with my mother and I do not recall a single pleasant hour they spent together in my life time,' Jack wrote in his autobiography. He respected his father but did not feel close to him. He could not feel close either to his sisters or to his elder brother Maurice, who was to become well known as an industrious non-fiction writer. In the neurotic family atmosphere 'a film of pain and bewilderment separated me from them'.

But he was emotionally tied to his twin brother Robert, later to become one of the world's leading paediatricians. A shadow, however, existed between them. Their birth had been a difficult one for their mother, late in her life, ending with severe labour pains, and Robert, the second twin, was born somewhat narcotised. When after a long struggle he started breathing and was handed to her, now changed from blue to pink, 'her maternal love poured out to me', Robert Collis wrote. 'The other twin, Jack, was forgotten and hardly seen for several days. From that moment she accepted me and rejected my brother.' Her exclusion of the elder twin from her life, like some motiveless malignity, was painful to see. 'I was never taken up in my mother's arms and kissed,' Jack wrote. He never received a word of endearment or an act of kindness from her. He learned to accept as normal her offers of second helpings at meals to Robert 'but not me', and her loving goodnights to him before she passed by his own bedroom without a word. 'She could not help herself.' His unhappiness was so penetrating that he suffered a virtual loss of memory before the age of nine.

His memory began when he left home for his preparatory school in Bray and his later schooling at Rugby in England. His formal education here was pitifully inadequate. 'I was a prime sample of classroom-fodder,' he admitted: 'unawakened, unoriginal, unprecocious.' In later years he would turn from an unquestioning victim of school knowledge into a passionate inquirer after personal knowledge. This process had already begun at Balliol College, Oxford, to which he gained entry with some judicious cheating at Latin Unseen. Here he perfected a technique for discovering something valuable within a system that was largely useless to him. He had already fallen under the spell of Shakespeare and been beguiled by the word-music of Tennyson. He also taught himself to understand the principles of prose structure by reading Macaulay. Above all things he warmed to the spoken word. 'I hankered after oratory,' he remembered. The chief gain he derived from Oxford was the practice of public speaking and the acquiring of a style. At the Oxford Union he heard Asquith, Chesterton, Lloyd George and W.B. Yeats speak, and also scored many oratorical successes himself.

After coming down from Oxford he briefly entered a theological college. In his dreams, he imagined himself a great preacher. But there had been another process at work in him. Riding his motor bicycle into the countryside each afternoon to examine his faith, he discovered that 'the more I looked at Nature, the less I needed theology. The more I loved the fields and skies the less I liked Doctrine.'

In London he managed to supplement an annual allowance of £150 from his father by writing for A.R. Orage's *New English Weekly* and Lady Rhondda's *Time and Tide*, as well as by teaching for the Workers' Educational Association and the Extra-Mural Department of the University of London. Much of this time he passed at the British Museum Reading Room where he continued the process of self-education and the search for a satisfying philosophy of life.

He also married. 'I met my wife in London and got married after a week.' But their married life with two daughters was oppressed by poverty during the 1930s. 'The financial problem was so appalling and so humiliating,' he records, 'that I could not even look at the flowers in spring so much did bills come between me and them.' His position was all the worse because he had been confident of success after the appearance of his first book, a perceptive study of Bernard Shaw, whose work had become an 'inspiration to me' and whom he elected as a spiritual father. This had been published in 1925 and was well received. But his subsequent books over the next fifteen years, which included a dramatic dialogue, an autobiographical novel, a work of philosophy and a literary pilgrimage round England, were largely ignored. They all testify to Collis's rigorous programme of reading, an untiring quest to find his own voice, and the form in which to use it.

The most interesting of these early books is *An Irishman's England* (1937). 'Isolation is the norm,' he wrote. But we, the readers, invisibly accompany him along his solitary way. There is no Beatrice to guide him. If he has any guide it is 'a man born almost dead' who is often near but whose name, Samuel Johnson, is never spoken or written down. The book contains several fine set pieces: on Kipling and India; on Armistice Day ('I happened to rise from the underground at Trafalgar Square . . . The Lions had practically disappeared – all except their heads had sunk beneath the crowd'); on the General Strike of 1926 ('I occasionally asked someone whether he did not think that the miners were in the right. I soon gave it up, for such a question caused visible embarrassment'); and on the Hunger Marches of the 1930s ('a thick river of men . . . flowed on for over an hour . . . I climbed down from my view-point . . . I was in the company of men who were doomed to live without routine, without purpose, without order, without enough to eat . . . I looked beyond the massed Marchers to the top of Marble Arch – a gateway leading to nowhere'). He writes as one whose self-employment too may be obliterated leaving him also without destination.

His place of self-employment was the round Reading Room of the British Museum. We see him there among the scholars and eccentrics. But which is he? He is neither. For he is an original. This is his home and his asylum. He works in company with desperate people: the 'small thin man' who 'takes innumerable notes in microscopic note-books until at last he walks with his head bent forward at a shocking angle'; the 'strange frock-coated gentleman who is unable to work for more than quarter of an hour at a stretch without getting up and talking to someone' before returning to work on his Chinese texts; the 'negro who studies Latin grammar'; the man who enters the Reading Room 'clothed only in a loin-cloth' and 'the man who went out carrying one of the chairs on his back'; 'the reader wearing rubber gloves and with a perforated enamelled mug strapped to his mouth' and 'the heavily veiled lady who used to raise her veil at intervals to stick a piece of stamp-paper on the end of her nose'. But, he concludes triumphantly: 'they are not excluded'.

Collis, too, had found a place of inclusion. *An Irishman's England* is his pilgrim's progress. He listens to the babel of voices at Speakers' Corner. 'Nearly all the speakers are talking about religion,' he writes, 'and the matter of their discourse is often incredibly puerile. There they stand, a long row of them, every day of every week, month after month and year after year, lifting up their voices. It is the voice of England that is being lifted up.' But is there any place for his own voice in this democratic hubbub? One man holds his attention.

I turned up one evening to find a beginner standing on his little ladder facing an audience composed of one. On each side of him a large crowd had gathered to hear another speaker. How then would he succeed in getting his audience? I wondered. He was a young man of about twenty-five, healthy-looking, and wearing an open collar and shorts . . . I moved off to listen to other speakers, but always found myself fascinatedly drawn back to watch this young man. He was not doing well. At one time his audience increased to three, but when I returned for the last time it had decreased again to one. He did not give up. Though very red and hot, he still preached on; and as I finally turned out of the Park away from the whole strange scene, I could still hear him answering his one heckler in clear loud tones to convince the great audience which was not there.

That young man is Collis's alter ego, and the questions he asks of him he must often have asked himself. But this book also provides some answers. For there are moments in *An Irishman's England* when Collis finds his voice and uses it eloquently. One supreme moment occurs on Hampstead Heath. 'Every year an elaborate Fair is held on Hampstead Heath. The latter is one of the most beautiful places in the world – and a typically English gesture,' he writes.

It is not a heath. It is a big stretch of wood and meadow land, a piece of the ancient countryside with hills and vales. London beats upon it from all sides . . . The overwhelming appeal of Nature at Hampstead Heath would be impossible without the existence of London beating upon it . . . From this green hill of hope we get a view of ultimate harmonies on a scale impossible to conceive elsewhere.

One Easter I stood on a slope in the blue of the evening haze. As I did so there reached me, not from above but from below, from beneath the soil, a strong, cold whiff of Spring, the *odour* of resurrection.

Passing on I rounded a corner and came upon a remarkable sight. In a small valley below dwelt a miniature city. It was glowing with stationary and moving lights, and sending up peals of gaiety and music. All was gladness down there, it seemed, a whoop of praise reaching to the sky. A thick mist nowhere else on the Heath had filled the valley and wrapped the town as in a shawl. The lights and movements in that mist belonged to fairyland and bore no relation to the life outside. The little city had evidently been let down from heaven in that shawl, and soon would be drawn up again.

Then I realised that it was connected with us. It was a fair, an Easter Festival. It was a gathering of men, now again as in ancient times, to celebrate the pleasures of revival, the joy in our annual resurrection from the dead.

Though Collis came down from his hill to find, in the fierce cynicism of the town below, with the mechanical music of its fairground and its threatening 'Wall of Death', its offerings of whelks 'spread with vinegar and steeped in gall', a very obvious place of punishment, he would remember that 'overwhelming appeal of Nature on Hampstead Heath' and see it as a sign on his quest.

In the Second World War, when his wife and daughters were evacuated to the United States, he began to work as an agricultural labourer. During this farming experience he gained the maternal love he needed from the land. 'I had got what I wanted at last,' he wrote, 'a complete participation in the ordinary work of the world.' It was as if a state of wellbeing, native and near to him, from which he had been mysteriously cut off, suddenly enveloped him.

These years marked a turning-point in Collis's career. 'I had a great literary chance to bring together the Fact, the Idea, the Process and the Person,' he wrote. 'Here was material upon which I could impose form.' The great work he fashioned from these experiences united his psychological and physical needs with the knowledge and training he had gained from the British Museum. 'The Reading Room days had not been entirely barren,' he was to write. 'There also I had sown; there also I had reaped to some extent.' But it was also true, as Richard Ingrams comments in his affectionate memoir of Collis, that until 1940 he 'bore the marks of someone who had spent too much time in the British Museum Reading Room, whose ideas about nature were derived, in part, from books by fellow writers. Now he found himself in the open, face-to-face with the rough reality.'

The Worm Forgives the Plough is the collective title Collis eventually gave to the two volumes, *While Following the Plough* and *Down to Earth*, that arose from these years. 'To work as a labourer on the land (not as a responsible farmer) had become a great desire of mine,' he explains. He swept away considerable obstacles and in 1940 went to live 'with my beloved dog Bindo' in an empty house in the far corner of a farm at Stonegate on the border of Kent and Sussex. The year he spent working here for J.G. Maynard forms the first part of *While Following the Plough*. Overcoming still more Hills of Difficulty, he then achieved his ambition to be a ploughman by going to a farm at Tarrant Hinton, near Blandford in Dorset. Gore Farm, which 'was one of the most difficult I could have found any-where and on that account one of the most interesting', became the subject matter of the second part of this volume. Throughout these farming years he kept a diary and his habit of writing down what had happened at the end of each day helped to give this work its authenticity and vividness.

Nevertheless twelve publishers turned it down and even Jonathan Cape, which did accept it, demanded revisions. Richard Ingrams records that Collis was proud of the tactics with which he fended off this criticism. After an interval he returned the manuscript pretty well unaltered. But he thanked Cape for the substantial amend-ments they had suggested, and Cape replied that they were 'delighted with the improvements'.

While Following the Plough was published in 1946, *Down to Earth* in 1947, and the two were brought together as *The Worm Forgives the Plough* in 1973. Acclaimed on their appearance, they have now become recognised as classics. Before his death in 1984, Collis would sometimes revisit the farms and woods of the war years. 'I go past fields in all of which I have had business,' he wrote; 'I go through Tarrant Gunville and up to my wood and see how it is going on, and it always has gone on; and then up to the high road towards Shaftesbury till I come opposite Gore Farm and see my long field. There I stop – amazed that I can say, "I have ploughed that field."'

In the late 1940s, after his wife and two daughters returned from the United States, Collis reluctantly came in from the country and recommenced family life. They lived at Carshalton, near Queen Mary's Hospital for Children, where his wife, a remarkable physiotherapist, now worked. Over this period, his career took second place to hers. 'I ceased to believe in my stuff,' he wrote. It was a wretched marriage sustained for the benefit of the children, who left home as soon as they were able. Then at last husband and wife were free to separate, and would have done so (she had a lover at the hospital) had she not in 1957 suffered a paralysing stroke. For the next dozen years, in an atmosphere of extreme bitterness fired by her frustration, he looked after her until her death at the end of the 1960s. Against this background, he wrote his devastating studies of Strindberg's, Tolstoy's and Carlyle's marriages.

Though he was to write other books about natural phenomena – trees, light and water, the human body (*Living With a Stranger*) – most of his books during the last twenty-five years of his life were biographies: besides his books on Carlyle, Strindberg and Tolstoy, the Lives of Havelock Ellis and Christopher Columbus, which may be read as metaphors for his own elaborate journey of self-discovery.

Collis was not an easy man, he was naturally awkward; he was not noticeably practical, but he had curiously good sense. He excelled at showing people what they already knew, or thought they knew until he made them see that they had merely taken it for granted. He had the childlike ability to see things as if for the first time, and the literary skill to make his readers rediscover the strangeness of the commonplace.

Though admired by other writers, he seemed destined to be categorised as an ingenious populariser who had a growing but never large or immediate readership. 'I have no doubt that future generations will see Collis as one of the most important and interesting writers of the twentieth century,' wrote A.N. Wilson in his *Spectator* obituary. But such recognition did not come to him in his lifetime. At the end of *Down to Earth*, having cleared and thinned an ash wood in Dorset for a forester, Rolf Gardiner, he wrote his farewell.

I look across at the growing and maturing trees now free from all entanglements . . . as far as I can see in any direction, a free plantation meets my eye, accomplished by the labour of my hands alone. Nothing that I have ever done has given me more satisfaction than this, nor shall I hope to find again so great a happiness. Realising something of what the work meant to me, and perhaps truthfully saying that he was very pleased with the result, Rolf entered this area of about twelve acres, in the books of the Estate, as COLLIS PIECE, and by that name it is now known. Thus then do I achieve what had never occurred to me could conceivably happen, that a piece of English earth and forest would carry my name into the future. Nobody is ever likely to confer upon me Honours or Titles or City Freedoms, nor will any Monument be raised to perpetuate and repeat my name. But this plot of earth will do it, these trees will do it: in the summer they will glitter and shine for me, and in the winter mourn.

1988

OSBERT AND OTHERS

The life of Sir Osbert Sitwell, who died in 1969 aged seventy-six, may seem remote to many readers today. Nothing would have delighted him more. For he strove to be remote from our age of 'the Common Man', and to make his remoteness richly enjoyable. Like a modern Columbus, he sailed across exotic seas in search of an Old World where he felt more at home. His books, in particular his multi-volume autobiography, beginning with *Left Hand, Right Hand!* chart these explorations in detail and celebrate the virtue of his discoveries.

The Sitwells (all three in one) were a splendid ornament of the Edwardian Age and of the 1920s in Britain. Though masquerading in the most aesthetic way as rebels, they were not politically rebellious. The modern political climate that sharpened or blighted the prose style of so many writers left the orchidaceous Sitwellian bloom untouched. In London, Sitwellism became a cause without a rebel. Edith, Osbert and Sacheverell were seen as a 'nest of tigers', but more for their feline grace and fine markings than for any innate savagery.

In *Who's Who* Osbert set out their programme:

For the past 30 years has conducted in conjunction with his brother and sister, a series of skirmishes and hand-to-hand battles against the Philistine. Though outnumbered, has occasionally succeeded in denting the line, though not without damage to himself. Advocates compulsory freedom everywhere, the suppression of Public Opinion in the interests of Free Speech, and the rationing of brains without which innovation there can be no true democracy.

What infuriated people was the Sitwell genius for self-advertisement, particularly Dame Edith continually confronting them with her poems of colour and sound (but where in God's name was the sense?) which reverberated through the halls and galleries of London.

The figure of Sir Sacheverell, architecturally wandering after nuns, monks, monasteries and other impedimenta of remote times, troubled Britain's puritans less keenly. But Osbert attracted enemies. He was the leader of the triumvirate. In the age of I.A. Richards and F.R. Leavis, it was not difficult to dismiss his squibs and satires, balnearics, inquilics as antiquated trifles. His tirades and panegyrics were never taken seriously at universities, and he was seen as an embodiment of obsolete *belles lettres*. What had he ever done except, in the false dawn of the Great War, within *Wheels* and at the Chenil Gallery, seen off a few emasculated Georgians with some barking-without-bite?

It was characteristic of such a man that his most sustained and expansive literary work should have been an autobiography – that growth of literature at which the English have excelled but have seldom valued. He was nearing fifty when, 'in the cruel and meaningless epoch behind the bars of which I now write', he began on this elaborate journey. It was to be his masterpiece, 'a work of art, upon which I can expend not only such gifts as I possess, but the skill acquired through many years of labour at my task'.

Like a great opera singer prodigiously controlling his breath, he delivered the rich rigmarole of his sentences, with heroic parentheses, stately asides, to safe grammatical, elegantly rhythmic culminations.

The tone, if not sanguine, was high-spirited, buoyed up with all the undismayed vitality and humour at his command. He laboured to ensure that it would not be an improving book, but beguiling, extravagant, valiantly old-fashioned. 'I want this to be *Gothic*,' he wrote, 'complicated in surface and crowned with turrets and with pinnacles, for that is its nature.'

In his introduction, Osbert likened his autobiography to a surrealist painting. I see it rather as a vast mediaeval tapestry. But what is this fabulous gothic creature over six feet tall that moves so rapidly across those woven vistas of pedigrees and coats-of-arms, long-tailed, black-waistcoated, its supple beard recording each delicate shift of mood as, with telescope and umbrella aloft, it promulgates 'a boat of stone upon the lake, or a dragon in lead writhing for a quarter of a mile through its level waters, or a colonnaded pavilion'?

Reader, it is his father.

Osbert paid his father the compliment of making him one of the most exorbitant eccentrics in literature. But I suspect that Sir George Sitwell, who knew of the literary man's requirements for extreme parentage and who allowed vigorous seasons for practical joking, sometimes engineered these feats for his children's benefit.

Some modern critics have suggested that an edited version of this massive digression of an autobiography would now read better. The five volumes (together with a postscript, 'Tales My Father Taught Me') contain pages of emotional congestion, stilted passages, *longueurs* where the peculiar locutions endemic in Sitwellism have failed. Nevertheless I disagree with these critics. No writer can be too particular over his faults. Only a pedagogue judges books by their perfection: a perfect corpse never puts a foot wrong. The faults of Osbert Sitwell's autobiography were part of the author's nature: they do not impede the quality of a work that, having achieved total irrelevance to contemporary life, can now be enjoyed to perfection.

Like a will with many codicils, his life has become involved after his death with new publications. *Queen Mary and Others* is a selection of minor Sitwelliana, some of which appeared in *Pound Wise* (1963). Though these essays cannot compare with, as Sir Harold

Acton puts it, 'his longer-winded prose', they all have the authentic Sitwell flavour. That stately tone, with its discreet irony, is well attuned to a subject such as Queen Mary. Her small formal world which, even in her prime, must have appeared curiously old-fashioned, is beautifully evoked. She was so robustly antiquated that time seemed to travel backwards whenever she made her appearance. A 'faint odour of ex-officio immortality' enveloped her, so that any illness came as a shock, as at some monstrous reversal of nature. At all moments she remained magnificently irrelevant to her surroundings and to the ordinary conditions of the country. In the Second World War, as Osbert Sitwell records, she took up with enthusiasm the national campaign to collect scrap:

> If she found a piece of bone deposited by a fox, or a fragment of old iron, she would at once pick it up and hand it, usually to a somewhat reluctant lady-in-waiting, to take home; though on one occasion I had to carry a really filthily dirty old glass bottle for several miles. Queen Mary's fanatical collection of scrap continued until the end of the war . . . one fine spring noon Her Majesty returned to the house in triumph after a walk, dragging behind her a large piece of rusty old iron to add to the royal dump. A few minutes later, however, one of her pages brought an urgent message from a neighbouring farmer. 'Please, Your Majesty, Mr Hodge has arrived, and he says Your Majesty has taken his plough, and will Your Majesty graciously give it back to him, please, at once, as he can't get on without it.'

No one was better qualified than Osbert Sitwell to appreciate the pure absurdity and disarming uselessness of such a life, or to orchestrate it, by his elaborate wit, more fittingly. From his meetings with Queen Mary, he creates a sumptuous comedy that exalts the unassailable redundancy of her career. The life she so rigidly led belonged to a past that had flourished 'before democracy swept Britain bare like a tide'. Like Osbert Sitwell himself, she was stranded in the twentieth century; but, also like him, she rose on wings of fantasy above its featureless uniformity.

Osbert Sitwell's natural allies were oddities. There is a splendid collection of them in this volume: from the man who met a strange death by sawing off the branch of a tree on which he was standing, to the stout woman who 'rang the front-door bell, and when I answered it, put her foot between the jamb and the door so as to prevent my shutting it, and demanded that I should take down in embroidery . . . colours that she would sing to me and, at this point, she burst into loud, unbidden song'. She is like a reflection of his sister, Edith.

Under Osbert Sitwell's florid treatment, the twentieth century becomes a foreign country, not much worth visiting. In its place, he spreads before us an imposing landscape, bathed in flawless sunlight, where strange creatures, both man and beast, riotously sport. In this kingdom of his imagination, rich in reverberating syllables, he has flung down the tycoons from their seat and raised up the obsolete in their place.

1975

Son and Father
J.R. Ackerley

As well as one play, some poems and a memoir of E.M. Forster, J.R. Ackerley also wrote four autobiographical books – all of them much praised by distinguished writers. In 1961 his novel *We Think the World of You* won the W.H. Smith Literary Award – it was, Raymond Mortimer wrote, 'a miniature masterpiece that will become a classic'.

Why then are his books – four or five of them in Christopher Isherwood's opinion masterpieces – mainly out of print and his name so little known to the reading public? Neville Braybrooke's interesting edition of *The Letters of J.R. Ackerley* (1975) suggests several answers.

These letters, which tell the story of Ackerley's career as editor and writer, his travels and friendships, complement the candid account of his family, his early homosexual adventures, and his experiences in the First World War which he gave in his autobiography *My Father and Myself*.

At Cambridge, where Ackerley paraded himself as 'free, proud and intellectually unassailable as a homosexual', he was (so he later acknowledged) 'profoundly riddled with guilt'. Tall and golden-haired, 'elegant to the point of dandyism, and fine-featured', as

William Plomer described him, with his expensive corduroys, voluminous black cloak and flowered waistcoats he attracted a good deal of admiring attention. 'I wish to God I had your looks,' a friend remarked. 'I'd have a love affair with anyone I wanted.'

With the problems of the rich and good-looking it is sometimes arduous for the rest of us to sympathise. Ackerley's advantages seemed to afford him little happiness. His literary talent thrived on misfortunes and crises.

In the First World War he had been wounded – 'the wound is not bad, but inconvenient, being in the bottom' – and led 'limping off into captivity, at bayonet point'. This experience was to provide material for his play *The Prisoners of War* – 'the most painful play I have ever seen', Siegfried Sassoon called it, 'and one of the most impressive'.

After the war, the good times revived and Ackerley languished among some unsuccessful Jamesian stories and an incomplete verse play about a fifteenth-century Milanese despot. It was E.M. Forster who came to the rescue by persuading him to go to India as companion-secretary to the Maharajah of Chhatarpur.

'Alan Quartermain has arrived,' he announced, looking wonderfully spruce in one of his 'new biscuit-coloured suits'. His letters from India, published in this book, reveal his gradual disenchantment – the dreadful Anglo-Indian women, the Maharajah's pathetic plainness, everyone's blind obedience to authority, the sickly atmosphere of intrigue.

'One wearies of it and yearns for vigour of mind,' he wrote to Forster. Though he gained no stability from this 'lifeless period', he had assimilated enough disillusionment for another literary work, his journal *Hindoo Holiday* – a book over which it was 'difficult to control one's enthusiasm', commented Evelyn Waugh, 'and to praise temperately'.

But good fortune soon struck again, and he retreated in 1927 into the BBC as a director of talks. Two years later his father died. Attached to his will, Ackerley found some correspondence disclosing that his father had kept two households and that most of his money had disappeared in providing his second 'wife' with a house and his three girls by this liaison with an education.

'This house of cards has indeed come tumbling about my ears with Dad's death,' he confessed to Forster. From this collapse he eventually constructed *My Father and Myself*, one of the most original autobiographies ever written. It was, he explained in one of these letters, an 'examination of his life and character, and of my own, to try to understand why we had so little confidence in each other, friendly though we were, and did not share each other's secrets. He led a double life . . . and so did I.'

From then on he could have attracted all the difficulties his talent could cope with. But his nerve failed and he retreated further into the womb of the BBC.

Between 1935 and 1959 he worked as literary editor of the *Listener*. The excellence of much of the BBC depends on people of Ackerley's calibre going there, yet it is impossible not to regret that he did so. His trials as a literary editor were partly artificial ones and, so far as his writing was concerned, sterile.

'How can you write when you have nothing to say?' he asked Herbert Read. The *Listener* – 'a paper on which I have rested too long and for which I have never had any great regard' – gave him the self-forgetfulness that can come from professional competence. In retrospect, regretting that he had never relinquished his salary for a freelance life, he was filled with 'a horror-feeling' over the waste.

If the *Listener* was the night in his creative firmament, when nothing grew, the love that developed in him for his Alsatian bitch Queenie was the day. Love, like a sense of humour (which he also had) complicates life devilishly, and from these complications came two remarkable books, *My Dog Tulip* and *We Think the World of You*. Both of them, clinical, amusing, 'indecent', examine mankind's oldest friend as if it were a new species.

Though puffed by the critics, these books had for the most part only a small public. 'It is a pity that sales and praise do not always go hand in hand,' he lamented. He was not sentimental, he did not flatter the reader. He believed that some people ought to be upset: 'I am not anxious to spare the feelings of the Philistines.' The description he once applied to a friend might also fit him: 'A man trying to be honest in a world of liars.'

Ackerley had a distaste for the limelight, but even before his death at the age of seventy in 1967 there was almost no literary limelight to avoid. If the readership of the *Listener* is any index, the reading public has shrunk since the pre-television era of the 1930s and 1940s to less than half its former size.

Since Mr Braybrooke is far too assiduous an editor to overlook such things, we must assume that Ackerley was offered no honour of any kind for services to literature after twenty-five years as an outstanding literary editor of the *Listener* – a nice example of the state's indifference to the arts.

The public tends to favour the prolific writer, and to read an author, not a book. Ackerley was a perfectionist, always seeking the just form, the exact word, right tone. But his immaculate prose originated in a lack of confidence, not in any relish for life on which he had 'no very passionate grip'. His books, like some eighteenth-century furniture, have a structural perfection; but they sometimes lack the narrative pull and warmth that come from a zest for living.

In retirement the darkness descended and the fumes of alcohol rose to meet it. Yet though he complained of the ghastliness of the world and of his self-dislike, though 'I am far more interested in animals now than I am in people,' Ackerley was no misanthrope and preserved, as these letters show, a number of enviable friendships.

From this correspondence, in particular there comes a tenderness not always exhibited in his books. He was an excellent letter-writer, and a debt of gratitude is due to Neville Braybrooke for producing such a worthwhile volume.

1975

ANTHONY POWELL

On several occasions in early childhood, Anthony Powell tells us, he was conscious of approaching the brink of some discovery. One afternoon in about 1911, when he was five or six, standing outside the door of his London home, 'the truth came flooding in with the dust infested sunlight', he writes. 'The revelation of self-identity was inescapable. There was no doubt about it. I was me.'

This parody of self-awareness, though amusingly described, leads nowhere. The Anthony Powell of this first volume of memoirs,* which ends with his leaving Oxford in 1926, remains as self-effacing a presence as Nick Jenkins, the central character of his twelve-volume sequence of novels *A Dance to the Music of Time*. Obliged for a few moments to contemplate himself, he is at a loss to account for his existence. 'Why, one wonders, did it all come about?' he asks, this journey 'tackled under the momentum of a slow pace, lowish blood pressure, slightly subnormal temperature'. It is Anthony Powell's achievement to have made such an unpromising journey into a dance of the most ingenious entertainment.

*Infants of the Spring: The Memoirs of Anthony Powell (1977).

He has given these memoirs a collective title of wry modesty, *To Keep the Ball Rolling*, which suggests that, with their similar pace, tone and rhythm, they will form a coda to the novel. The quotation comes from Conrad's *Chance*: 'To keep the ball rolling I asked Marlow if this Powell was remarkable in any way. "He was not exactly remarkable," Marlow answered with his usual nonchalance. "In a general way it's very difficult to become remarkable. People won't take sufficient notice of one, don't you know."'

His parents had nothing in common except their ability for taking little notice of their son, who came to feel closer to a number of mediaeval Welsh ancestors than to his father, a military gentleman of foaming and cantankerous temper, or to his mother, who busied herself mildly with good works. Of their decision not to send him to a preparatory school where one of the boys had been injured by the headmaster, he comments (characteristically in parentheses) that 'nothing much short of loss of a leg would surely have been noticed'. Such is his fastidious lack of self-pity, and the excellent polish and patience of his punctuation, that we are made to feel nothing worse than humorous appreciation.

At Eton, he ponders amiably over his school reports: 'a little apart from other boys but I think they respect him'; 'his quiet reserve and dignity may prevent him having any strong influence with others'; 'a cold superiority or frame of mind too judicial. It may of course be simply due to shyness.'

Or, more probably, due to a lack of self-esteem instilled by his parents' indifference. Powell's method of adapting himself to his past neglect has been subtle and vicarious. At both Eton and Oxford he pursued his unobtrusive way as a passionate observer, apparently invisible to others, who nevertheless found himself in company with some of the most remarkable people of his generation.

Powell excels at his portraits of these contemporaries. Here is George Orwell, looking 'rather distinguished' in his tattered tweeds, his voice a curious rasp, his moustache (a concession, perhaps, to dandyism) provoking 'thoughts of France', who emerges as a curiously complicated man, ambitious yet unworldly, sceptical yet given to self-dramatisation, fond of seeing himself as a man of action, thriving only in comparative adversity. 'Like most people "in rebellion" [Orwell] was more than half in love with what he was rebelling against. What exactly that was I could never be sure.' Here too is the extravagant aesthete-homosexual Brian Howard, reputedly the original of Evelyn Waugh's Ambrose Silk, who, 'in spite of modishly intellectual fireworks in conversation', comes through as a preposterous adman manqué, 'the essence of that self-propagation for its own sake which has nothing to do with creative ability'.

We see the hypnotic, alarmingly omniscient Cyril Connolly, whose face, though it appeared to have been kicked by a mule, became such a perverse feature in the elaboration of his personal myth, 'one of those individuals – a recognised genius – who seem to have been sent into the world to be talked about'. And there is the unpredictable Evelyn Waugh, so intensely funny when drunk, though disillusioned with human conduct when sober and given to fantastical hatreds; Henry Green, a novelist who leaned towards obscure diction, famous (like the equally elusive William Gerhardie) for being under-rated; the Acton brothers, like understudies to the Sitwells; the rackety Duggan brothers, stepsons of Lord Curzon. Among the many others relentlessly and hilariously remembered was Maurice Bowra – 'noticeably small . . . [he] looked a little like those toys which cannot be pushed over because heavily weighted at the base: or perhaps Humpty-Dumpty, whose autocratic diction, and quickfire interrogations, were also paralleled'.

Powell himself moves imperceptively from the isolated child through a period as potentially bright schoolboy on to a slightly dazed undergraduate. The book ends with him coming down from Oxford equipped with a Third and ready to 'dive head first into the opaque waters of London life'.

'More often than not,' he writes, 'it is better to keep deeply felt views about oneself to oneself.' He does not gaze 'into the personal crater with its scene from Hieronymous Bosch activities taking place in the depths'; nor does he inflict on us impolite details of the melancholy that clouded some of these years. He is never alone in this book; there is no horror or anguish in its pages. The girl he once saw kneeling in front of an empty seat, her face buried in her hands, haunted him until he decided she had been playing hide-and-seek. Sexual matters remain tentatively mysterious, though he remarks of his first sexual experience that 'total fiasco was evaded'.

Powell replaces all melancholy, anguish and fiasco with a stately and sophisticated humour that clothes his observations of others and brings them brilliantly to life. Unlike his father, these remarkable people included him in their charmed circles. From these circles he has described a beautifully constructed world where, as the observer-creator, he has himself 'become remarkable'.

1977

INTRODUCING MR CRISP

It is a brave writer who attempts a preface to *The Naked Civil Servant*. In one sense the book needs no introduction: it says everything with extraordinary precision and force. Mr Quentin Crisp has been well-known to himself for so long that he suspects he is now internationally famous as one of London's works of art. He is unlikely to recognise the need for an introduction to American readers.

Yet he first came to the attention of the United States public only in the autumn of 1976 when a dramatic documentary of his life blazed across American television sets. This programme produced an astonishing reaction, and rightly so, since it had been based on this most astonishing autobiography. I was in New York the week after it was shown and everyone seemed not simply to be talking about it, but asking me about him. I told them nothing. A writer is like a weighing-machine: words come only when you put money in. This is a condition of literature which Mr Crisp has had no difficulty in grasping.

In fact I told them nothing not through professionalism, but ignorance. I have never met Mr Crisp. Although I am introducing him to you, no one has introduced him to me. This is proper. I am not doing a friend a favour: I am attempting to do you one.*

Perhaps you will never meet Mr Crisp. He doesn't believe in 'abroad' except as a nightmare place where everyone makes absurd sounds all round you until, once you have moved out of earshot, they revert to standard English. On his travels, wherever he may have imagined he was going, he appears never to have reached much beyond High Wycombe (a hamlet thirty miles from London). So his gaunt and mincing figure will never pitter-patter in menacing retreat from you on the sidewalk; you will never be dazzled by the blue hair, orange face and vermilion lips, or deafened by the roar of his amulets. You are safe from having ludicrously to feign indifference, or from being tempted into savage philistinism. You meet him in his most convenient shape which nevertheless conveys the essence of the man. For though he represents himself as a diseased oyster, he has here produced his pearl.

It is open to you to see Mr Crisp as uniquely English, the Queen of Queer Street and a most vivid embodiment of the era of eccentricity that followed the decline of the British empire. If it were only that, his story would be part of history and of sociology, and no more. Unfortunately he writes so well that his life grafts itself on to ours. If we are not affected by these pages then we must be partly dead. For Mr Crisp does not write exclusively of homosexuality, but of the outcast state in whatever form it may take anywhere at any time. Like King Lear, he has exposed himself to 'feel what wretches feel': and we have taken too little care of that. He challenges our response to anything we think is deeply and unfashionably non-conventional.

The response to him in Britain has been terrible, and this has afforded Mr Crisp some satisfaction. It is his form of revenge. The wonder (and for himself the disappointment) is that he is still alive. God knows how, though his frail body is full of stamina and his

---

*This essay was commissioned in 1977 by Quentin Crisp's hardback publisher in the United States. It was printed as an introduction to *The Naked Civil Servant*, which went into paperback the following year. Mr Crisp soon became a celebrity. When we appeared together on television in the 1980s, he was obliged to return the compliment and explain to viewers who I was.

spirit wrapped around with cunning and iron politeness. But he should have been killed: that would have ended the business in the most logical way. Fielding's London lives again in these pages, with its squalor and violence. Civilisation retreats as Mr Crisp daintily steps forward.

The Naked Civil Servant was first published in Britain in January 1968, and it is interesting now to see what reviewers made of it then. They came, certainly not to praise the book, but to bury it with respectability. Simon Gray in the Listener called it 'a brave little tale'; Paul Bailey, writing more enthusiastically in the Observer, thought it 'entertaining'; John Whitley gave it marks for 'candour' and 'charm' in The Sunday Times. There is bravery, entertainment, candour, charm. But the discomfort of those critics who did not like the book was preferable to the tepidity of many who did. B.A. Young in Punch called it 'a book full of self-pity'; the critic of The Times Literary Supplement, revolted by the 'intolerably arch and jaunty manner', read it with 'total absence of compassion' – as did Mary Conroy in the London Times. Accepting it 'without emotion', she complimented the author on having exploited so well his gift for unpopularity. These critics had felt the threat. Best of all was the Scotsman, which optimistically placed it among the week's fiction. Only Irish reviewers recognised the bleak wit and insight, and did not look away: and it is with an Irish writer that I see The Naked Civil Servant having affinities. To the English, Mr Crisp has appeared as one of the more flamboyant inventions of Evelyn Waugh; but his world is closer to that of Samuel Beckett:

> My relations with Jackson were of short duration. I could have put up with him as a friend, but unfortunately he found me disgusting, as did Johnson, Wilson, Nicholson, and Watson, all whore-sons. I then tried, for a space, to lay hold of kindred spirits among the inferior races, red, yellow, chocolate, and so on. And if the plague-stricken had been less difficult of access I would have intruded on them too, ogling, sidling, leering, ineffing and conating, my heart palpitating. With the insane too I failed, by a hair's-breadth.

Mr Crisp would, I believe, recognise this scene as being very near to his own life. He shares with Beckett this desolation and disgust and the wonderful ability to free it from all sentimentality, to breathe vitality and humour into it, to give it style. Mr Crisp is a master of the inverted cliché. He stands the world of the 'dead normals' on its head: he makes it truly dead.

In his first sentence, Mr Crisp refers to himself as having been 'disfigured' by homosexuality. He has not hidden this disfigurement, but tried to find a way of turning guilt and humiliation, fear, hatred and all his other crippling disadvantages into enviable assets. He converted his body into a fantastic vehicle called 'Quentin' (he had been christened Denis), fashioned for propaganda and amusement. If he could not command love, at least he could get attention. By dressing up so as to attract hostility, he transferred the guilt and hatred to ordinary conventional people. He set great store by their bad opinion and became a connoisseur of different classes of enmity. 'Nobody escapes my love,' he tells us – but almost everyone has tried. There are 'no sympathetic characters in real life'.

In the 1920s Mr Crisp became a walking tutor to London and was kept going by his evangelical zeal. Though girls could be boyish, men still had to be men and homosexuality was felt to be something classical and far-distant, vaguely Greek. Mr Crisp brought it up to date and gave it a bad name – like cancer. Freud's works were then for the first time being translated into English, and as the climate changed Mr Crisp hurriedly jumped off the bandwagon and switched from reform to entertainment. Peace came to him with the Second World War. Utopia had temporarily arrived – imported by Americans in uniform. Mr Crisp 'adores' Americans. 'I was by nature American,' he writes. So over to you.

Since the war the Quentin vehicle has apparently overshot its mark. By the 1960s fancy dress had become *de rigueur* and it was only by advertising himself as a grotesque and ageing caricature of the new teenager that Mr Crisp continued to attract adequate contempt. The book stops in 1967, the year in which legislation following the Wolfenden Report on Homosexual Offences and Prostitution was introduced. This legal relaxation came too late to

make much difference to him except as an obstacle to gaining that
state of alienation he sees as desirable.

To bring the story up to date. Mr Crisp, now in his seventieth year,
has risked his self-sufficiency by becoming a minor cult personality.
People commiserate with him on the number of parties to which
he's invited: but he tells them it's wonderful. He has achieved his
purpose of making the enemy appear harmless. When they telephone and threaten him with death, he gives them an appointment.
They know where to find him. He has been living in the same
Chelsea room now for thirty-three years: after the first four, the dirt
and dust have got no worse. He receives cake from a distant admirer
in Hampton Court; he gives Wine and Crisp Evenings, 'a Straight
Talk from a Bent Speaker'. He has two television sets at cinerama
angles to each other: one is inert and the other 'comes off the water
supply' – but no one is fooled. For the truth is that Mr Crisp is
reaching his prime in the television age. In an interview for the
Guardian, he told Alex Hamilton that people are continually
informing him that they have seen him on television, 'rushing up to
you in the street to say it, when you think they would hurry by with
their faces averted. The essence of style is to be predictable and television rapidly established predictability. People say, "Oh, you would
say that," or quote you and add, "as you would say", and if this is
what they like, you must do it. If people can predict you, they own
you, and they love you.'

If he had known what television would do, he confessed to Alex
Hamilton, he would have told his mother that he didn't mean to
learn to read and write. He would wait for television.

Mr Crisp's career has been a strange boxing match with the world
where each blow that struck him counted as a point scored in his
favour. The rules were his and he has come out an easy winner. But
the contest is over now. At the end of this book he threatens to
commit a murder: instead he has been led away into success and is
now ready for the United States.

This monster of depravity is also the author of a poem about a
kangaroo, a novel on the welfare state and a volume on window-
dressing. Does this *oeuvre* have any message for us? I think there is

one: that we should all have the courage to develop our own feelings and form our own opinions, and not take on second-hand thoughts and emotions. Mr Crisp stands for postjudice versus prejudice.

But if you want to irritate him, if you can't resist it, then, bearing in mind his hostility to all 'culture', join me in proclaiming *The Naked Civil Servant* a classic of autobiography.

1977

PETERLEY HARVEST

Peterley Harvest was first published on 24 October 1960. The book had a mysterious history and, shortly before publication, stories began to appear in the press declaring it to be an elaborate hoax.

The jacket of the book contained the information that David Peterley was the only son of an old Quaker family that had 'lived in the Chilterns and been neighbours of Milton and the Penns'. He had left college in 1924 at the age of twenty-two and, despite 'having been trained to no trade or profession', gone to work in a solicitor's office. To escape the tedium of this work, and as an alternative to marriage with a woman of his father's choice, he set out to see the world and, after staying some four years in Australia, returned to England in 1930.

From 1926 to 1939, when he went back to Australia, Peterley kept an extensive diary, rewriting the personal passages so as to produce a 'more or less continuous autobiographical narrative' which, we are told, the editor Richard Pennington further abbreviated for publication. The first four years of this diary were dissolved into Mr Pennington's introduction, and *Peterley Harvest*, 'the private diary of David Peterley now for the first time printed' opened in June 1930 as David Peterley disembarks at Liverpool.

This framing of the book provoked much bewilderment. Readers were not told whether or when David Peterley had died or how his papers came to reach McGill University in Canada. They were told that since 1946 Richard Pennington had been head librarian at McGill University. But by including an anonymous drawing in profile of David Peterley as frontispiece, and a photograph of Mr Pennington on the inside flap of the jacket, the publishers were giving away too many clues. The drawing showed the young man whom Mr Pennington describes in his introduction as having the 'slight irregularity of face that women find handsome, especially when matched with blond hair and blue eyes'. The photograph of Mr Pennington revealed a dark-bearded, middle-aged man who was described as having been at different times a publisher, sailor, printer, university lecturer and frequent speaker on Canadian radio and television. Yet were these not likenesses, light and dark, of the same man? If so, it would give point to such jokes as the Peterleys having been near neighbours to the Penns (which, when added to Milton, almost gives you Pennington), and the remark made by a friend to Peterley while on a visit to Prague 'that it was a pity my name was David, and that if it had been Richard I could have become the second Richard of Prague'.

Confirmation of this single identity appeared to have been provided by the copyright line, which simply read: © Richard Pennington. It seems unthinkable that a sometime publisher and printer would have allowed such a line to appear had he wished to float a forgery – he would have used the more discreet tactics of *Madame Solario* or *Letters of an Indian Judge to an English Gentlewoman*. *Peterley Harvest* is not in fact a forgery but one of those 'fakes' that present autobiographical material with the foreshortening and ambiguity of an imaginative work – what Wordsworth meant by the phrase 'to throw over incidents and situations from common life a certain colouring of imagination, whereby ordinary things should be presented to the mind in an unusual aspect'.

The unusual aspect of *Peterley Harvest* gave its first reviewers an appalling headache. They did not know what to make of it, 'Unless, of course,' hazarded *The Sunday Times*'s literary editor, 'the diary is really the work of Richard Pennington.' Even then, how was one to evaluate such a strange enterprise? Some papers gave it cautious notices ('has atmosphere' noted the *Guardian*) or retaliated with venom: 'The harvest of David Peterley was sour grapes,' commented *The Times*. Others left it alone. It is easy to feel sympathy for those literary editors who at short notice found themselves in this predicament, but their fears of becoming the dupes of a sinister literary plot now seem exaggerated. Philip Toynbee, for example, who declared that he had never really been taken in for a minute, his scepticism having been awakened early on by the frontispiece (you can't get much earlier in a book than its frontispiece) obviously *had* been taken in and felt let down. 'While I could still believe that it was dealing, through however many curtains of romantic gauze, with a real life and a real person,' he wrote in the *Observer*, '. . . I wanted very much indeed to know who he was. But as soon as I had concluded that he was nobody at all I found *Peterley Harvest* a serious strain on my patience. Did the author foresee such a reaction? . . . how could he imagine that the hoax would work? How could he dare to introduce his figment to men and women of authenticated flesh and blood?'

Toynbee was particularly sensitive to the danger of literary victimisation, having been much mocked in the late 1950s for the generous welcome he gave to Colin Wilson's *The Outsider*. Determined not to be taken in again, he was aggressively on guard against some of his own best instincts. There was, too, a genuine problem of category. Was *Peterley Harvest* a novel autobiography or an autobiographical novel? And does it matter whether the book is a memoir or fiction or an ingenious amalgam of the two?

Short of the *Hitler Diaries*, this question has seemed to matter less in the last twenty-five years partly because there has been considerably more cross-fertilisation between fiction and non-fiction. This process has enriched our recent fiction, most remarkably perhaps the novels of Peter Ackroyd, Beryl Bainbridge, Julian Barnes, D.M. Thomas and Thomas Keneally, whose *Schindler's Ark* was marketed in the United States (under a slightly different title) as non-fiction and in Britain as a novel. Writers of light fiction, too, have added to the enrichment of their work by introducing people from history to fictional characters from the books of other novelists – a notable example being the co-operative sleuthing of Sherlock Holmes and Sigmund Freud in Nicholas Meyer's adventure *The Seven Per Cent Solution.*

Many American and British novelists, from Truman Capote to Piers Paul Read, have taken on the non-fiction thriller. But the benefits of fictional devices to serious non-fiction, from the days of André Maurois's romanticised version of Shelley to Norman Mailer's pastiche of Marilyn Monroe, seem more dubious. With *Peterley Harvest* there was an additional problem because, unlike recent fictional diaries such as *Nazi Lady: The Diaries of Elisabeth von Stahlenberg 1933–1948*, or fictional autobiographies such as Robert Graves's *I, Claudius*, or *Danny Hill: Memoirs of a Prominent Gentleman* (edited by Francis King) and Margaret Forster's 'edition' of Thackeray's *Memoirs of a Victorian Gentleman*, the book mingled well-respected literary figures still alive in Britain with private characters who, if not invented, were surely concealed like the author himself under pseudonyms. *Peterley Harvest* therefore seemed suspended between the fictional diary that has a well-established place in English literature and such fraudulent productions as *The Whispering Gallery*, those anonymous 'leaves from a diplomat's diary' whose author had been prosecuted in the late 1920s on a charge of attempting to obtain money under false pretences. The author of that hoax, reputed to be Lord Birkenhead, turned out to be an actor named Hesketh Pearson. In a subsequent book of breezy reflections on the craft of biography called *Ventilations*, Pearson gave examples of how the non-fiction writer may use his fancy to improve on fact – a perversion of Wordsworth's prescription which Pearson renounced for solid Johnsonian principles of biography once he became a professional biographer himself in the 1930s.

It seems to have been Mr Pennington's aim to shake these Johnsonian conventions, which had become somewhat fossilised by the twentieth century, and to use more ambiguous combinations of methods to achieve his particular artistic ends. He writes in his foreword that the justification of *Peterley Harvest* is to be found 'in the revelation of the inner life of fugitive images in the mind and fitful impulses of the heart, that inner life which with most of us goes unrecorded and which it is the aim of the official biography to conceal'. This is very similar to Virginia Woolf's view of traditional life-writing which she parodied in her fantasy-biography *Orlando*: 'Directly we glance at eyes and forehead, we have to admit a thousand disagreeables which it is the aim of every good biographer to ignore.'

There had been a number of experiments in the late 1920s and early 1930s – among them Harold Nicolson's delightful vignettes *Some People*, Lytton Strachey's psychological melodrama *Elizabeth and Essex* and A.J.A. Symons's detective mystery *The Quest for Corvo* – all designed to find more imaginative and adventurous ways of writing non-fiction. What these authors were trying to do was to release biography from the mechanical processes of the card-index, the confinement of chronology, the heavy impedimenta of reference notes and bibliographies as well as from all the pompous paraphernalia of nineteenth-century Lives and Letters that had made the getting of information their chief priority and locked up biography in the reference library. *Peterley Harvest* does not even have an index. We are told that it is 'strangely one-sided', that 'all the memorable things are omitted' and that 'as a record of living it is absurdly false'. 'I do not believe that the choice of entries for a journal is made *à votre insu* by your subconscious,' writes the author, 'and therefore is a true revelation.' But this declaration cunningly prompts a reaction that the diary nevertheless is a fantastical revelation, since the entry goes on to describe all those convivialities that it states go unrecorded. Of course, the biographer must respect facts, and these may be independently authenticated; the novelist seeks a truth that may be verified by his own vision and the imprint that the novel comes to make on the minds of readers. By finding legitimate ways of managing the facts and incidents of life with the imaginative techniques of novel-writing, Harold Nicolson, Lytton Strachey and A.J.A. Symons had wanted to put biography back on the English literature shelf. *Peterley Harvest* is another attempt to combine the advantages of both worlds by attaching the substance of biography to the freedom of fiction.

A number of the facts may be checked. It is a fact, as Peterley writes, that in 1937 Graham Greene was chosen to edit an English imitation of the *New Yorker* called *Night and Day*, and it is a percipient comment, in view of the coming success of *Horizon* and the brief existence of *Night and Day*, that Cyril Connolly's talent might have better fitted him to be its editor. The bibliographical information concerning the British poet Robert Nichols's career is factual; the biographical asides surrounding that drunken social outcast, the Australian poet Christopher Brennan (whom J.C. Squire believed to be an invention of David Peterley's, and who is now recognised as Australia's first poet of international significance) may be checked against a long manuscript in the Mitchell Library at Sydney – by Richard Pennington. Gwen Ffrangcon-Davies did take the part of Etain in Rutland Boughton's opera *The Immortal Hour* in 1922 with Peter Shelving's designs; and since she also acted in a play called *Spring Tide* which opened at the Duchess Theatre on 15 July 1936, we may safely bet that this play was, as Peterley reveals, co-authored by J.B. Priestley under the pseudonym Peter Goldsmith. Richard Pennington's slip here, by failing as editor to move Peterley's diary from June to July, is almost an invitation to the critic to misunderstand his methods. For in terms of such events we are reading an accurate account, including some unorthodox items that find no place in official biographies and academic bibliographies. It follows that Peterley's record of the Czechoslovakian crisis in the late 1930s is historically true, and Harold Nicolson's attitude, though more sympathetically presented in his diaries, not unfairly shown. But there is no mention of Peterley or Pennington in Nicolson's diaries or in James Lees-Milne's two-volume biography of Nicolson.

There is no mention of them, or of this book, anywhere. They do not appear in the biography of Arthur Machen by Aidan Reynolds and William Charlton, though *Peterley Harvest* has some vivid pages on Machen. From this biography, published three years after *Peterley Harvest*, the facts of Peterley's narrative may be verified. There was, for example, a dinner held in his honour at the National Liberal

Club on 29 October 1937. Pennington can introduce Peterley to it because Pennington was actually Gladstone librarian at the National Liberal Club. He gives a fuller description of the event than the biography, which contains nothing so wonderfully evocative as 'the night of Machen's punch'.

The most arresting picture of a writer in *Peterley Harvest* is that of A.E. Housman delivering his Leslie Stephen Lecture, 'The Name and Nature of Poetry'. Every fact that Pennington uses, from the date and the time to the presence of Quiller-Couch and Will Spens, the vice-chancellor, may once more be checked from works subsequently published such as *The Letters of A.E. Housman* (1971) and Richard Perceval Graves's reliable biography *A.E. Housman* (1970). *Peterley Harvest* has been overlooked by Mr Graves (who uses the evidence of commentators such as Frank Harris): but who can doubt that the non-existent Peterley was among the audience at the Senate House that May afternoon in 1933, and that we are reading an exact, first-hand account from this invisible man?

Housman rose, placed a brown-covered small octavo pamphlet (of paged proofs?) upon the reading desk and immediately began to read. He spoke slowly, with precision, in a pleasant, even, low, but clear and well-modulated voice, not raising his eyes, and frequently twitching the pamphlet up to the top of the desk, and holding it there with one hand. Even at the witty points he did not look up or change his tone, but kept the outward severity of face and the evenness of voice. Only twice or thrice did his voice falter or change: when he read the stanza 'Take, oh take those lips away' and Blake's verse about the lost traveller's dream under the hill, and once when he recalled the time long past when he had composed the last poem of *A Shropshire Lad*; then he was checked for a moment, and brushed his eye with his hand. And there was a solemnity at the end when he bid adieu to literary criticism – and to the world – with the words 'Farewell for ever.'

Housman is of middle height, spare of figure, with severe, sharp-cut, well-complexioned face, with thin white hair and white Edwardian moustache and dark black eyebrows. In profile the head is remarkably elongated at the back. He wore a very dark-grey suit, with stiff upstanding collar folded right round the throat, and long stiff cuffs. He spoke for seventy minutes, and the applause at the end was fervent and enthusiastically prolonged, and repeated after the formal thanks of the Vice-Chancellor; and throughout the whole reading there had not been the least stir in the audience, so intent was it upon each word, so conscious of the importance of the occasion, so enthralled by this marvellous discourse. I am immeasurably the more content with life after having heard and seen Housman, and am certain that there can be no comparable experience possible now. I am sure that this greatest of living Englishmen will be great even among the dead.

Housman is especially a poet for the young and it is appropriate that he should appeal so deeply to the Peterley who doubts at the end of this journal whether he has grown more mature. 'One develops a worldly wisdom for the struggle for existence; but this is cunning rather than maturity,' he writes. 'I am in danger of staying too long in the aesthetic stage, where one should not linger too much.' Housman, no less than the Welsh wizard Arthur Machen with his magical brews, was a splendid solitary figure from the past who had become stranded in the twentieth century, as Peterley feels himself to be, and was consoled in his isolation by the timeless sounds and sweet airs of our literature. He valued poetry as Peterley values the music that fills so much of this journal: by its non-intellectual power to 'transfuse emotion', as Housman expressed it, bristling the skin, shivering the spine, constricting the throat, watering the eyes: and by its power to summon up 'something older than the present organisation of his [man's] nature, like the patches of fen which still linger here and there in the drained lands of Cambridgeshire'.

Peterley too feels the need of something older than twentieth-century organisation, something represented by the eighteenth-century house which carries the same name as himself and which, he writes,

'I cannot help thinking nobler because less commercial, and because rooted in the soil'. With Peterley himself we reach another layer of this book, which cannot be authenticated against records but must be measured by its imprint on our minds and emotions. What Richard Pennington attempted to do was to create an Englishman of the imperial decadence, a contemplative aesthete, incapable of action, who self-consciously reflects the mood of an inglorious period of English history. 'Peterley [the house] seems now to be merely the symbol of an England that is lost for ever,' Mr Pennington makes David Peterley write before casting off for Australia early in 1939. 'The *entre-deux-guerres* is joining the Edwardian age and the nineteenth century as history. There does not seem to be any present, apart from this waiting for the first shots of the second war. Time and a future may still exist abroad; but here there is only suspension of time and movement, a mere waiting. I shall go abroad.'

To establish David Peterley as a figure pinned to this transitory period of decline, and mirroring it through his idle and unpurposed life, Richard Pennington makes him come and go from the other side of the world, and assigns him to that class with most opportunities for 'downward mobility', the upper class. But this invention of an historical character is superseded by something more personal, a Yeatsian image or mask of the anti-self. 'We are made up of all the things wished for as well as all the things achieved,' he writes. One may imagine the people whom Mr Pennington saw while employed as librarian at the National Liberal Club; and imagine how in his mind's eye he followed them from the club into the country and a different world – a world he comes decorously to inhabit as David Peterley and which, being longed for passionately, becomes not something merely outside himself, but a part of his being. 'Do you know, I had the feeling at Peterley of being in another century,' one of the visitors to this make-believe house remarks. It is a romantic past, like an extended evening, gentle and melancholic, that Mr Pennington conjures up around his alter ego. In David Peterley he gives us, not someone simply caught between two wars, but a character adrift between two centuries.

Peterley feels that 'the eighteenth century was right in its horror of mountains, as in most things. Civilisation is connected with the river valleys.' He loves the dead ceremonies of the Church that, having had all meaning rubbed away by the twentieth century, 'have gained instead a pacifying perfection like that of Byzantine frescoes or Raphael paintings, that soothe but not inebriate'. He wants transportation to be 'slowed down rather than speeded up', suspecting that there may be an inverse relationship between speed and the cultivation of the mind. Like Wordsworth, he distances himself from a world that

> *is too much with us; late and soon*
> *Getting and spending, we lay waste our powers:*
> *Little we see in nature that is ours.*

With his own cultivated mind and from his privileged (if reduced) situation, he understands the word 'uneconomic' to mean something that, while not making money, is capable of fulfilling our human needs: 'My advice would be: if it's uneconomic, let's do it. Most things that have given most satisfaction to human beings have been uneconomic – cathedrals and gardens, plays and paintings.' Peterley's interests lie in the rural society built upon an agricultural economy. 'The life of the village and of the small country town I know and love, and think the only life worth living,' he writes. 'The life of the industrialised world is a blank.'

David Peterley's romantic preoccupation with the past pulls against his romantic attraction to Polly, a middle-class musician living in London and belonging very much to the twentieth century – 'the only woman for whom I have any passionate feeling'. It is, as he admits, 'the attraction of the unknown', and it makes him come alive in the present. But 'marriage would be unthinkable: one does not go to Sydenham for wives'. At the beginning of the narrative he has married Jane, a lady better suited to the style of the house than the personality of David Peterley himself. But after this empty and passionless union is ended, it seems as if he will repeat the error by sacrificing Polly to his obsession with the past and

marry another well-cast mistress of the house. The emotional sus-
pense is tightened by Peterley's exquisite hesitations. 'I viewed this
theoretical future all the way back to London,' he writes at one
moment in the event-plot, 'and found the pros and cons so nicely
equal that the scales refused to kick the beam and solve my hesitations.' As the story develops, Peterley shows himself to be a
connoisseur of indecision, procrastination, and all the sensations of
vicarious experience. 'Life is cruder and simpler than you imagine,'
Polly rebukes him. But it is not simple for Peterley, a creature of the
imagination, who hovers agonisingly between his hopes for the
future and regrets for the past, knowing life to be the risk of choosing, 'and having that choice we are the slaves of the anxiety it
occasions'.

Eventually he is impelled into action by Hitler, who both opposes
order deriving from the eighteenth century and threatens existence
in the twentieth. The Nazi element in the diaries is introduced early
through Peterley's 'Cousin Richard'. David Peterley is not taken in. 'I
bought a paper and read of a blood-bath of more than oriental
amplitude that the National Socialists have been enjoying,' he writes
in the summer of 1934. 'There seems to be less of the Puritan
Ironsides about this new party than Cousin Richard would have us
believe.' Cousin Richard, 'who's always as full of the hot gospel from
Munich as of Niersteiner', asks Peterley whether he would like to
receive an invitation to a party rally at Nuremberg, but 'I felt bound
to refuse this so flattering offer, and rejoined Polly in the street
below.'

Until the later years of the decade it is the pleasures of private
life that absorb Peterley. 'We lingered amicably my charming companion and myself in the deserted lounge behind the closed
shutters,' he writes during a visit to France in 1934; 'and if Hitler
had at that moment been reported crossing the Rhine I doubt if I
should have been disturbed.' But the shutters must eventually open.
The journal skilfully plots the change of emphasis from private to
semi-public life. There is a horribly convincing account of the
effect of Hitler's speech-making on a Viennese audience in the
autumn of 1938.

I knew that voice. I had heard it before in days when it held an appeal and had a fascination. Its power was still there to charm men's ears, and I had to admit that I was listening to one of the greatest orators of the world . . . the venom in the mind of the orator spilled over into his voice and my companions of the Viennese café were in a murderous heat. The spells of the enchanter were still terrible, and these fat lazy pub-crawlers had turned into man-haters, with their blood pounding in their arteries, their eyes strained and bloodshot, and their sagging muscles tightening under the stimulation of the chemical secretion of their glands.

This must have something of the effect produced on 'Cousin Richard'. But the Munich Crisis opens his eyes: he is disenchanted with his Führer – and Cousin Richard joins David Peterley, the two in one, in forming a political group for the defence of Czechoslovakia.

The politics of *Peterley Harvest* offer an unfashionable counterpoint to *The Orators* or *Down and Out in Paris and London*. 'The young Auden, the young Orwell, longing for signs of change, angry and impatient at the persistence of ingrained forms of social injustice or inequality of wealth, speak of the same world as Peterley's but seen from the opposite angle,' John Wain has written. 'There is no evidence that Peterley worries about social injustice, or thinks about it at all, for that matter.' With whatever undertow of self-disapproval, Richard Pennington rises from an inferior social position through the phantom figure of David Peterley. His Peterley wants reaction rather than reform, 'and books on economics and sociology therefore have no meaning for me,' he writes, 'and the plays of Mr Galsworthy bore me, and I cannot share the conscious worries of Fabian reformers.' He sees himself as an individualist and spectator of the current scene, though he belongs very much to that age of Proust and Dunne's *Experiment With Time* as he calculates the effect on his emotions of the present drifting into the past, and tries 'not to think of the future'.

Much that is severely hostile to this position and critical of Pennington's 'frozen caricature of yourself' comes through the letters of Peterley's friend Alice Peers or 'AMP', who blames him for his empty egocentricity and terror of commitment. Peterley's political views are expressed with deliberate arrogance. 'I am sitting in cafés and enjoying the life of the sense and the mind,' he writes as late as June 1938.

But, after all, that is exactly what all politics are: only the administrative machinery for making possible. The only justification for Mr Chamberlain, Herr Hitler, and M. Beneš is that they enable me to sit under the castle of the Winter Queen on a summer night drinking wine, and wasting time, and enjoying that strange game of arranging words so as to form an image for the listeners to guess the meaning of, and feeling that emotion of contentment and quiet desire that comes from watching handsome women.

This view of politics would sound more sympathetic if it insisted on everyone's right and opportunity to sit in cafés, for it is not so far from Dr Johnson's

> *How small of all that human hearts endure*
> *That part which laws or kings can cause or cure.*

Like Johnson, Peterley has inherited a vile melancholy – 'that very paralysis of will which prevents your voluntary escape from it'. As the record of these years grows darker, so Peterley's accidie intensifies and his speculations on the elusive nature of happiness become more rarefied. Walking through London in the spring of 1938, with the sense of being on the snow-line of a new ice age, depression overwhelms him like a black wave. 'Whitehall is a gloomy street,' he writes, '. . . and at night dead as the Acropolis; and my own past and the past history came up like a darker cloud in the dark night, and I seemed to be walking in the ruins of a buried civilisation.' Whitehall was Mr Pennington's place of work at the National Liberal Club – the club where the mysterious Peterley sometimes drops in to brood or entertain his guests. The formality of belonging to this disappearing world oppresses him, but 'when it passed away I am not sure,' he writes in the autumn of 1938; 'nor whether it was merely my world that has vanished, or the world of all the people around me. I suspect the latter; and that it was almost certainly the Führer who uttered the spell that dissolved the baseless fabric.'

It is a tribute to the strength and sensitivity of Richard Pennington's writing that Peterley's journey through the 1930s does not irritate or depress. The structure of the book is many-layered. It includes an anonymous diary within the diary, letters from known and unknown people, a ghost story by 'Cousin Richard', a short story and a few poems by David Peterley, more than one love affair, some travellers' tales and an intermittent narrative of historical events. These layers of fantasy and actuality give the work a complex satisfying texture, and reinforce the central theme at private and public levels. Listening to the King's abdication speech on 12 December 1936, Peterley records: 'I shall long remember the shudder that ran through the celebrities . . . when the phrase "the woman I love" came so awkwardly out of the mechanical box. I felt it too.' He feels and will remember it because the King's moral dilemma has been a magnified version of Peterley's own risk of choosing.

To solve all the riddles of *Peterley Harvest* would need a preface by Mr Richard Pennington himself: and perhaps, after all, that would only add to them. Shortly after the book's first publication, and greatly to the publisher's dismay, Mr Pennington had it withdrawn and destroyed. Such an act recalls Arthur Machen's words to Peterley: '"The job of the literary man – at least I've found it so – is inexpressibly painful, nervous, laborious, with more of disappointment and despair than happiness. Only your belief in the value of the written word supports you; and it needs all your strength of will to cling to that belief in this country." He showed me a book of newspaper cuttings: "These are the unfriendly reviews." It was quite a large book.' It may be that adverse criticism had some effect, but there are likely to have been other reasons for its withdrawal, some of which (in the spirit of Peterley) were vicarious and some regretted. In any event, a few copies had been bought and others sold abroad before the edition was suppressed, and these so appealed to the common reader that rare copies were soon fetching greatly inflated prices. In 1963, Mr Pennington issued a small new edition in Canada without the frontispiece and with the title page slightly amended. Until now, there has been no other printing.

John Wain has likened Peterley to Boswell – 'not the Boswell who hero-worshipped Johnson but the Boswell who filled volume after volume with the fascinated shredding-out of his own moods and emotions, who once noted "I should live no more than I can record," as if the only value of experience were to provide pabulum for this delighted connoisseurship of the vintages of his private cellar. Of such grapes is the Peterley Harvest composed.' What the brew lacks in Boswellian robustness it makes up for with its ingenious sensibility, its urbanity and gamesmanship. It may also be seen as one of those rare hybrid works, blending realism with romanticism, the serious and the tongue-in-cheek, of which the forerunner was George Borrow's *Lavengro* – a book that also had in its beginning few appreciative critics and some vituperative ones.

1985

EVELYN WAUGH

'A disgusting common little man,' was Rebecca West's description of Evelyn Waugh. He was common, she explained, in the sense that 'he had never been taught how to avoid being offensive'. But Dame Rebecca (whom few would call inoffensive) has reason to feel grateful to Waugh. Not once throughout Mark Amory's edition of his letters* is her name mentioned. So she escapes the vocabulary of abuse – 'ugly as hell', 'dull as mud', 'insufferable', 'beastly', 'progressive', 'nasty little', 'sub-human', 'Lesbian', 'tart'.

Waugh was a deeply humorous, deeply pessimistic man. His battery of invective, often wittily and fantastically fired off, came from a deep capacity for unhappiness. In 1960, at the age of fifty-six, he recalled the unhappiest day of his life as having been Ascension Day 1917. 'My first term, first month at Lancing. I had never heard about Ascension Day before . . . I overheard boys talking of this mysterious day and when it came they all disappeared. It was a whole holiday. I had nowhere to go and no friends.'

Though still shy and lonely, and despite a miserable homosexual phase that increased his sense of ostracism, he felt he was going to be

*Mark Amory (ed.), *The Letters of Evelyn Waugh* (1980).

'immoderately happy' at Oxford. The 'mayonnaise and punts and cider cup all day long' made life there beautiful. Oxford was 'all that one dreams' and 'immensely different' from Lancing. He began learning how to revenge himself on those who had excluded him: 'for gods sake be unpleasant to Woodard'.

A rather dim career as schoolmaster, during which he learned to 'preside at a sausage tea and say grace for it', was offset by a bright social life. He felt better in the company of the upper classes, especially when dismissing the rest of the population: if you must be part of a minority, make it an élite. 'The sad thing is,' he told Ronald Knox, 'that "Metroland" is my world and that I have grown up in it & I don't know any other except at second hand or at a great distance.' The break-up of his marriage in 1929, after only a year, pierced his defences and again brought unhappiness cascading in. The wit evaporates and there is real pathos when he writes to his parents: 'May I come & live with you sometimes? . . . So far as I knew we were both serenely happy.' To his friend Harold Acton he admitted: 'I did not know it was possible to be so miserable & live but I am told this is a common experience.'

Hatred of this life and the conception of a next life as retribution (heard posthumously in these letters) became his formula for escaping further misery. He was received into the Catholic Church, believing that 'there is no justice in this world & that one must look to a life beyond the grave to regulate the accounts'. Catholicism also became a means of purging his self-dislike. 'I know I am awful,' he wrote to Edith Sitwell. 'But how much more awful I should be without the Faith.' He turned this dislike on to others, defensiveness into the offensiveness of which Rebecca West complained – a reflection, he thought, of 'my ugly nature' which was responsible for a number of unsuccessful love affairs ('stiff upper lip and dropped cock').

But one person was exempt from the world's awfulness: his second wife Laura. In a letter proposing marriage he confessed: 'I can't advise you in my favour because I think it would be beastly for you . . . I am restless & moody & misanthropic & lazy and have no money . . . I have always tried to be nice to you and you may have got it into your head that I am nice really, but that is all rot. It is only to you & for you.' His letters to Laura are, in their fashion, genuine love letters in which the prevailing tone is one of gratitude. The happiest days of his life were with her and she changed him to the extent that 'I could no longer look at death with indifference'.

'A letter should be a form of conversation,' Waugh believed. His own letters fulfil that criterion very well, though it is probably more comfortable to read this book than to have been drawn into the conspiracy of conversation with him. He avoided actuality by absorbing himself into the 'furious fancies' of his novels. Among other novelists he admired were Graham Greene ('the greatest novelist of the century'), Angus Wilson ('awfully clever'), the master P.G. Wodehouse and William Gerhardie, from whom 'I learned a good deal of my trade'. His dislikes were more eccentric. Proust was a 'mental defective'; the reputation of D.H. Lawrence had been 'made by an illiterate clique at Cambridge'; W.H. Auden he found 'dull and awkward'. The verdict on Winston Churchill – 'lost when least excited' – is the most wittily succinct of all.

Waugh's style depends for its perfection on the exclusion of much human experience. The pressure of that exclusion, aided in later years by deafness, was kept up by his belief in the world's hostility. When his defences faltered he was overcome by 'Pinfold feelings of persecution'. Criticising John Betjeman's Protestantism, he had written: 'If you try to base your life & hopes on logical absurdities YOU WILL GO MAD.' From a different point of view something similar might be said of Waugh's Catholicism. For the most part he did not succumb to his sense of being 'a victim of the malice of others'. But his barricaded world, though exquisitely constructed, was small and eventually it bored him. He had avoided unhappiness, but at a cost. 'I am not unhappy,' he wrote not long before his death. 'I just do not much like being alive.'

1980

From the Life

THE MAKING OF
BERNARD SHAW

In the late 1960s, the Shaw estate decided to commission a new biography of Bernard Shaw, and the Society of Authors, which acted as agent for the estate, was asked to sound me out. I was then thirty-four, had published a biography of Lytton Strachey the previous year, and had already agreed to write a biography of Augustus John. To my eyes, the legendary GBS appeared a gigantic phenomenon with whom I felt little natural intimacy.

He seemed one of the most perplexing, perhaps even forbidding, figures in modern literature. He had produced, by common consent, some of the finest music criticism ever written, introduced the theatre of ideas to the English-speaking stage, and, with a series of brilliant political pamphlets, converted many nineteenth-century aesthetes into twentieth-century radicals. He had composed more than fifty plays. His collected works extended over almost forty volumes (and were well exceeded by his uncollected writings). There were libraries of books about his work and also huge deposits of unpublished papers around the world. He wrote ten letters every day of his adult life and his correspondents kept his letters. I suspected that, with his shorthand and his secretaries, GBS could actually write in a day more words than I could read in a day. Since he lived into his mid-nineties, writing vigorously almost to the end, this was an alarming speculation.

Lytton Strachey had taken me almost ten years. *Augustus John* lay before me. I therefore prevaricated, replying that while I would in principle be delighted to write Shaw's life, I could not in practice begin until I had finished the book in hand.

To my surprise, the Society of Authors appeared almost more pleased by this postponement than by my acceptance. 'The slower the better,' replied Elizabeth Barber, the general secretary. 'We feel perfectly happy about the delay.' Here was someone with whom I could do business. My appointment was confirmed by the end of 1969 and a formal letter of agreement was drafted in the spring of 1970. As I look at it now, that letter appears an amiable work of fiction, signed over a sixpenny stamp, and envisaging much sympathetic consultation with Shaw's hardback publisher – Max Reinhardt, at the Bodley Head – as the biography calmly progressed to its publication, scheduled for 1976.

I remained largely ignorant of how the Shaw estate operated and reached its decisions. But in this ignorance lay my strength. I never felt overburdened by any bureaucracy or impeded by demands from different parties. It seemed an easy-going regime. It was true that they could withdraw their authorisation if they judged the work to be poorly written, but they could not prevent its publication as an unauthorised Life, merely charge fees for Shaw quotations which would otherwise be free. My appointment was made public during the summer of 1970. In London, *The Sunday Times* accurately reported my mixed feelings. 'At present he's trying not to think about it,' Philip Oakes wrote, adding that I nevertheless recognised GBS as being 'far too good a subject to miss'. *The Times* was meanwhile telling its readers that I would have access to 'a mountain of unpublished Shaw material', including 'all the Shaw letters in the British Museum, as well as many in the hands of Professor Dan H. Laurence (professor of English at New York University) whose edition of Shaw's collected letters is being published by the Bodley Head'.

Only after finishing *Augustus John*, when I was able to turn my attention to Shaw, did I begin to understand the importance of Dan

H. Laurence in Shaw studies, and sense how greatly such a newspaper report could have upset him. Dan Laurence had begun his career as a junior colleague of the great Jamesian scholar Leon Edel, with whom he published a bibliography of Henry James in 1957. But already, in the early fifties, he had committed himself to Shaw, on whose behalf he entertained many noble plans, among them preparing a four-volume edition of his letters, compiling a comprehensive bibliography, providing editorial supervision for a complete edition of the plays with their prefaces, and also a facsimile edition of the early play texts in manuscript, then writing a study of Shaw and the American theatre, and gathering into various volumes some previously uncollected writings by Shaw on Ireland, on music, and on politics. So formidable was his knowledge that he had been appointed the literary and dramatic adviser to the Shaw estate in 1973 (a position he continued to hold until his seventieth birthday in 1990). But he had not been asked to write the authorised biography. It was a traumatic oversight.

Although there were a few noted Shaw scholars in Britain and Ireland at the time, most of the best work on GBS was being done by scholars in Canada and the United States. Dan Laurence was pre-eminent among these scholars, and it was scarcely surprising that he should have expected to crown his career by writing the authorised life of Shaw. That the prize should have gone to someone in England who had no academic qualifications whatever and no record of having written on Shaw simply beggared belief. It was incredible. It was also an insult.

The Society of Authors was inclined to treat Dan Laurence as a prima donna who, after many tantrums and rumpuses, always sang beautifully on the night. It was true that he had fallen silent with Max Reinhardt, and would, it seemed, rather plunge into the traffic than pass on the same side of the street as him. Nevertheless good sense seemed to be prevailing as the Bodley Head brought out the first two volumes of his Shaw letters very successfully, in 1965 and 1972. When he arrived in London in the summer of 1974, Elizabeth Barber set up a meeting between us at the Society of Authors offices, discreetly absenting herself, like a matchmaker who is confident that some alliance, if only a marriage of convenience, will be reached.

It might have been better had she stayed. Dan Laurence did not want to meet me. If a meeting was so vital, why had I not got in touch with him on receiving my appointment – an appointment he had come to hear of from a third party, who had read about it in a newspaper? Now he had been trapped into this awful business. He walked into the office and saw me for the first time, some fifteen years younger than he was, and seated in an imposing chair behind a desk while indicating an inferior chair for him – and he a scholar of international reputation! Later on, he said that he wished he had spat in my face and left.

He told me that his first impulse had been to invite me to his home in the United States, where I could use the Shaw material he had acquired and had been working on for the last quarter of a century – provided I promised never to allow Max Reinhardt to publish my book. But because I had not sought him out or asked for his co-operation, he had changed his mind. He intended to publish his own, unauthorised 'Quest for Shaw', and considered me his rival as well as a usurper.

In much that I said that day, I was guided by advice from those who in their work for the Shaw estate felt that they had got to know Dan Laurence's 'complicated nature'. I suggested that he had not been considered as a candidate for the biography because he had already committed himself to a lifetime's work on GBS. He simply wouldn't have had time. That being so, I argued, it must be in the interests of Shaw scholarship for the authorised biographer and the bibliographer (and editor of the letters) to work in harmony. I saw us not as rivals but as colleagues in the same field of work. My difficulty, I added, was that I had so little to offer him in exchange for the generosity I was seeking. But if he would agree to assist me perhaps I could credit his help in some way on the title page and perhaps also negotiate extra financial support for his work from the Shaw estate itself. What else could I do?

Silence descended, and he left.

I had no response to any of this for six months. Only after I wrote a letter attempting to clarify my position did I hear from him. In January of 1975, Dan Laurence replied from his home in Texas.

Reading his letter, it became clear to me that he believed he was being subjected to pressures that bordered on intimidation. I was made to understand that if he were to accede to the proposal of becoming my research assistant, collaborator, flunky, or whatever I chose to call it, he would lose all academic freedom, impair his health, and further delay the work to which he had dedicated himself. He was obviously angry at having such callous demands made of him. What business had I accepting the job of biographer if I was not competent to do it without him? Yet if I withdrew I gathered that he would under no circumstances put himself forward as a contender for my replacement as the 'authorised' biographer.

I was dismayed by this reply, and greatly discouraged. But to my surprise, Elizabeth Barber considered it a rather promising letter. She accepted, more readily than I did, his assurance that all signs of 'anger, vindictiveness or acrimony' were unintentional. She believed that it would be impossible for me to 'embark on something of this magnitude in the teeth of hostility from Dan Laurence', and what had encouraged her in his letter, she wrote, was the statement that he would do nothing to impede my work, would assist me in gaining access to material if I encountered resistance, and, were I to need it, would cheerfully let me have the date of a birth here, a death there. He did, in fact, encumber me with a little help. He gave me the names of manuscript libraries with Shaw papers, though these had already been published; he let me have the name of a distant relative of Shaw's who had never known him; and he enclosed a statement for my use to the effect that he had no personal objection to my obtaining copies of Shaw correspondence for my biography – copies which were not an infringement of his own work. As the authorised biographer, with copyright clearance from the Shaw estate, I found it bizarre that he felt I might encounter resistance from professional manuscript librarians or need this additional permission.

I would have needed to trouble Dan Laurence far less and bring less vituperation down on myself if by the mid-1970s his scholarly volumes were available, as I had been assured they would be at the time of my appointment. The Society of Authors had long been

seeking ways of helping him complete these works, and now redou-
bled its efforts, pressing assistance upon him. Their efforts were
utterly unsuccessful. He refused the offer of clerical or secretarial
help; he refused a research team; he refused a paid sabbatical year.
He was on his own – or nowhere.

I was beginning to form my own opinion of Dan Laurence. In
scholarly matters, the very letter of scholarship, he had absolute
integrity. You could not bribe, flatter, coax, or bully him. Indeed, as
I eventually discovered, I could not even reason with him. He
wanted no one's help beyond the minimum that one scholar is
obliged to give another. He wanted to be in nobody's debt. He didn't
mind difficulties; he didn't mind enemies. What he minded was
lack of admiration and understanding where it was properly due. He
was determined to climb his mountain alone – alone with GBS. He
suspected the Shaw estate even when it brought gifts. Such help
would only diminish his lonely achievement. He would rather sell
everything he owned, he declared, except his typewriter and the
clothes on his back, and go to live in a dungeon, than undermine his
great work by making compromises with fifth-column agents within
the Shavian ranks. He was creating a masterpiece that would, he
said, 'stand as a model for ages to come'. In preparation, too, such
work was timeless. So he needed exclusive access to Shaw material
for an almost unlimited time.

Around this core of integrity, it seemed to me, was a minefield of
anxieties and aggressions on to which it would be unwise to advance
further. The best thing I could do, I thought, was to soldier on. Early
in 1975, I crossed over into Dublin and began my research. I lived in
Rathmines, strategically placed between a convent and a barracks,
and a mile or so from Shaw's birthplace in Synge Street.
Intermittently, I worked in the National Library of Ireland (to which
Shaw had donated the manuscripts of his novels), and I visited
Dalkey, where he had passed his happiest hours while he was growing up. I also met a number of writers – John O'Donovan, Monk
Gibbon, Vivian Mercier – who were encouraging. The atmosphere
was thick with goodwill. Yet, however hard I try, I cannot account for
my time in Ireland very coherently. There was almost no one who,

even when he or she had no information at all, would not be prepared to volunteer something over a jar or two. People I had never heard of came to inform me that they knew nothing, and then stayed on awhile. I was swimming in the wake of the great Shavian legend: swimming and almost drowning.

The financing of a long biography for a self-employed writer can be a complicated and perilous business. Because of the falling out between Dan Laurence and Max Reinhardt (I never knew what it was over), I had not signed a contract with the Bodley Head, but I had made an agreement in the United States with Holt, Rinehart & Winston, the publishers of my *Lytton Strachey* and *Augustus John*. I was to receive some $10,000 a year for a period of five years. Somewhat prematurely, I had also sold, sight unseen, the serial rights to my biography to Harold Evans, the editor of *The Sunday Times* in London – a deal that over the years would earn me the best part of £20,000. This money from the United States and Britain helped to pay for extensive trips I had to make – in particular, to large deposits of Shaw papers in North America. I also hoped to add a little to my income by giving lectures and writing theatre programme essays and newspaper reviews about GBS. The Shaw estate was keen to have me do such things, and in the summer of 1975 I was commissioned by the *Observer*, in London, to write a substantial, two-part article to commemorate the twenty-fifth anniversary of Shaw's death. Rather to my surprise, the Society of Authors asked me to mark unpublished quotations in red and published quotations in blue before handing in the manuscript. I was then asked to calculate the number of words quoted in the article which came from correspondence that might appear in the last two volumes of Shaw's letters covering the years 1911 to 1950. Such exercises were new to me. The number of words came to fewer than 275. Having made this calculation, I set off from Ireland on the first of several research trips to the United States, unaware of having put a match to a high explosive.

Not until I reached the Humanities Research Center at the University of Texas at Austin did I find out the extent of the crisis that had flared up. As I worked alongside other researchers there, a rumour reached me that Dan Laurence had been among us. I felt a horror of cutting him unintentionally since, following our one meeting in London eighteen months back and my rather blurred period in Dublin, I could not recall exactly what he looked like. Perhaps I had already failed to notice him in the act of cutting me dead. To avoid this impossible situation, I left a message for him with the librarian saying I was working there and would like to say hello whenever he had a few spare minutes. He appeared before my desk the next morning and led me to a soundproof room, so that what he had to say would not over-excite the scholars or embarrass the staff. What he had to say was that he had resigned as the editor of Shaw's *Collected Letters*.

The ostensible reason for his resignation was those 275 words. But it was not really the exact number of words that troubled him; it was the breach in principle. There was no scholar in modern times, he told me, who was not protected by the licenser. Let me try publishing a letter by D.H. Lawrence or W.B. Yeats while scholarly editions were in progress and see how far I got.

Dan Laurence had been trained in a stern school. The Henry James executors froze all James's papers for a quarter of a century while Leon Edel was writing his official biography, and, further, they protected James's correspondence while Edel's edition of the letters was in preparation. Dan Laurence believed he should have been invited to build a similar empire in Shaw studies. He had felt angry and despondent when the authorised biography was handed to someone who 'knows bloody nothing about Shaw'. Now he felt betrayed. I was seeking to underwrite my expenses with 'some goddamn articles in newspapers' that cut right across his work. He was entitled to absolute protection against such audacious raids – protection against the contamination of quotations, paraphrases, and sometimes even references to material that he must keep fresh and unsullied. Otherwise it would all be as dead as mutton.

He had poured the sweat and blood of fifteen years into this project, he reminded me, so that, instead of the miserable routine volumes of correspondence that had sufficed for Aldous Huxley, for D.H. Lawrence, and even for James Joyce, he would be able to bring

Shaw's *Collected Letters* to a brilliant fruition. But he had been harried by the Society of Authors with an appalling lack of sensitivity – they should be taken to court for their disgraceful ethics. It was true that he had promised publication of both the letters and the bibliography 'this year or next year' for several years. No one regretted the necessary postponements resulting from the complexities of the work more than he did. But he would not compromise. He felt he could trust hardly anyone. He would see me in hell before he would lavish more help on me. The trouble was he had been 'too goddamn reasonable', covered up his wounds, overlooked my boorishness, turned the other cheek. And where had it got him? He would do it no more. Publication of his bibliography would take place at some time of his own choosing, and publication of the letters probably never.

He concluded by saying that the Shaw estate had 'one hell of a lot' more to lose than it had bargained for. He would work on his so-called unofficial biography, which would have the distinction of being the definitive book that I was incapable of producing. Publishers would line up at his doorstep for this book, and there would be 'money galore'. He would chuck the literary advisership, too, and break the news to *The New York Times*. Finally, he would set off in his garden the largest conflagration of literary documents since Dickens's bonfire at Gad's Hill.

As I listened to this agonised outcry, I said very little in our soundproof room. I really did not know what to say. It seemed to me that whatever I said, wrote, or did would be wrong, according to his lights. I felt shell-shocked. But Dan Laurence seemed to feel better after what he called our 'candid talk'. It had, he believed, 'cleared the air somewhat'. In any event, he could now admit to feeling some 'personal animosity' toward me, and this admission seemed to cheer him. He decided to play the gentleman, air his principles of hospitality, and carry me off the following Sunday to San Antonio, his home town. It was a generous and excruciating gesture. At his apartment, encased with books by and about GBS, he could, at the switch of a button, flash Shaw's words on to a screen. He was pleased with this device, which, if he chose, he could operate while lying down.

But to me it presented a frightful warning. I began to see the lengths to which a lonely obsession could, in the pursuit of excellence, lead any of us.

Elizabeth Barber's place at the Society of Authors had by 1975 been taken by Roma Woodnutt. She shared her predecessor's heart-breaking optimism. They had been through worse tidal waves in the past, she assured me, and were used to such stormy stuff. All the same, it took some two years of complex negotiations, involving meetings of committees and flights in jet aircraft, to woo Dan Laurence back to the editing of Shaw's letters. To assist the negotiations, I was asked to suspend work on my biography during this period. In consideration of this, the Shaw estate offered to pay me a retainer, or contribution to my expenses, backdated to the beginning of 1975. These annual instalments, starting at £750 and rising by 10 per cent increments each year, were to reach a total sum of £10,185 by 1984, the year I was now expected to deliver my completed type-script. This arrangement was drafted into a new letter of agreement, signed in December 1977. It is a more sophisticated and tantalising work of fantasy than the original letter of April 1970 which it super-seded, decked out as it is with several discreet subplots and variant narrative sequences, all of them nevertheless moving towards a happy ending.

During my enforced time off, I edited an illustrated symposium, *The Genius of Shaw*. This added a little to my income, which during the eighties grew very erratic. I still hadn't signed a contract for the biography with Max Reinhardt at the Bodley Head, and, partly because of the ever-lengthening delay, I had cancelled first my con-tract with Holt, Rinehart & Winston (which my Anglophile editor, Tom Wallace, had left), and later the serialisation agreement with *The Sunday Times*, of which Harold Evans was no longer editor. In both cases I repaid my advances. I was to some extent dependent on the support I was receiving from the Shaw estate – a position not so dif-ferent from that of Dan Laurence himself. 'Of course we must keep him going,' said Terence de Vere White, the Shaw estate representative from the National Gallery of Ireland. He was referring to me. 'Caution however is needed,' he added. Shaw 'is an almost endless subject', and he did not want to see the estate subjected to my whims, as he believed it had been to Dan Laurence's. Yet, as the years ticked by, this was perhaps what happened.

By 1981, a new *modus vivendi* appeared to have been established. In celebration, the Society of Authors held a lunch for Dan Laurence and for me, during which we gave, I believe, a very pretty display of manners, like an exhibition of fencing after the real fighting. There was no question of spitting now. Dan declared that he had been very rude when we first met. I countered this statement by saying I would probably have done the same thing in his position. Then I presented him with a bundle of photocopied Shaw letters from Belfast which he had not seen; he mentioned some papers in Cambridge and offered me proofs of his Shaw bibliography and letters as soon as they were printed and ready to be seen. 'Well, now my conscience is clear,' he sighed at the end of the meal. Roma Woodnutt, presiding over this lunch, was almost in tears at the beauty of our exchanges.

I was still urgently awaiting this bibliography which, as Dan Laurence plausibly asserted, would be worth ten volumes of Shaw's correspondence. 'His bibliography of Shaw,' I wrote at the end of 1981, 'is awaited by all those engaged in Shaw studies with something of the frenzy of telephone subscribers without directories.' It was published by the Clarendon Press in the autumn of 1983, and I reviewed it early the following year in the *London Review of Books*. I did not hesitate to praise it highly. 'He compels salutation from us all,' I wrote. This tribute was sincere and written without irony. But he also invited some teasing, I suggested, by likening himself to Robert Browning's supernatural knight Childe Roland, blowing his own slug-horn and sustaining himself on his savage trample to the dark tower with an angry determination that vented itself in tirades against lesser scholars for being 'appallingly negligent'. This teasing was not welcomed and I had apparently gone and ruined our new accord.

In truth, however, neither of us had altered our positions. In Britain, my piece was read as a very favourable review flavoured by some Shavian comedy. The publishers, who took me to lunch and inquired whether they might publish my biography, were delighted. But among some Shaw scholars in the United States (to quote one such) my review was perceived as 'a brilliant piece of barely disguised malice, masquerading as praise of genius'. No doubt cultural differences partly account for these different readings, but there were also personal factors. To Dan Laurence himself my review seemed an almost libellous personal attack. He had expected nothing better, he said, having always known that I was a 'spiv' and an 'incorrigible fool'. Now everyone could see that I looked like 'the horse's rear end' I truly was. It was obviously a relief being able to speak naturally again. He could breathe once more. As for Shaw's *Collected Letters*, he gave instructions that I was to be sent nothing that any other reviewer would not receive. I was also to be shown no letters that had been deleted from the volumes.

Nevertheless, when the third volume of these letters appeared, in the spring of 1985, I went ahead and reviewed it in *The Times Literary Supplement*. Nor did I hold back. 'The conventional tributes to an editor of letters seem inadequate in the case of Dan H. Laurence,' I wrote, and went on to liken him to that admirable creature the truffle hound. One criticism I did allow myself was aimed at his habit of dedicating Shaw's letters to groups of his own family and friends. Was this appropriate, I asked, in view of Shaw's dislike of dedications which, deriving from the beggar's petition, he believed 'should be discontinued except in cases where there is very special personal relations between the author of the subject of a book and the dedicatee'? It seemed to smack of possession rather than scholarship.

I also tried to address the problem, as I saw it, of the dictatorship of solitary perfectionism that had ruled over this manuscript material. Many years back, Dan Laurence had pointed to the Pilgrim Edition of Charles Dickens's letters as an example of excellence achieved through an uncompromising investment of time. This was good evidence. But scholarly practice had been changing. The two volumes of E.M. Forster's letters (edited by Mary Lago and P.N. Furbank) had been published within three years; the four volumes of Beatrice Webb's diaries (edited by Norman and Jeanne MacKenzie) were being brought out within four years; Virginia Woolf's correspondence (edited by Nigel Nicolson and Joanne Trautmann) appeared in six volumes over seven years; and the Cambridge Edition of D.H. Lawrence's letters, to be published in seven volumes during fourteen years, was to have a different co-editor working with James T. Boulton for each volume.

'I do not know what my expectation of life is, but it seems very improbable that I shall be able to read the book!' exclaimed Cyril Russell, a legal representative of the Shaw estate, referring, in the mid-eighties, to my biography. It is impossible not to feel some sympathy with the estate and its agent, the Society of Authors, caught as they were between the fell incensèd points of mighty opposites. But what could they do? Recognising that my snail's pace had been conditioned by Dan Laurence's stately advance, they tore up our second letter of agreement and continued my retainer until 1987, the year I finally signed a contract with Chatto & Windus for my book in Britain.

My contract with Chatto & Windus was to provoke an uproar in the press, on account of the startling size of its royalty advance. What was not reported was the fact that I had already 'advanced' the publisher many years of research and many thousands of words. In return, and calculating the sales and subsidiary earnings from three volumes of hardbacks and paperbacks (plus a final, miraculous three-in-one edition), Chatto & Windus was to guarantee me £625,000, to be paid in instalments over a dozen years. This was hardly the lottery cheque described by some newspapers, but a generous middle-age pension that, by releasing me from reviewing, lecturing and broadcasting, was to buy enough time for me to complete the book. Even after sharing this money with my literary agent and the Inland Revenue, I could still boast of some £40,000 a year. This was a fine sum for a writer, though not I hope the 'obscenity' trumpeted by some commentators – especially when compared with the incomes of footballers, film stars, bankers and other business people in their prime. Nevertheless, it was yet another red rag in the face of poor Dan Laurence.

My three volumes of biographical narrative eventually appeared between 1988 and 1991. Of my fifteen years with GBS, half were spent travelling the world in his footsteps (to the Soviet Union, Italy, New Zealand, South Africa, and other countries) and also pursuing him to places where he never went but which have acquired his manuscripts. In the handling of personal letters or diaries or the drafts of plays, I seemed to get almost literally in touch with him. My biography presents a darker GBS who has something in common with Swift and Beckett but who struggled against pessimism. Much of what I wrote as social history now appears to me to have gained a peculiar relevance to contemporary politics. The break-up of the Soviet Union, the 'end of communism' and of 'history', the spread of privatisation – and of nationalism – across the world, the fear in Britain of the very word 'socialism' (as fearful as 'liberal' in the United States) have made Shaw's beliefs deeply unfashionable. Many of the battles in which he had fought were being fought again and with opposite results. Yet being out of fashion, wilfully marching in an unpopular direction, was a Shavian speciality – and perhaps a democratically useful one. It is a lonely business, being in Shaw's army, and keeping company with him so long has probably made me more isolated.

What can I write that may bring comfort to the Shaw estate over its choice of biographer and bibliographer? To my mind Dan Laurence did not have the perspective of Shavian humour and imagination. As with Annie Besant, comedy was not his clue to life and no truth presented itself to him as a joke. Quite the contrary. Yet he has been a tireless and faithful scholar, which is perhaps what Shaw needed. As for me, my very existence irritated him enormously. That is undeniable. But his irritation may well have sharpened that 'angry determination' he needed to finish his great work. Not that he has ever finished with GBS.

Now that I have completed a one-volume abridgement of my biography, my GBEssence, I shall be leaving this Shavian territory. That is the opposite course set by Dan Laurence, who is now a great patron of Shaw studies, selecting with infinite expertise the editors of newly published Shaw volumes. Under his supervision, GBS has become a most prolific posthumous author. Besides compiling the Shaw bibliography and editing the *Collected Letters*, he has edited a book of selected correspondence called *Theatrics*, and co-edited with various scholars Shaw's correspondence with Lady Gregory and the sixteenth volume of *The Annual of Bernard Shaw Studies*, as well as a three-volume edition of Shaw's prefaces. It will never end until he is ended. I do not envy him. I cannot work with him. I have no more wish to see him than he has to see me. But between these boulders of disfavour moves an exasperated admiration. In the calm of retrospect, I salute him.

Dan Laurence's publications have been of great value to me, as to all readers of GBS, and the slowness of their preparation may have been an additional benefit. The time I was obliged to live with Shaw on my mind gave me the sense of intimacy I lacked at the beginning of my research. Between Shaw's work and his life, I found, moved an unexpected current of passion. With the extra time I had been granted, I sought to navigate this complex stream of energy. Shaw covered up his vulnerability with dazzling panache: I tried to uncover it and, without losing the sparkle of that panache, show the need he had for such brilliant covering. He became a saint of the lonely and a fugleman for those who were out of step with their times. He gave them a heartening message. For every disadvantage, in Shavian terms, becomes a potential asset in disguise. Perhaps Dan Laurence and I had been working all that time under the spell of this heroic paradox.

2001

A Romance in
E Flat Minor

When Rupert Brooke went to Rugby in the early 1900s, he noticed that a girl about half-a-dozen years older than himself would sometimes come and join the boys at meals. Her name was Erica Cotterill and she occupied a special place at Rugby, her aunt having married William Parker Brooke, Rupert's father and the housemaster of School Field.

Erica was not popular with the boys. She had a habit of telling Mr Brooke which of them had taken 'too much pudding'. She was not a shy girl: rather someone who provoked shyness in others. But Rupert got on well with her and by 1904 the two of them had started a correspondence in which he took on the pose of a disillusioned decadent, and she volunteered to have wrung from her 'Wonderful Secrets' involving the possibility of duels between foreign gentlemen.

From his role as a nineties bohemian Brooke was largely converted by the plays of Bernard Shaw on which he would drop in during flying visits to the Court Theatre in Sloane Square. 'My present pose is as a socialist,' he concluded. In 1905 he had seen *Major Barbara*, 'a brutal sordid play, difficult to understand and very interesting,' he told Erica. 'One of the characters utters a scathing invective against public school masters at which I applauded very suddenly and loudly in the midst of dead silence.' Even better was *John Bull's Other Island*. 'It is unspeakably delightful . . . exquisite, wonderful, terrific, an unapproachable satire on everything.'

It was while listening to this play in the autumn of 1905 that Erica herself felt suddenly filled with Shaw's ejaculation of words. Having conceived this new literary enthusiasm, she poured out her passion in a letter to Shaw, signing herself 'Miss Charmer'. Following twenty years of neglect in Ireland and another twenty years of rejection in England, Shaw had been left with a need for attention: any kind of attention, even attention he desperately didn't want. So now, despite not knowing his correspondent's name and having no address other than 'Poste Restante, Godalming', he couldn't help replying. He told her that her romantic notions were the 'greatest nonsense' and recommended her to 'marry and have children: then you will not ask from works of art what you can get only from life'.

The effect of this letter was decisive, and Erica immediately transferred her infatuation from the plays to the playwright. She was twenty-four; he nearly fifty: and over the next dozen years she aimed at him erratic bursts of unpunctuated, strangely compelling letters. So, Shaw explained, 'I started giving her a little advice.' He advised her to join a socialist society ('There are always envelopes to be directed and tracts to be distributed'); and he advised her to 'get some business to do that is specially your own business'; otherwise (he continued to advise her) she could go 'quite cracked'.

From her other literary mentor, Rupert Brooke, Erica had unintentionally switched on a parallel current of advice. 'For God's sake let me advise you,' he appealed. 'I'm glad you've been among people who live for Art. It must be very good for you. I love Art myself; especially in the evenings. But why are you not a Fabian? Which kind of non-Fabian are you? The Feeble-minded, or the emotional?'

By provenance it was Erica (not Brooke) who should have been a Fabian. Her father, Charles Clement Cotterill, was an outspoken schoolmaster and socialist. He had signalled his revolutionary stance by refusing to wear a beard and by producing such books as (ambiance Brooke) *Suggested Reforms in Public Schools* and (ambiance Shaw) *Human Justice for Those at the Bottom*. Erica attempted to join literary ambition to Fabian interests by publishing a play called *A Professional Socialist*. She arrived with a copy of this play at Shaw's house. He nervously handed it to his wife who, while agreeing that it was 'remarkable', advised Erica to 'cut it'. In this play the character of Ursula Windridge straightforwardly states Erica's own quest: 'I want to find *real* passion ... I want great blazing racing feelings that flame round you like a glorious wind; I want some gorgeous thing to live for with every atom of my own soul.'

That was certainly what Erica wanted: and her 'gorgeous thing' was GBS. She was intoxicated with romance – something that Brooke, with his tidy rhymes, was understood to celebrate and that Shaw believed he had been sent into the world to trample on with thick boots. Erica provides an ironic commentary to both their careers, exposing the vacuity of Brooke's early poetic fancies and the inability of Shaw to enact his own ideas. Like a searchlight, she glances into their worlds, lighting up the respectability of the bohemian and the timidity of the revolutionary. Erica feels, thinks, lives through the page as if it were her body; her writing is an orgasm of emotional experience. By contrast, the professional poet and professional dramatist appear to pluck their material from its natural ground, remove it indoors and press it on to paper. Shaw did this with Erica herself, adapting her first pseudonymous approach to him for use in his play *Getting Married*. When this disquisitory drama opened to a hail of critical denunciation at the Haymarket on 12 May 1908, Erica asked Brooke to the opening night and after a palpitating pause, he accepted her 'alluring' invitation. 'You are strangely practical,' he hazarded. 'I shall come. (Mother will swoon if she hears.) Only you are to behave and *not* "clutch my arm at thrilling moments" ... Bring an umbrella & clutch that, if you must clutch ... you must be very good & patient, & only speak when you explain the jokes to me.'

But *Getting Married* was more than a volley of jokes: it appeared to set forth all the dangers, injustices, anomalies in the institution of marriage; demonstrating that sex was the most gloriously impersonal part of human relations, and asserting the right of women to bear children without bearing the additional burden of a husband.

Since Shaw had already advised Erica to have children, to experiment in life rather than in art, the lesson of this play was obvious. She would have *his* children (with Rupert Brooke as their godfather) – and she dashed off a note to Shaw to advise him of this. His response disappointed her. 'Now it is clear that you cant marry me, because I am married already, and too old anyhow,' he urged.

> But please do not suppose that your loving me is the smallest reason for your not marrying someone else. On the contrary, it is an additional reason for doing it as soon as you can. To begin with, a great deal of *pain* in youthful love is purely physical. Every complete and vital person wants to fulfil the sexual function . . . and one will do as well as another for purposes of physical fulfilment.

What seemed curious to Erica was that the author of *Getting Married* should use the word marriage as a synonym for sexual intercourse. To ensure that he had not misunderstood her she wrote again, and then again, until Shaw's advice grew more peremptory. Why not, he urged, 'marry somebody with a short temper and a heavy fist, who will knock you down'? She must, he insisted, occupy herself with work and babies. Without these she would end up 'a nagging prig'.

There was something about the way in which Erica accepted his advice that unnerved Shaw. Believing it was time her parents took some notice, he demanded that she make her love known and she obliquely agreed by threatening to write to H.G. Wells about it. In fact she seems to have confided her wonderful secret only to Rupert Brooke. 'I grieve for your nerves,' he responded, but cautiously restricted his Shavian reference to literature, singling out as 'the best play in the world' *Candida*, in which the youthful poet renounces domestic love (with a wife and children) for the solitude of literary inspiration.

Some of Erica's difficulties, Brooke diagnosed, came from her style (likened by Shaw to Dora Copperfield's) which rose and fell with unflagging conviction. She did everything too hurriedly and should have cultivated a little Fabian gradualism. 'The great thing is to *make other people understand what one means,*' Brooke hinted. 'So merely to blurt it out and understand it oneself, does not do . . .'

> I think it is good to shock people a little, & speak out to them, but one must be careful to do it gradually, as a rule, so as to get them accustomed by degrees. Only, I think, if one really feels 'inspired' – feels it *absolutely necessary* to tell out some burning thing – if one is sure of this feeling, to speak out is right at all costs. It is a matter to settle with one's own conscience, I think.

Erica's conscience left her untroubled since her normal condition was one of burning 'inspiration'. She was full of the necessity to speak out her total love for Shaw. He had calculated that she was one third mad and always therefore on the verge of rousing his hatred for mad people whom, nevertheless, he seemed increasingly to attract. Her letters bored him terribly yet their power was undeniable and though he longed to fling them into the wastepaper basket, he often found himself glancing at them, beginning to read them, then actually replying, using the force of his own style to combat hers. He told her she was a 'luxurious young devil, with the ethics, and something of the figure, of an anteater'; that if she dared try to crawl over him as she doubtless had crawled over Rupert Brooke, she would be 'hurled into outer darkness'; that whenever he received anything in the nature of a love letter, he handed it straight to his wife.

Erica's reaction to this was to make her letters more easily available to Charlotte Shaw. Shaw himself (who was used to having his advice ignored) challenged her to type her letters and make her love public. So, in 1908 and 1909, using a printer in Sydney Street, Chelsea, she privately published her correspondence to Shaw. To this first series of about 60,000 words she subsequently added during the First World War (after Rupert Brooke had died and his restraining influence been removed) another 200,000 printed words entitled 'An account' or 'An Account through Letters' which she dedicated to Shaw 'whom I love': over a quarter of a million words of self-indulgent, oddly eloquent, stream-of-consciousness prose.

I am conscious from the beginning of writing this to you that it will be printed, but yet everything I write I shall write to you alone, and in the same way as I've written to you before, out of a feeling that I am speaking to you, more than I am writing to you. You know how Ive written, over and over in different forms, that it felt that so long as I consciously held back from giving one thing that I could give for this thing which is my love for you that I should be held back from everything, and you know how nearly from the beginning a thing has come back and back in me, a feeling that I needed to go, and kneel down to you in front of people . . . I spread things out through writing, I didnt hide them, nor the form they came in, and I kneeled down to you before people in my imagination, but held back from kneeling down to you with my body . . .

It is from her imagination that she writes. She is obsessional, relentless, ecstatic, insistent: and as unstoppable in her fashion as Shaw himself. She repeats and repeats. Her prose is hypnotic, like a chant, a litany, ascending in exaltation, curling about itself monotonously and sinking so it may rise again, again, again. The ritual of this writing was the vehicle for her love, fuelled by religious fantasies of sex: of conception and birth. She summons Shaw to look round and confront all he had deliberately turned his back on.

What is coming is coming my dear hearts stretch out to meet what comes out of some part in you which is deeper than what you mostly stretch out of to meet things which come through words . . . can you feel a dim dim knowledge in you that behind a single separate thing are things which are struggling to push out through you – and will you pray for me my dear ones not only out of dim feelings in you but still more out of everything that laughs and dances in you – its as if if inside you you stretched out your hands and took my hands out of everything that laughs and dances in you I should reach my love.

Shaw's weapon against passion was iron politeness. He was magnificently armed with good manners, jokes, witty advice, reverberating words: and he banged them all off at her. But she had as many words in her armoury as he did and used a different vocabulary. Her talent was 'as irresistible as Shelley's & Tolstoy's rolled into one' and she would 'either die a lunatic before you are 33', he prophesied, 'or be the greatest English woman writer – indeed one of the greatest of English writers – before you are 40'. This tribute Erica sensibly preserved and had printed almost thirty years later wrapped round her anonymous 1939 novel *Form of Diary*.

How strange were women! What did they really want? Shaw had taken the trouble to give her notice of his Fabian lectures, send her theatre tickets, introduce her to friends, demand information about her home, inform her about publishing contracts and promise to 'exude wisdom at every pore': and still she did not feel rejected. Charlotte, his wife, actually accused him of encouraging the girl! Was it his fault if she rented a neighbouring cottage and came racing up to his house on a motor bicycle? Eventually they were forced to threaten her with the police. 'I would not stand it from Cleopatra herself', cried Shaw, who drafted a stern letter for his wife to write which explained that he 'is quite friendly and sympathetic with everybody, from dogs & cats to dukes & duchesses; and none of them can imagine that his universal friendliness is not a special regard for them. He has already allowed you to become far more attracted to him than he should; and I do not intend to let you drift any further into an impossible position.'

Yet behind the boredom and impossibility of it all, there was some 'special regard' between them. Erica's account of their relationship, though choked with her own symptoms, has clear insights into his nature and, when it touches on fact, is accurate, comparing closely with his correspondence. 'One day when I was in a train with you,' she writes, 'you suddenly leaned forward and said – Now Ill tell you what Id tell few women, you told it and I answered you and presently you said – Ill leave the country.' Shaw's version of this episode is perhaps used in Act 2 of *Heartbreak House*, where Captain Shotover (Shaw) and Ellie Dunn (Erica) go to the sofa and talk.

CAPTAIN SHOTOVER. What did you expect? A Saviour, eh?
Are you old-fashioned enough to believe in that?

ELLIE. No. But I thought you were very wise, and might help
me. Now I have found you out. You pretend to be busy, and
think of fine things to say and run in and out to surprise
people by saying them, and get away before they can answer
you.

CAPTAIN SHOTOVER. It confuses me to be answered. It dis-
courages me. I cannot bear men and women. I have to run
away. I must run away now [*he tries to*].

ELLIE [*again seizing his arm*]. You shall not run away from
me. I can hypnotise you. You are the only person in the
house I can say what I like to. I know you are fond of me. Sit
down [*She draws him to the sofa*] . . . Dream. I like you to
dream. You must never be in the real world when we talk
together.

CAPTAIN SHOTOVER. I am too weary to resist or too weak. I
am in my second childhood. I do not see you as you really
are. I can't remember what I really am. I feel nothing but the
accursed happiness I have dreaded all my life long: the happiness that comes as life goes, the happiness of yielding and
dreaming instead of resisting and doing, the sweetness of the
fruit that is going rotten.

ELLIE. You dread it almost as much as I used to dread losing
my dreams and having to fight and do things. But that is all
over for me: my dreams are dashed to pieces. I should like to
marry a very old, very rich man. I should like to marry you.

Erica lived in 'a fanciful world of her own', Shaw wrote; and in
the fanciful world of his plays she has a special place for she was, he
acknowledged, 'an exquisite sort of person'. But in the world of
facts and actions all was impossible. When over fifty, she adopted
two baby boys whom she was reputed to feed largely on peanut
butter. She changed her name to Mrs Saye and gave that name to
the children, whom she brought up as farmers in North Devon. But
nothing went the way of her dreams – one of the boys forged her

signature on a cheque and ran off with a married woman much older than himself whom Erica had thought of as her friend.

Though fulfilling neither of Shaw's extravagant prophecies, Erica lived what by Shavian standards was a lunatic life until her seventieth year. She died in 1950, the same year as Shaw himself. 'What a relief!' he exclaimed when he heard the news. She had been a terror and a nuisance and he had never wholly got over his dread that she might roar up again on her motor bicycle one night. Yet he would have been happy to see her on what he called 'reasonable terms', that is, pressed on to paper as an ingredient for his fantasy. So now that she was safely dead, he wrote to ask a friend: 'Are any photographs of her obtainable?'

1983

ARTIST IN EXILE
Gwen John

Nothing of importance had happened to her, Gwen John told Rodin, until the age of twenty-seven, when she came to live in France. 'England has become quite a foreign country to me,' she wrote. 'I don't want to see any English pictures again except the work of two or three artists.'

She had been born in 1876 on the west coast of Wales, one of four children and the elder sister of Augustus John. In 1884 her mother, an amateur painter, died; and the children were brought up by their father, a sanctimonious solicitor, assisted by various governesses optimistically described as 'Swiss'. It was a bleak upbringing in a dark house with a silent and unsympathetic parent. All the children associated happiness with what they saw outdoors, with the countryside and especially the sea; and they dreamed of exiling themselves when grown-up from the land of their father. Thornton, who had ambitions to be a gold prospector, escaped to Canada; Winifred, who was musical, gave violin lessons in California and married one of her pupils there; Augustus, whose mind had wavered between China and 'Red Indian' country, went in 1894 to the Slade School of Fine Art in London; and, the following year, Gwen joined him there.

Like Augustus, she was an exceptionally gifted draughtsman, winning a certificate for figure-drawing in her second year and, in her last year, the Melvill Nettleship Prize for figure composition. This was the beginning of a grand epoch in the Slade's history, a School of British Promise being established there in the 1890s under the guidance of Henry Tonks and Frederick Brown, and through the rigorous teaching of figure-drawing. But during her three years as a student Gwen grew more interested in oil painting. From Ambrose McEvoy (once known as the Shelley of British Art) she learned the Old Master technique of putting on fluid paint in layers, modifying the underlying colour (a green monochrome wash) with a series of semi-transparent glazes.

In choosing Ambrose McEvoy as her mentor Gwen seems to have been aiming for someone to displace Edwin John, her father. 'We are the sort of people,' Augustus once boasted to Nina Hamnett, 'our fathers warned us against.' The dandified, short-sighted figure of McEvoy, with his monocle, Phil May fringe and insatiable absinthe-drinking might well have earned the disapproval of Edwin. But McEvoy's personality was too immature for Gwen; and his paintings, which eventually veered to stardust portraits of society women, were of a sort particularly relished by her father. Besides, he was at that time greatly under the spell of Augustus.

McEvoy and Gwen belonged to a group of Slade students that was to include Edna Waugh, Ursula Tyrwhitt, Ida Nettleship (who married Augustus), Gwen Salmond (later the wife of Matthew Smith) and William Orpen. Many in this group were Tonks's favourites; but they gave direct allegiance to Augustus John, the Slade School 'genius', whose personality ruled these years. From a distance, the figure of Gwen John did not stand out and she was not independently well-known. One student remembered 'someone pointing her out to me as she crossed Gower Street: "That's Augustus's sister." '

Augustus was always an admirer of Gwen's work, but his presence dominated and distracted her. Something of what she felt was expressed by another contemporary painter, Wyndham Lewis. 'I feel that if I were left alone, I could both write and paint just now,' he told his mother: 'but near John I can never paint, since his artistic personality is just too strong, and he is much more developed, naturally, and this frustrates any effort.' This was peculiarly Gwen's predicament at the Slade and in her middle twenties. 'I should like to go and live somewhere,' she wrote to Ursula Tyrwhitt, 'where I met nobody I know till I am so strong that people and things could not affect me beyond reason.'

People and things: to women, children, men, cats, flowers she was acutely sensitive. 'I was born to love,' she wrote. Though extremely confident of her work and delighting in the visible world, she was pessimistic about human relationships. Her social elusiveness disguised considerable self-esteem. When asked her opinion of an exhibition of Cézanne watercolours, she replied in a scarcely audible voice: 'These are very good, but I prefer my own.' On a later occasion she expressed herself as 'pleased and proud' to see her *Portrait of Mère Poussepin* among the American patron John Quinn's collection, adding: 'I thought it the best picture there, but I liked the Seurat landscape.' She was docile but determined. To Ursula Tyrwhitt she confided: 'I cannot imagine why my vision will have some value in the world – and yet I know it will . . . I think it will count because I am patient and recueillé in some degree.'

It was this patience and singlemindedness that differentiated her from Augustus. Describing a holiday the two of them spent with McEvoy at Le Puy, Augustus wrote: 'Gwen, like me, had been crossed in love, but, unlike me, was inconsolable, and spent her time in tears.' This capacity for absorbing rather than dissipating pain was part of her strength and she transferred it to her pictures. Of a show the two of them held in Chelsea in 1903 (forty-five pictures by him, three by her, of which one may have been withdrawn) Augustus told William Rothenstein: 'Gwen has the honours or *should* have – for alas our smug critics don't appear to have noticed the presence in the [Carfax] Gallery of two rare blossoms from the most delicate of trees. The little pictures to me are almost painfully charged with feeling; even as their neighbours are empty of it.' Both of them were extremely responsive to the work of other artists, but whereas Augustus surrendered himself to one influence after another, displaying with extraordinary virtuosity a diversity of styles, Gwen took only what she wanted and assimilated it into her own style. To achieve this integration she had to control the excitements she shared with her brother – what she called the 'impatience and angoisse'. She would prepare for a picture slowly – then paint it with fearful rapidity. 'I think a picture ought to be done in one sitting or at most two,' she later told Ursula Tyrwhitt.

Behind the serenity of Gwen's pictures lay a painstaking struggle for composure that fascinated Augustus. Far from being opposites they were 'much the same really,' he judged, 'but we took a different attitude'. Making himself the target of vast publicity, he became the hollow man who, though recognised everywhere as the standard celebrity, was without identity; and a painter whose canvases, as they grew larger, finally grew emptier.

> *Shape without form, shade without colour*
> *Paralysed force, gesture without motion.*

Gwen drew attention to herself through the severity of her self-neglect, and the size of her pictures gradually diminished until, a few years before her death, she seems (except for a few 'nervous jottings') to have given up painting altogether. Some inherited factor – exuberance combined with a melancholy that (like Dr Johnson's) made them 'mad' all their lives, 'at least not sober' – cut them off from other people. But Augustus could not endure the isolation to which Gwen implacably was to submit herself, and he tried to rid himself of strong feelings in the uproar of a perpetual party.

> *And if I drink oblivion of a day*
> *So shorten I the stature of my soul.*

Gwen turned the other way and eventually edited her vulnerability to men and women by eliminating them from her life. 'Leave everybody and let them leave you,' she noted in her diary. 'Then only will you be without fear.'

Gwen's removal from England to France may be seen as an expulsion from the family territory from which Augustus merely played truant. 'We don't go to Heaven in families any more – but one by one,' she wrote. Against her father's wishes, she set off for Paris in the autumn of 1898, staying with Ida Nettleship and Gwen Salmond, who smuggled her as an afternoon pupil into the Académie Carmen. This newly opened school was run by a one-time model of Whistler who himself took two lessons a week. 'Whistler has been twice to the studio – and Gwen finds him very beautiful and just right,' Ida reported. 'He's a regular first rate Master and, according to Gwen, knows how to teach.'

Whistler's school was a perfect corrective to that of Tonks and Brown at the Slade – 'a tonal modelling not a drawing school'. Far from being a fellow artist in shirt-sleeves, Whistler appeared before them as the master visiting his apprentices. He offered no magical short-cuts and would have liked to send them back to the beginning, even to the grinding and mixing of colours. 'I do not teach art,' he declared, 'I teach the scientific application of paint and brushes.' The palette, not the canvas, he insisted was the proper field of experiment; and to emphasise this he would sometimes ignore his pupils' pictures altogether and make a performance of examining their palettes and the order in which they had arranged their colours. Art, he told them, was the *science* of beauty. Under his influence Gwen developed her individual technique, preparing her canvases and colour mixes, and inventing a system of numbering tones. 'But it is a strange confusion of the intuitive and the scientific that emerges from her notes on painting,' Mary Taubman has written. 'A typical extract begins "April faded Panseys on the sands at night," and goes on "Tones, sky 22 clouds 13, house & bushes & grass 23 & 13."' Within this shorthand of descriptive notes and mathematical indexes are variously phrased rules, reminders, formulas. One list, headed 'The making of the portrait' reads: '1 the strange form 2 the pose and proportions 3 the atmosphere and notes 4 the finding of the forms (the sphere the hair the forehead the cheek the eye the nose the mouth the neck the chin the torse) 5 blobbing 6 the sculpting with the hands.' Another recipe, called 'Method of observation', lists '1 the strangeness 2 colour 3 tones 4 form'; and there is 'Rule 1: The drawing is the discord.'

Such schemes for pictures, unintelligible to others, helped to bring Gwen John the painstaking tonal accuracy her original vision needed, and she developed her methodicity, Augustus wrote, 'to a point of elaboration undreamt of by her Master'. Rodin, he recorded, acclaimed her gifts. '"*Vous êtes belle artiste*", were the words she reported to me with natural elation.' Augustus, seeing Whistler in the Salon Carré of the Louvre one day, remembered he had introduced himself as Gwen's brother, saying that he thought her drawings showed a feeling for character. But Whistler corrected him: 'It's *tone* that matters. Your sister has a fine sense of *tone*.'

It was her friend Gwen Salmond who had provided the tuition fees for her to study at the Académie Carmen. During these four months Edwin John arrived in Paris to check on his daughter and, after a quarrel between them, made sure that she would receive no money from him. So in February 1899 Gwen came back to England and, though she returned briefly to France for a holiday in the autumn of 1900, she did not finally go to live there until the late summer of 1903 – and then in the most unlikely manner. 'I have never seen her so well or so gay,' Albert Rutherston wrote that summer. 'She was fat in the face & merry to a degree.' The source of her happiness was a new friend, Dorelia McNeil, later to become a mythical figure in the life and paintings of Augustus.

To the beauty of Dorelia both Gwen and Augustus were equally responsive. Dorelia 'seems to be a great friend of all the Johns', Albert Rutherston confided. 'I think John must have a secret agreement with that lady and Mrs J – but not a word to anyone of this – it is a notion and a mad one at that.' But it was true. Augustus had fallen deeply in love with her and she was strongly attracted to him. It was probably to escape from an increasingly difficult position between Augustus and Ida John that Dorelia consented that summer to what seemed a mad proposal of Gwen's: to leave London and walk to Rome. The two girls were as excited as if by an elopement, though Augustus, like an angry parent, was appalled, relenting only so far as to offer them a pistol. Gwen's motives were not so different from Dorelia's. She also wished to escape from the John clan. It was essential that she cut herself off emotionally and geographically from her past; and it was characteristic that she did it in such an impetuous fashion. Brushing aside all Augustus's objections, she got together a few belongings and a good deal of painting equipment, collected Dorelia, and boarded a steamer on the Thames that took them to Bordeaux. It was a difficult journey. They started walking up the valley of the Garonne, drawing portraits (and sometimes singing songs) at bars and cafés to make some money, sleeping in fields close together with their portfolios as bedclothes. 'We shall never get to Rome I'm afraid,' Gwen admitted, 'it seems further away than it did in England.' But by the autumn they did reach Toulouse and it was here that Gwen completed various drawings and three exquisite paintings of Dorelia – *Dorelia by Lamplight*, *Dorelia in a Black Dress* and *The Student*. These beautiful pictures represent the culmination of her English painting. Though they glow with love, Gwen's feelings never spill over the form of the paintings into sentimentality. The form, however, is not so strange and there is not much discord in the drawing. The pictures belong to the best of the new English art of this period and may be sympathetically compared with, for example, the softer portraits of Rose Pettigrew done in the early 1890s by Wilson Steer, who taught painting at the Slade.

Also belonging to this period are two self-portraits. The first, which was bought by Fred Brown of the Slade, shows all the gentleness and sensitivity that was one part of Gwen's nature. Painted in 1900, it presents a plain, neat, rather spinsterish and slightly apprehensive image of herself: a Jane Eyre governess. But the second portrait, painted anything up to five years later, is far more self-assertive, the pose defiant, the face revealing another side of her nature to which Augustus gave the word (in its English sense) formidable.

It was this formidable aspect that Gwen was to develop in Paris, where she and Dorelia went from Toulouse early in 1904. 'I am getting on with my painting, and this makes me happy,' she reported to Alice Rothenstein. But Dorelia, who had become involved with a young unmarried Belgian artist called Leonard, was not happy. There was a crisis, and she left secretly with him for Bruges. She had decided to stay with him there for three months, or a lifetime, depending how things worked out.

How things worked out depended largely on Gwen. The decisive way in which she took over the management of everything is extremely self-revealing and provides an index to the story of her own life during the following ten years. In a series of letters she successfully appealed to Dorelia to leave Leonard and link her destiny to Augustus. 'You are necessary for his development and for Ida's, and he is necessary for yours – I have known that a long time – but I did not know how much,' she wrote.

> Dorelia you know I love you, you do not know how much. I should think it the greatest crime to take with intention anyone's happiness away even for a little time – it is to me the only thing that would matter . . .
>
> I am sorry for Leonard, but he has had his happiness for a time what more can he expect? We do not expect more. And all the future is yours to do what you like. Do not think these are my thoughts only – they are my instincts and inspired by whatever we have in us divine. I know what I write is for the best, more than I have ever known anything . . .
>
> Strength and weakness, selfishness & unselfishness are only words – our work in life was to develop ourselves and so fulfil our destiny. And when we do this we are of use in the world . . .
>
> I love you so much that if I never saw you again and knew you were happy I should be happy too.

There is extraordinary authority in Gwen's advice ('I know what I write is for the best . . . If you are perplexed, trust me'). She believes in a divinity that shapes our ends and in the proper usefulness to our work of deepening and developing our emotions. Never promiscuous, puritan in many of her attitudes, she was nevertheless a believer in the religion of love for art's sake.

This confidence reflected a happiness that had come to her this year after meeting Rodin. He was as necessary for her destiny, she believed, as Dorelia was for Augustus's. The story of her love for Rodin, and their love affair, has been told by Susan Chitty in her biography of Gwen John. At sixty-three Rodin was a legendary figure who became god-the-father to Gwen. Earlier in 1904 she had written of getting homesick for London: 'Fitzroy St and Howland St seem to me more than ever charming and interesting,' she had confessed to Alice Rothenstein. 'We shall be going home in the Autumn I think or before.' After falling in love with Rodin the old life in England that had clung to her so damply tumbled to pieces like an old shell. She was out of it, could do what she liked and go where she wanted. She did not want to go to England. Apart from a few weeks in 1927 when she was preparing a 'lovely' cottage in Hampshire that Augustus had helped her to buy, she did not return during the remaining thirty-five years of her life. 'I don't mind seeing Gus now or the family,' she was to assure Ursula Tyrwhitt. 'It is such a beautiful place . . . I sometimes want to be there very much.' But her instinct overrode this decision and she continued to anchor herself in Paris, where she had experienced love and where she made her unconventional home-from-home.

Until 1913 she lived in a series of rooms round Montparnasse, where she painted a number of *intimiste* interiors. The most haunting of these show some corner of the room, usually with light from a window, perhaps a curtain, sometimes a chair, a table with teapot or flowers, but no person; others contain a single figure, most often herself, standing reading or seated in a chair or on a bed. Originally she tried to make the figure look like a Vierge of Dürer, but decided that this was a 'very silly thing' to do. 'I did it,' she told Ursula Tyrwhitt, 'because I didn't want to put my own face there.' Later she did put her own face in ('it is more fitting') and would take some of these pictures to Rodin to show him where she was living. 'My room is so pretty,' she wrote to him in 1907. 'I will draw it for you in the wardrobe mirror with me doing something in the Dutch manner.'

To earn money she modelled for Rodin and for a number of women artists. When one of the lesbian artists she posed for asked her whether she wasn't *ashamed* to stand naked before Rodin, she answered: 'Oh no. I like it very much.' She had, as Rodin said, '*un corps admirable*'. From Rodin she learned to study nature with a 'humble and patient love' and to observe 'the grace of life, make it without timidity – not be preoccupied with details, but not leave gaps either'. But where Rodin's work is dramatic, Gwen's lies 'between the acts'. Under his influence she learned how to concentrate her powers of observation by the repetition of images and how to simplify her work with strong contours.

Rodin added to her self-assurance. In London she had been (in her own phrase) 'shy as a sheep'. In Paris she grew into the person Augustus was to describe as exuberant. 'She wasn't chaste or subdued, but amorous & proud,' he wrote. 'She didn't steal through life but preserved a haughty independence which people mistook for humility. Her passions for both men and women were outrageous and irrational. She was never "unnoticed" by those who had access to her.' Dorelia, too, had observed that she was both 'hard' and 'rather vain'. Under Rodin's spell she spent hours on her appearance, pinching her breasts to make sure they did not diminish, buying new clothes, reading books he liked and learning by heart the whole of Euripides's *Iphigenia* to recite to him (though this performance, owing to her bad French, was cut short). The governess of the early self-portrait was now reborn as an obsessive, rather brazen female speaking of 'things I never thought of before' and commanding Rodin not to waste his energy on condolences to someone else but save it up for their next love-making. But, as Susan Chitty has written, this love-making which rejuvenated Gwen was ageing for Rodin. 'Love is my illness,' she told him, 'and there is no cure till you come.' She wore him out with her obsession, haunting the café opposite his studio, camping almost naked in the bushes outside his fence when he was out. She wrote to him, often three times a day, feverish, gross, adoring letters, some of them addressed to an imaginary 'Julie'. She had no self-pity and did not complain at sharing their bed sometimes with another girl.

On the whole Rodin seems to have treated her with tenderness and generosity. '*Vous avez de grandes facultés de sentir et de penser,*' he wrote to her. '*Courage, petite amie, moi je suis si fatigué et vieux . . . mais j'aime votre petit coeur si dévoué, patience et pas de violence.*' At her request Rodin organised the timetable of her days. Like Augustus, she had been drastically affected by her mother's death and by what they both felt to be the loveless life with their father. Augustus's obsessional theme as a painter was of a mother-and-children in the womb of a mythical landscape; Gwen's need too was for a new childhood and she created it in her life with Rodin. By means partly flirtatious, in part threateningly vulnerable, she brought out the father in him. 'He scolded her for not looking after herself,' wrote Hilary Spurling, 'urged her to eat, wash, work, brush her hair, tidy her room, go for walks, told her, in short, all the things a little girl needs to hear.' After her first break with Rodin, her handwriting changed (in Rosemary Dinnage's words) 'from crisply adult to pathetically schoolgirlish'. Her dependence on Rodin co-existed with the 'haughty independence' Augustus had attributed to her. There was 'a quiet part of her mind' somehow not engulfed by the shocks and fevers of her emotions. She needed love: and this need gave the serenity of her pictures their peculiar intensity.

Her solitary life emphasised rather than protected her from the stress and torment of this passion. At each rupture in their love, she recoiled further into this solitude. 'I had a tiring life for some years and so seem only now to begin to paint,' she wrote in 1914. After Rodin's death in 1917 she trained herself to 'put all that energy of loving into my drawing'. It sustained her, at terrible physical expense, for another dozen years of work. She had thought, after he died, she might go mad. 'I don't know what I am going to do,' she wrote incoherently to Ursula Tyrwhitt. 'When one gets tired one loses something which one never gets back.' But after the war she revived, describing herself as like a 'plant that was dying and nearly dead and begins to grow again'. It was 'almost unbelievable and what a joy it is to live'. She had managed to recover the 'quiet part of her mind', safeguarding it with the Catholicism to which (since it was Rodin's religion) she had been converted in the winter of 1912–13 – this was a 'journey to Rome' she appeared to have completed. She also surrounded herself with cats that absorbed some of her loving; and protected herself with the nun-like abstinence of an eccentric, exiled, half-starved, English spinster. In a sense her life was over. She had had her happiness for a time. What more could she expect? So far as possible she filled the days with her work and her religion. 'I think I shall do something good soon,' she had promised Ursula Tyrwhitt. 'If I'm left to myself and not absolutely destroyed.'

Though 'God's little artist', as she called herself, could be coy and self-regarding in her perception of herself, her confidence in her work grew more rigorous and well-defined. 'Impose your style,' she instructed herself. 'Let it be simple and strong. The short strong stalks of flowers. Don't be afraid of falling into mediocrity. You would never.' Already by 1908 this style had begun to change. She began experimenting in gouache. 'I am doing some drawings in my glass, myself and the room, and I put white in the colour so it is like painting in oil and quicker,' she wrote the following year to Ursula Tyrwhitt.

> I first draw in the thing then trace it on to a clean piece of paper by holding it against the window. Then decide absolutely on the tones, then try and make them in colour and put them in flat. Then the thing is finished . . . I want my drawings, if they are drawings, to be definite and clean like Japanese drawings . . . the practice of putting things down with decision ought to help me when I do painting in oils – in fact I think all is there – except the modelling of flesh perhaps.

A feature of her later work, which she derived from Rodin, was the practice of working in sets. 'Not only paintings and gouaches but many of the portrait drawings are repeated over and over again with hardly perceptible variations, and with no loss of vitality,' Mary Taubman wrote. She was abandoning her fluid technique of oil painting, using instead a quick-drying medium (Mary Taubman suggests petrol, which had been recommended by Whistler) and laying on the canvas a dry, chalky paint in a mosaic of tiny brush-strokes. This new technique, which achieved greater breadth and simplicity, relied on thick paint, careful preparation and rapid painting – a method and medium that brought together the patience and impetuosity of her nature. In the early 1920s, too, she increasingly refined her range of tones so that her pale blue and yellow and rose all look like subtle variations of a muted grey.

Her subjects were women, children, flowers, cats, occasionally a street scene of the house where she was living. Sometimes one of her wide-awake cats will confront you with a stare, but usually her subjects are glancing down, looking to one side, or simply turning their backs in prayer. She is an autobiographical artist, showing us the people she saw near the place where she lived, revealing her susceptibility to their beauty and the strength with which she contained that susceptibility. In her portraits of Dorelia, the emotion had been directly stated; the feeling in her later work is implied, allowing, with detachment and accuracy of observation, more anguish and poignancy to appear.

Though the idiom is traditional, it is this obliqueness, this experiment in 'the discord' of drawing, and her search for 'the strange form' that make her work modern. Because she seldom showed her pictures and lived a life of such obstinate seclusion she has been represented (by Wyndham Lewis for example) as islanded from the influences of her times. She did, however, exhibit between 1919 and 1925 at the Société du Salon d'Automne, and saw as much painting perhaps as she needed to see. Like her brother, she greatly admired Puvis de Chavannes and Picasso, to whose Blue Period some of her pre-war work has similarities. Occasionally in her correspondence she mentions a picture she has seen and liked – something by Rouault, Segonzac or Chagall, and a whole collection by a naïf painter in a different style, Rousseau. Her last watercolours and gouaches 'display a change in handling which seems to indicate an awareness of Cubism', Cecily Langdale has written; 'there are hints of Derain, for example, in her tiny late still lives. In the last figure pictures . . . she employed the heavy outlines that one associates with Rouault.' Several critics have linked some of her work with that of Modigliani. In a summary of her career, Mary Taubman concluded: 'In her concern with order and solidity, her obsessive desire to perfect her statement of the simplest image . . . Gwen John takes her place with Seurat and Cézanne among the great modern classical painters.'

The years between the beginning of the First World War to the late 1920s, which registered the spectacular decline of her brother's talent, were to be the most fruitful period of Gwen John's working life. At about the time of her conversion to Catholicism she took an attic (*'cette maison est si humide, les murs suitent et des petits ruisseaux coulent des murs des escaliers'*) at 29 rue Terre Neuve, in Meudon, a south-west suburb of Paris, where Rodin lived. The anonymity and calm of the place, near a Dominican convent, suited her, and she continued to rent this room even after buying a hut, still in Meudon, on a piece of waste ground in the rue Babie during the late 1920s. Nuns and orphans in the church (the nuns at Meudon ran a school for orphans) were the subjects of many of her pictures for over a dozen years. 'It was in art,' Augustus insisted, 'that she found true happiness.' Her religion, which dignified self-neglect as mortification of the flesh, was a method, loyal to Rodin, by which she sought to avoid being 'absolutely destroyed' and which redirected her passion from people to an invisible God. But Catholicism as represented by the nuns and by her spiritual adviser (signing himself 'Y[our] M[aster]') was hostile to her art and Gwen often 'fell into a discouragement'. Her niece, Vivien, remembered her in 1926 'like a miniature Augustus, with eyes that filled with tears almost continuously as she talked, very pale, bluey eyes and she wore dark, dark clothes'.

She appeared on the verge of a depression. In 1928 she was again gripped by an over-mastering passion, this time for Véra Oumançoff, the sister-in-law of the Catholic philosopher Jacques Maritain. Véra was a plump, motherly woman who thought to exercise over her a thwarted ambition for nursing the poor. Her attentions released in Gwen something of the same devotion that had been aimed at Dorelia. 'She loved Véra, she told her, as she loved flowers,' Susan Chitty wrote. 'She loved her so much that she dared not look into her eyes.' Such passion dismayed Véra who, in self-protection, reproved her:

Avez-vous réellement besoin de m'écrire presque tous les jours? Je ne le crois pas – et je crois même que c'est très mauvais pour votre âme – car vous vous attachez trop à une créature, sans même la connaître pour ainsi dire. Je sais bien que vous avez une grande sensibilité, mais il faut la tourner vers Notre Seigneur, vers la Sainte Vierge.

'You told me my letter was too long,' Gwen replied. 'Too long for what? I think souls in Purgatory must feel like me. I don't live calmly like you and the rest of the world.'

Gwen was allowed to see Véra only on Mondays, when she would present her with one of her drawings. It was characteristic that she should hand over so much of her work to someone who cared for it so little. After they stopped seeing each other in the early 1930s and Véra moved away, these drawings (*Les Dessins de Lundi*) also stopped. 'You must continue,' Gwen had noted to herself in 1927. Late in the 1920s, with her pencil and gouache studies of *Little girl with a large hat and straw-coloured hair* and *Boy with a blank expression*, she had found a new simplified style 'definite and clean like Japanese drawings'. But not long afterwards she seems to have lost her equilibrium. During the 1930s her Catholic faith began to fade and her vitality for painting ebbed away. Feeling too 'tired' to finish her paintings, she could not fulfil her destiny and, by her own standards, was not of use in the world. She had once told Véra that the orphans at Meudon charmed her so much that if she 'gave up all that there would not be enough happiness in my life'. Without this sunlight the plant did not grow again. She had longed for solitude and found isolation. 'People are like shadows to me and I am like a shadow,' she had written to Michel Salaman. 'I don't think we change, but we disappear sometimes.' During the last three years of her life she seems to have disappeared into the shed in the rue Babie.

On 1 September 1939, 'feeling the old compulsion of the sea upon her', she took a train to Dieppe, but collapsed in the street there. Having no possessions she was taken for an indigent and removed to the Hospice de Dieppe where, at 8.30 am on 18 September, she died. No cause of death was given on the certificate.

The previous year she had not turned up at her father's funeral in Wales, and none of her family now came to Dieppe. Augustus had thoughts of designing a gravestone but 'never got round to it' and the whereabouts of her grave is now unknown. She had banished herself from Britain, orphaned herself from the family, sought recreation through her power of loving, grown into the child of her work. The quality of this work has gradually become better known since her Memorial Exhibition at Matthieson Ltd in 1946. Augustus had always known it. 'Few on meeting this retiring person in black,' he wrote, 'with her tiny hands and feet, a soft, almost inaudible voice, and delicate Pembrokeshire accent, would have guessed that here was the greatest woman artist of her age, or, as I think, of any other.' He had recognised, too, if sometimes as a form of self-criticism, the courage she needed to maintain and increase her susceptibility to 'people and things'. In his concern for her welfare he had threatened her independence, offering her a half-and-half existence like his own. But she was not tempted. 'I told you in a letter long ago that I am happy,' she assured him. 'When illness or death do not interfere, I am. Not many people can say as much . . . If to "return to life" is to live as I did in London – *Merci, Monsieur!* . . . There are people like plants who cannot flourish in the cold, and I want to flourish.'

1982

THEMES AND VARIATIONS
Augustus John

'You are reflecting whether it is not time to throw Augustus John, who has clearly become compromising, overboard,' wrote Walter Sickert in the *Burlington Magazine* in 1916. 'Take my tip. Don't!'

Yet Augustus John has been thrown overboard by many art critics today. In the first fifteen years of the twentieth century he was looked to, with admiration or opprobrium, as a leader of much that was progressive in British art. But recently he has vanished from the history of art in Britain to the extent of appearing only as the subject of a portrait by Matthew Smith in the exhibition *British Art in the Twentieth Century: The Modern Movement* held by the Royal Academy in 1987. It is as if what Virginia Woolf had called in 1908 'the age of Augustus John' never existed.

In the current climate it is probably as well to remind readers of how critics and fellow artists regarded John's early work. 'We hardly dare confess how high are the hopes of Mr John's future which his paintings this year have led us to form,' Roger Fry wrote in the *Athenaeum* towards the end of 1904. He would have to 'go back to Alfred Stevens or Etty or the youthful Watts', Fry added, to find a fair comparison. Three years later John was sharing a notice with

Rubens and Delacroix which Laurence Binyon contributed to the
Saturday Review. In the United States, reviewing the famous Armory
Show of 1913, James Huneker pointed to John, along with Matisse
and Epstein, as the three big European talents.

Reacting to what *The Times* called John's 'uncanny notes of form
and dashes of colour', reactionary critics were equally extreme. 'At his
worst he can outdo Gauguin,' one of them complained in 1910. For
many he was the last word in incomprehensible modernity. 'After
Picasso, Mr John.'

But John's fellow artists, among them surrealists, futurists and
vorticists, looked on him as their fugleman. He had a magnetic power
over his contemporaries. 'I think John's talent and daring is an excellent example for us,' the portrait painter Neville Lytton wrote to
William Rothenstein in 1908, 'and shows us in what direction it is
expedient for us to throw our bonnets over the windmills.' Paul Nash,
who singled out his 'technical power', confessed to 'a deep respect for
John's draughtsmanship especially when it was applied with a paint-
brush'; C.R.W. Nevinson, who called him 'a genius', wrote that
'though I am always called a Modern, I have always tried to base
myself on John's example'; and Wyndham Lewis, despite mocking
him for having become 'an institution like Madame Tussaud's',
praised John for having, as the legitimate successor to Aubrey
Beardsley, buried 'the mock naturalists and pseudo-impressionists'.

John's work began to change in the First World War and went rapidly downhill in the 1930s. He found no new subject matter, no new
vocabulary, and he abused his technique. 'I have always been an
enthusiastic admirer of John's work,' Roger Fry had written in the
Nation in December 1910. But seven years later Fry was telling
Vanessa Bell that he found John 'almost entirely stupid' about modern
pictures after a visit to the Omega Workshops. For the most part,
however, John's later inferior work did not blind critics to his earlier
merits. Looking back over forty years of his draughtsmanship at the
National Gallery in 1940, Herbert Read paid tribute to his 'superb
mastery of form', his 'balance of psychological insight and formal
harmony', and concluded that it was 'doubtful if any other contemporary artist in Europe could display such virtuosity and skill'.

One of the first writers to attempt a survey of John's career, reconciling the apparent contradictions, was Anthony Blunt. 'Everyone is agreed on the fact that Augustus John was born with a quite exceptional talent for painting – some even used the word genius – and almost everyone is agreed that he has in some way wasted it,' Blunt wrote in the *Spectator* in 1938. John's greatest works, akin to those of masters from the past, were his portrait heads, usually done in two coloured chalks at the beginning of the century, Blunt argued. 'These early drawings have a sort of industrious observation which distinguishes them from all the later productions. For even in the oil sketches of the next period John is already letting himself go in a sort of mannerism, though the mannerism is so brilliant that one is at first willing to accept it as a serious basis for painting.' What Blunt finally objected to was the accelerated, almost baroque, method of painting John adopted which helped him to outpace the growing doubts and hesitations from which he sometimes attempted to divert attention by over-emphatic gesture and rhetoric – most famously in the full-length profile portrait of Madame Suggia of 1920–3. John's technical brilliance 'will stand the most minute study, and even study over a long period, without becoming thin', he wrote. 'It is only in his methods of dealing with the psychological problems presented by his sitters that his shorthand appears.'

The portraits and figure studies from the 1920s onwards lost the brilliance of the earlier paintings without regaining the meticulous care of the early drawings. 'It is only because his gifts are so great that one is forced to judge him by the very highest that he seems to fail,' Blunt concluded.

In contrast to Fry, Read and Blunt; to Paul Nash, C.R.W. Nevinson, Wyndham Lewis and others in the first half of the century came the wholesale dismissal led by Geoffrey Grigson in the mid-1970s. John was transformed into a *pasticheur*. His oils were seen as 'flashy and inferior' and his draughtsmanship no more than 'simulacra of the genuine'. Under such treatment, John dwindled into a 'vulgar art-school draughtsman with a provincial mind' whose drawings were uncreative and impersonal and whose paintings lacked imagination.

At the turn of the century we are left in a quandary. Was John's high reputation a product of the insularity and delusion of the English art world which lasted into the 1930s? Or has the posthumous decline of that reputation been, in the words of Grey Gowrie, 'a quirk of our own time'?

There are several factors that have dramatised this decline. The very necessary re-evaluation of his sister Gwen John's work, which began seriously in 1968 with a touring exhibition organised by the Arts Council, has been conducted somewhat unnecessarily at the expense of Augustus John – not by Gwen John scholars such as Cecily Langdale or Mary Taubman, but by journalists obliged to submit to the aggressive simplicities of a competitive age. In addition, the mass of indifferent work dumped on to the market through the posthumous studio sales of 1962–3, which has continued haphazardly to surface ever since, further depressed estimates of his worth.

In his monograph on Augustus John published in 1979, Richard Shone likened his career to those of Thomas Lawrence, David Wilkie and John Everett Millais, all 'artists who began very well and ended very badly'. John's talent was predominantly lyrical, Shone argued, and he interpreted the English, Welsh and French landscape through poetic or visionary eyes. 'This lyrical mode belongs essentially to youth (as so often in poetry) and it is rare,' Shone wrote, '. . . for the artist to effect a successful transformation as he grows older.' W.B. Yeats was, of course, an outstanding exception to this rule. But what would have happened had Keats lived on? And would Shelley, as Maurice Baring proposed in his *Unreliable Histories*, have swelled into the Tory MP for Horsham?

A successful transformation was made more difficult by the misapprehension of John's talent and temperament by his contemporaries. As early as 1900, Charles Conder decided that 'large decoration . . . seems to be his forte'. Nine years later, Roger Fry was writing in the *Burlington Magazine*: 'In Watts we sacrificed to our incurable individualism, our national incapacity of co-operating for ideal ends, a great monumental designer. A generous fate has given us another chance in Mr John.' There are one or two good examples of John's large-scale composition, notably the impressive if incomplete *Lyric Fantasy* and the more eloquent *Childhood of Pyramus* once owned by Clive and Vanessa Bell. But for the most part these big decorations were disappointing and sometimes disastrous. The mural he was commissioned to paint for the Irish art patron Sir Hugh Lane, called '*Forza e Amore*', he went on to destroy; and the vast triptych over which he laboured many of his last years came to nothing. Those that were completed, such as *The Mumpers*, often appear as artificial essays in the manner of Puvis de Chavannes, unhappily blended with some aspects of modernity, revealing John's inability to organise large groups of people. Yet he went on longing to paint on the heroic scale. 'When one thinks of painting on great expanses of wall, painting of any other kind seems hardly worth doing,' he said to John Rothenstein in 1939. No wonder Joyce Cary used John as one of his models for the bohemian artist Gulley Jimson in his novel *The Horse's Mouth* (1944).

In fact John was happier drawing and painting single figures on a comparatively small scale – his oil panels are seldom larger than 15 × 12 inches. In this he resembled his sister Gwen, acknowledging late in life the strange fact that 'Gwen and I were not opposites but much the same really, but we took a different attitude'. What they shared was an unbridgeable loneliness interrupted by desperate infatuations – at least once for the same person. Gwen tried to come to terms with her solitude by living alone, almost in exile, in Paris. Augustus tried to lose his sense of loneliness with a large complicated family and amid a crowded London life. They also shared a sense of impatience, both believing that a picture should be finished in one or two sittings. But Gwen prepared for this fast working practice with meticulous care, while Augustus attempted to achieve it through an intense 'fit of seeing'. His paintings, when they became larger, became emptier; hers grew smaller and eventually vanished altogether. It was as if they had the same telescope but were looking through different ends of it.

Gwen was aged eight and Augustus six when their mother died. She had been an amateur painter, and the determination with which son and daughter took up her gift says something about its origins and their obsessive choice of subjects. In Gwen's empty chair beside an open window, in her vacant rooms, we can feel her isolation; her women alone, her children sometimes facing away from us in church, have a poignancy enhanced by their obliqueness; her flowers and cats are containable love objects. All are indoor subjects. Augustus used outdoor subjects: women poised against the sky with their children or planted like trees in the landscape, raggle-taggle families of wanderers, all reflecting an ideal life as in some ballet, the focus of his wish fulfilment.

Neither of them were anecdotal artists, but Gwen's subjects leave you with the impression of a story told, a story with a sad ending in which all of us are implicated. Augustus's pictures are aesthetic statements, sudden sightings of the *dramatis personae* before the drama begins. Contrasting them in her survey of the fortunes of women painters and their work, *The Obstacle Race*, Germaine Greer explains that Gwen John moved away from the virtuoso beginnings she shared with her brother 'forever compressing and concentrating her art and her feelings to one inner end', while Augustus John's 'marvellous facility' stranded him in 'superficiality'. In literature, superficiality is almost inevitably a pejorative term, but in painting not so. It was the profundity of the superficial Augustus John explored. For as Oscar Wilde reminds us: 'It is only shallow people who do not judge from appearances. The mystery of the world is the visible, not the invisible.'

In his *Modern English Painters*, John Rothenstein recalled seeing Augustus peering fixedly, 'almost obsessively, at pictures by Gwen as though he could discern in them his own temperament in reverse; as though he could derive from the act satisfaction in his own wider range, greater natural endowment, tempestuous energy, and at the same time be reproached by her singlemindedness, her steadiness of focus, above all by the sureness with which she attained her simpler aims'.

The testimony of Augustus's admiration for Gwen's pictures extends over fifty years. 'I am flummoxed by their beauty,' he wrote to his son Edwin a year after her death in 1939. But what did she think of his pictures? 'I think them rather good,' she wrote to their

Slade School friend Ursula Tyrwhitt at the beginning of the First World War. 'They want something that will come soon!'

Did the quality soon come? Or was it there, cumulatively, from the beginning, only to fade with time? *Themes and Variations*, the exhibition of Augustus John's drawings over thirty years (1901–31), is an attempt to answer these questions. John's full-length drawings of Ida, one hand on hip, another held parallel to the ground and disappearing off the paper, out of the frame; and of Dorelia, with one arm draped over her head and the other leaning against the frame, are preparing to take their places in the rhythmical arc of figures for the large decoration called *The Way Down to the Sea*. Similarly, the Equihen fishergirl sitting with her elbows angled out or standing with her back to us is destined for another decoration planned on the north coast of France. All of them resemble dancers in rehearsal, preparing for the curtain to go up. All of them, metaphorically, belong to the same picture.

His portrait heads speak for themselves. But a series of variations tells us something new. They replace the legendary facility of someone who, with a swish of the pencil, went from one flash in the pan to another, and present in its place evidence of an obsessive observation and industry, like the drawings 'often repeated dozens of times, with slight variations' of his sister Gwen. The large-scale decoration which others had hoped for, and over which he dreamed, may be seen, with its recurring themes and variations, in combinations of his many small compositions when hung together on an exhibition wall. For what he had taken for moments of rehearsal reveal themselves, whenever they are gathered together, as parts of a finished production, a single picture on which he had been working all his life, and which is his cumulative achievement.

1996

BLOOMSBURY

In the early years of the twentieth century, the Bloomsbury Group stood for everything that was progressive. They introduced post-impressionism into Britain before the First World War, and the writings of Sigmund Freud between the wars. They reformed the novel, revolutionised biography and, through the work of Maynard Keynes, altered our concept of economics, making it an art rather than a science.

Above all they replaced Victorian values with a new creed that encouraged sexual tolerance and religious scepticism, placed self-fulfilment above self-advancement, valued art and philosophy more than action and politics. They waged a crusade against philistinism.

It is the fate of successful pioneers to become outdated. But whenever Bloomsbury is put down as a snobbish and self-admiring middle-class club, the group rises vigorously up again. It is as if it gains strength from its enemies.

Among the first and most ferocious of its critics was that adept in the art of making enemies, Wyndham Lewis. Before the First World War, Lewis began aiming his invective at this 'Pansy-clan' in his polemical, puce-coloured magazine *Blast*. Through the 1920s and 1930s, he went on satirising their 'not very robust talents', singling out with special relish that 'orthodox idealist' and tremulous 'peeper' into life, Virginia Woolf, creator of the occasional pale sketch or pretty salon fragment; and also the 'revolutionary' pseudo-man with the affected anarchical gait, Lytton Strachey, whom he presented uttering his platitudes with 'a nasal stammer modelled upon the effects of severe catarrh'.

As for the Bloomsbury painters, 'their darling star performer' Duncan Grant, the not-worth-mentioning Vanessa Bell, and that 'painter and publicist' Roger Fry, they struck him as being 'of almost purely eminent Victorian origin, saturated with William Morris's prettiness'. Lewis acknowledges Fry, 'their honoured leader', to be the most important of the Bloomsbury artists. 'But he has the distaste for reality of the scholar, and some of the spoilt-child qualities of the Rich Man'.

This was the burden of much anger against Bloomsbury. From the neat little novelist E.M. Forster to the big empty critic Desmond MacCarthy, they were timid academics manqués, with too much privilege and not enough talent.

No less devastating, though politer in manner, was the despair lavished on Bloomsbury by Bernard Shaw. These people were nice enough, he allowed, but they were futile. In his wartime play *Heartbreak House*, he presents the Bloomsbury Group as the alternative to British philistinism with its tedious dedication to sport, horses and warfare. But Bloomsbury's never-ending love charades which, during periods of relaxation, appeared so delightful, became a moral vacuum at times of national crisis when the earth was bursting with dead bodies. 'Shaw visits upon the age of Bloomsbury,' wrote one critic of *Heartbreak House*, 'with its cult of sentimental personal relations the same scorn Carlyle visited upon the age of Brummel with its Byronism.' And, it could be added, the same scorn that Winston Churchill visited upon GBS himself before the Second World War.

A third powerful enemy was D.H. Lawrence, who unsuccessfully tried to rescue the young novelist David Garnett from Bloomsbury's 'horrible and unclean' atmosphere. After seeing Maynard Keynes in his pyjamas at Cambridge one morning in 1915, Lawrence had dreamed of black beetles and thought he might go mad. 'I am sick with the knowledge of the prevalence of evil, as if it were some hideous disease,' he warned the Bloomsbury hostess and patron Ottoline Morrell. 'I *will not* have people like this . . . Sometimes I think I can't stand England any more.' For Lawrence, as for Shaw, Bloomsbury represented the decadence and decline of the country.

After the deaths of Lytton Strachey, Roger Fry, Virginia Woolf and Maynard Keynes, the opposition to Bloomsbury was taken over by the redoubtable teacher and critic F.R. Leavis. In 1951, in his journal *Scrutiny*, Leavis questioned how Cambridge philosophers and men of letters like Henry Sidgwick and Virginia Woolf's father Leslie Stephen could have been overtaken by the coterie power of Bloomsbury. Could we imagine these great nineteenth-century thinkers 'being influenced by, or interested in, the equivalent of Lytton Strachey?' he asked incredulously. 'By what steps, and by the operation of what causes, did so great a change come over Cambridge in so comparatively short time?'

Leavis believed that Bloomsbury represented a pernicious form of upper-middle-class triviality that was articulate but never serious. Hiding this lack of seriousness under an ironic poise, and their conceit under a masquerade of sophistication, they produced some disastrous consequences. One of Leavis's pupils remembers him telling his students that Lytton Strachey, through his malign influence on Maynard Keynes, had been partly responsible for the outbreak of the Second World War.

In more recent times, by an academic irony, Leavis's peculiar hostility to Bloomsbury was taken up by Paul Johnson, who went on to criticise the group for having created a sterile place in which patriotism withered and homosexual espionage flourished. But can we imagine Leavis being influenced by, or interested in, Paul Johnson? The opposition was gaining momentum as it went downhill.

By 1960, when I signed a contract to write a biography of Strachey, the reputation of Bloomsbury had reached a very low point. Strachey's own books, *Eminent Victorians*, *Queen Victoria* and *Elizabeth and Essex*, were not available in paperback; students were then reading not the novels of Virginia Woolf, but Herman Hesse;

E.M. Forster's standing as a novelist and Maynard Keynes's as an economist were in the doldrums. As for the paintings of Duncan Grant and Vanessa Bell, they had been removed to the cellars of many galleries; while the art criticism of Roger Fry and Clive Bell was no longer regarded as significant. It looked as if Wyndham Lewis, Bernard Shaw, D.H. Lawrence and F.R. Leavis had finally knocked Bloomsbury out for the count.

But although no one realised it, the Bloomsbury Group was shortly to launch a dramatic revival that would grow into a fashion, then an industry, and finally a potent influence on the next generation.

Two works published in the 1960s were to begin this revival. The first was Leonard Woolf's multi-volume autobiography, which came out between 1960 and 1969. The second was Mary Ellmann's *Thinking About Women*, which appeared in 1968.

Leonard Woolf went some way to answering Dr Leavis's question as to how Strachey and Keynes had become so influential at Cambridge at the beginning of the century. His first volume explored the origins of Bloomsbury in the work of the philosopher G.E. Moore and through a famously secret society known as the Apostles. Moore gave 'increased depth and meaning to our relationship', Leonard Woolf recalled. For Lytton Strachey, the publication of Moore's *Principia Ethica* in 1903 marked 'the beginning of the age of reason'. The nineteenth-century values of Henry Sidgwick and others seemed 'utterly mangled'. For Keynes, who described the impact of *Principia Ethica* as being like 'the opening of a new heaven on earth', the effect was equally dramatic. 'We repudiated entirely customary morals, conventions and traditional wisdom,' he later wrote. 'We were, that is to say, in the strict sense of the term, immoralists.'

Leonard Woolf did not explain what form this immoralist heaven on earth had taken. But in succeeding volumes he presented with engaging lucidity an account of his marriage to Virginia Stephen, her recurring illness, their setting-up and management of the Hogarth Press, Bloomsbury's pacifism in the First World War and Virginia's suicide during the Second World War.

These volumes, which became a key text for future Bloomsbury studies, made the first map of the territory. When I published *Lytton Strachey* in 1967–8, and Quentin Bell brought out the biography of his aunt Virginia Woolf in 1972, we had a ready-made reading public.

Mary Ellmann's *Thinking About Women* produced a more indirect effect on Bloomsbury. It marked the beginning of a resurgence in feminist writing, and a new comprehensive awareness of what feminism meant in literature, politics, economics and sociology. Crossing into 'the thorny region of feminism' back in 1934, Wyndham Lewis had ascribed Virginia Woolf's exaggerated literary significance to 'a purely feminist phenomenon' which was already declining because 'feminism is a dead issue'. Forty years later, the raising of female consciousness was giving her novels and other writings a renewed significance both historically and in contemporary life. The once avant-garde blaster of reputations, Wyndham Lewis, appeared suddenly old-fashioned; while another macho critic of Bloomsbury, D.H. Lawrence, with his belief in 'the great living experience of every man' being 'his adventure into the woman', also came under siege.

The Bloomsbury revival of the 1970s and 1980s was largely sustained by its non-fiction: by the diaries and letters of Virginia Woolf and the diaries of Ottoline Morrell; the autobiography of Gerald Brenan; the letters of E.M. Forster, Roger Fry, Lydia Lopokova and Maynard Keynes, and more recently Vanessa Bell.

This non-fiction also introduced some remarkable new characters, mostly women, to the public, which got to know Frances Partridge through her fascinating diaries, Angelica Garnett from her revelatory autobiography *Deceived With Kindness* and, perhaps most remarkable of all, the mysterious painter Dora Carrington, whose letters were edited in 1970 by David Garnett. It was as if the reading public were witnessing a long and complex archaeological excavation at which a lost way of life was gradually being revealed.

This rediscovered life seemed to have a special relevance to Britain after the sixties. In a celebrated broadcast, Leslie Stephen's biographer, Noël Annan, declared that the modern world saw Bloomsbury not as an alternative to philistinism, as Bernard Shaw had suggested, but to Shaw himself, and his fellow Fabians Sidney and Beatrice Webb. Searching for a new way in which to regard conduct, Noël Annan said, we had come to see it 'through the eyes of Mrs Webb or Mrs Woolf'.

'I cannot get over my distaste for the Fabian type,' Virginia Woolf had written in her diary. The Fabians were sociologists, the Bloomsbury Group were artists; Fabianism was collectivist, Bloomsbury individualist; the Fabians had looked to Marx for inspiration, Bloomsbury had moved on from G.E. Moore to Freud, whose works were translated into English by Lytton Strachey's brother and sister-in-law James and Alix Strachey and published by the Woolfs' Hogarth Press. Finally, the Fabians were a generation older than Bloomsbury, which put its faith in the cult of youth.

'We all aim at maximising human happiness,' Beatrice Webb wrote. 'Where we differ is how to bring about this ideal here and now.' Shaw and the Webbs thought that a better life could be achieved through a reduction in private property, the dismantling of the English class system and a more equitable redistribution of the country's capital: in short, a conversion from personal inequality to common wealth.

But such wholesale restructuring of society seemed to threaten the charmed privacy of Bloomsbury – the room of one's own, the room with a view. Bloomsbury believed that the good life depended upon aesthetic sensibility and freedom in personal relationships, particularly sexual relationships.

A number of excellent biographies published in the last twenty years – P.N. Furbank's *E.M. Forster*, Frances Spalding's *Vanessa Bell* and *Duncan Grant*, Robert Skidelsky's *Maynard Keynes*, Hermione Lee's *Virginia Woolf* – have shown how intricate and strange these sexual relationships were. Bloomsbury's experiments in gender roles made the group of increasing interest not only to academics but also to gay and lesbian campaigners.

Lytton Strachey, for example, was seen to have taken the nineteenth-century cult of aesthetics, made notorious by the trial of Oscar Wilde, and turned it into a twentieth-century weapon of revolt. His *Eminent Victorians* had long been recognised as an attack on parental authority which exposed the unholy nineteenth-century marriage between commerce and religiosity and led to the explosion of the First World War. What had not been recognised until recently was the way in which he had smuggled into his irresistibly readable narratives of English history what was called 'sexual perversion'. Unorthodoxy was now part of our national heritage.

It was the sexual element in Bloomsbury that broke out of academic disciplines into popular entertainment. After a succession of E.M. Forster novels had been filmed by David Lean or Ismail Merchant and James Ivory, David Garnett's novel *Aspects of Love* became an Andrew Lloyd Webber musical, Virginia Woolf's *Orlando* a Sally Potter film, and the 'triangular trinity of happiness' precariously formed by Carrington and Lytton Strachey a Christopher Hampton film, we were all Bloomsbury 'scholars'.

Had it not been for the casting of Emma Thompson as Carrington, the first major retrospective exhibition of Carrington's pictures, shown at the Barbican in 1993, more than sixty years after her death, would have been still further delayed. Jane Hill's *The Art of Dora Carrington*, published the previous year, turned out to be a useful guide for the critics in unfamiliar territory, and they greeted the show with cautious enthusiasm. But then, as if regretting such generosity (or blaming Bloomsbury for her neglect), they turned and savaged Richard Shone's *The Art of Bloomsbury* shown at the Tate Gallery in 1999. The sound and fury of this attack was so extreme that an art historian searching for some equivalent might have been forced back to the two post-impressionist exhibitions of 1910 and 1912. Critical orthodoxy appeared to have spun 180 degrees. So Bloomsbury, which had been assailed so vehemently early in the century for having imported modern French painting into the country, was being assailed at its end for being so far removed from contemporary British art competing in adjacent galleries for the Turner Prize. The work of Duncan Grant, Vanessa Bell and Roger Fry was compared disastrously to that of Cézanne, Matisse and the French post-impressionists, and never to other British artists of the period. The validity of domesticating the avant-garde was dismissed and then criticised as an uncomprehending, tame, non-creative act, never as an experimental exercise that, for example, in the pre-Rachel Whiteread building, Charleston, forms an historical work of art in which the spectator (for the price of an entrance fee) may appear.

In another twenty-five years the foaming intemperance of this critical attack, rising in places to wonderful incoherence, may itself become an object of wonder. For at its best, Bloomsbury derided all such manufactured outrage, whether in art or politics, religion or sex. It has been assailed with equal ferocity by conservatives and radicals, which is an uncomfortable but not necessarily a dishonourable place in a democracy. Though regarded as insular, the Bloomsbury Group punctured English insularity with French and Italian culture. Biographers today may not copy Lytton Strachey, but they make use of the freedoms he won in non-fiction writing. Similarly, though often criticised for her narrowness (no less narrow than Jane Austen), Virginia Woolf extended the boundaries of the novel by raising female awareness of a male-dominated world, and that world's awareness of women, in ways that will increasingly be taken for granted. So, when the commotion dies down, Bloomsbury will be invisibly suspended in our future.

1999

Enthusiasms and Alibis

PATRICK HAMILTON

Patrick Hamilton's apparently conventional, upper-middle-class family background in the south of England seethed with tragicomic extravagance. Bernard Hamilton, his untrustworthy and vainglorious father, was himself a novelist, a truly awful novelist, who pursued an astonishing variety of additional roles: as an occasional soldier, part-time theosophist and bewigged though non-practising barrister; also an impressionable traveller, amateur actor, fascist (he was an ardent admirer of Mussolini), and dogged religious controversialist ('What a low comedian you would have made!' exclaimed Henry Irving after one of his monologues on religion). At the age of twenty-one he had inherited a fortune and then married a prostitute who threw herself in front of a train at Wimbledon Station. His second wife, the sexually frigid daughter of a fashionable London dentist, filled her time copying oil paintings, singing music-hall songs and writing romantic fiction. She found compensation for a loveless marriage in the possessive love of her three children, of whom Patrick was the youngest.

Patrick Hamilton's first novel, *Monday Morning*, described by his brother Bruce as 'a joyous miscellany of scraps of autobiography shaped to the needs of a novel', was published when he was twenty-one. It was followed a year later, in 1926, by *Craven House*, which made his reputation as a realistic novelist. He was seen as being in a line of descent from Dickens, and compared in Britain to George Gissing and in the United States to Sinclair Lewis. Both books were largely autobiographical. *Monday Morning* chronicles the awkwardness of an early unconsummated love affair and provides it with a charmingly unconvincing fairytale ending. The novel presents, his biographer Nigel Jones suggests, 'a self-portrait of a young author newly liberated from the smothering possessiveness of his mother and the tyranny of his father'.

Craven House, which was written in a guest house at Kew where his mother had protectively taken him, is a precursor to *The Slaves of Solitude*. Both novels chart with meticulous, almost plodding care the banality of lodging-house life in England during wartime, the dullness and horror of which Patrick Hamilton's macabre imagination converts into something between an asylum and a torture chamber. In *Craven House* we glimpse the beginnings of a break-up in English social life that took place after the First World War. This change was to be bewilderingly accelerated in the Second World War by the 'twanging, banging invasion' of United States soldiers – embodied in *The Slaves of Solitude* by the broad uniformed figure of 'Lootenant' Pike, whose wide American grin, gorgeous American teeth and insurmountable American talk dazzle and bemuse the other characters. But whereas *Craven House* is endearingly sentimental in its optimism, *The Slaves of Solitude* is a black comedy of manners that reaches its climax with a great cry from the soul echoing through the empty universe: 'God help us, God help all of us, every one, all of us.'

Patrick Hamilton's lodging-houses, with their meagre gas fires, their dim light bulbs hanging from the ceiling, and the oppressive silences of their exhausted tenants, have something of the same nightmare atmosphere as Dickens's boarding schools. As an escape from their imprisonment in these sullen institutions, he ushers his characters into the lighted world of the public house, where they can lose their private inhibitions, and lose themselves, by entering for some time a parallel world of fantasy and illusion. Pubs feature in almost all Patrick Hamilton's novels, most particularly his marvellous London trilogy *Twenty Thousand Streets Under the Sky* (1935), which makes brilliant and poignant use of his own disastrous infatuation with Lily Connolly, a young prostitute, during the late 1920s.

This must have seemed an escape from the confining world of his parents. But it followed the pattern of his father's first marriage to a prostitute. The affair with Lily seemed both a copy of, and perhaps an exculpation for, that marriage – since here it is the prostitute who educates and takes revenge on the gentleman. By moving into a lower social sphere, Patrick Hamilton did not shed the insecurities implanted by his upbringing: his emotional vulnerability helped to make him one of the chronically dissolute and distressed who wander the dingy London streets and find refuge in its pubs and dosshouses.

The first book of this trilogy *The Midnight Bell* (1930) is an account – in places almost a transcription – of Patrick Hamilton's disastrous romance with Lily, who appears in the novel as Jenny Maple. When first published it had the subtitle 'A Love Story'. But the word love, though desperately repeated in the many blurred conversations, loses all particular meaning and becomes a vague shorthand for what the characters imagine they want – the possession of beauty, money or security: in essence, the possession of the unattainable.

The Midnight Bell is a study of infatuation. We are spared none of its detailed tortures or griefs, betrayals and deceits, in this anatomy of humiliation that brings us to the frontiers of Patrick Hamilton's famous psychological thrillers for the stage, *Rope* and *Gaslight*, and his classic murder novel *Hangover Square*. 'Her perfect cruelty and egotism appalled him . . . He would kill her.' But there are to be no murders in this trilogy, for it is the endurance of ordinary life that we are being shown. What *The Midnight Bell* loses in detachment, it gains in intensity. The appalling monster bores of this pub are excruciatingly observed and intimately known. As we follow the intricately plotted inanities of their tales, which divert us by driving the other characters to distraction, we do not overhear them from a distance, but are brought into their very presence.

The Siege of Pleasure (1932) is the story of Jenny Maple's first step down from respectable servant girl towards prostitution. 'Jever hear of Bernard Shaw? . . . He wrote a book called *Mrs Warren's Profession* – an' showed it was all economics,' Bob, the waiter of The Midnight Bell, tells her – to which she replies: 'I guess he was just about *right*.' The economic point is well made in *The Siege of Pleasure*, which portrays the meagre and pleasureless conditions of Jenny's servant life as a form of socially acceptable, class-regimented prostitution. By describing as the place of her employment his own suburban home in Chiswick, and giving portraits of his nerveless mother and eccentric aunt as her employers, together with a fearful silhouette of his father (pathetically fallen away after a stroke and the unwelcome double success of *Rope* and *The Midnight Bell*), he aligns his own escape with Jenny's to make it all the more comprehensible.

Jenny is a shallow character – her shallowness makes all the more remarkable the power of her beauty which so profoundly impresses Bob. 'He decided he would really die for such beauty.' This sexual-aesthetic longing, and a longing for the freedom of financial security, are the two motivating forces in all these novels. Jenny herself has no eye for beauty and is even blind to her own looks, believing Bob is 'a bit mad' to be so 'crazily in love' with her. It is one of the ironies of the trilogy that the prostitute is sexless and the bar-maid, Ella, does not drink. Both have little understanding of their clients, though a good deal of professional expertise. As a servant, Jenny has been 'arduously trained in the practice of pleasing strangers' and it is this skill she has taken on to the streets. Her own pleasure comes through drink, which gives her access to wonderful sensations and the feeling of being in harmony with her environ-ment. 'She never believed it was possible to be so happy.' For Jenny, drink is the replacement for everything that her existence itself has prevented her from enjoying naturally. 'Love, of which some spoke, was a closed book to her, and she honestly believed it would remain a closed book all her life. It was a closed book which she had no desire to open.'

But love seems an open book to Bob and as real as his literary aspirations. When, intoxicated by her murderous beauty, he puts his arms round Jenny and wills himself to believe that she loves him, happiness feels very close. Led into a hell by this alluring and irresistible pilot, he comes to use drink as a way of forgetting a 'vile and disappointing planet', where such promised happiness is only a mirage.

Between the writing of *The Midnight Bell* and *The Siege of Pleasure*, Patrick Hamilton managed to free himself from his debilitating passion for Lily. He was helped in bringing his life under control by a sensible, if passionless, marriage in 1930 to a woman who was also in retreat from an unsatisfactory romance. Having reduced his drinking, he was in good spirits when, in January 1932, walking along Earl's Court Road with his wife and sister, he was knocked down and critically injured by a car. For a time his life was in danger, but after some months he made the best recovery possible, despite plastic surgery on his face, particularly his nose, which had been almost torn off. He added the accident to his final draft of *The Siege of Pleasure*, equating those who had done him emotional damage with those who had damaged him physically.

For almost two years following the completion of *The Siege of Pleasure*, he was unable to write anything new. Then, in a sudden concentration of creative energy, he completed the trilogy with a wonderfully balanced and accomplished novel developing a subsidiary plot from *The Midnight Bell*. Also centred in the pub, *The Plains of Cement* (1934) is Ella the barmaid's story, which complements Bob's story and brings a deeper perspective to the themes of *Twenty Thousand Streets Under the Sky*. Although apparently disinherited from the privileges of romance by her plain looks and financially disadvantaged by her background of lower-class poverty, this sensible girl is not without her dreams of a better emotional and economic life. But, unlike Bob and Jenny, she struggles to keep these tempting fantasies under control. She is secretly in love with Bob but endeavours to keep this a secret even from herself. She has it in her to feel for him what he feels for Jenny, for although 'a placid and efficient girl, she also worshipped at the shrine of pure beauty and romance'. Knowing nothing of Jenny, she believes that 'any girl with eyes in her head would be after' Bob, but schools herself to accept that she can never hope to attract his attention. 'She was, she found, incapable of inspiring his tenderness.'

Because of the social divisions between men and women and the incompatibilities of male and female sexuality, there is truth in Ella's sober assessment. To Bob's mind, Jenny, with her ingenuous expression and clear blue eyes, is a heavenly creature who 'with the child's weight of her body' seems magically uncontaminated by the world; while the humming buoyant figure of Ella, his frank and admirable companion in toil, who really *is* uncontaminated, appears no more than 'a jolly good sort'. Jenny is the child who must be owned, and Ella the mother who is taken for granted and eventually will be left. His intelligence tells him that this is false; but we do not act through intelligence, reserving it for commentary on our actions:

> Particularly did he feel he was betraying Ella. She so deserved his respect, but all his homage went to another. Poor Ella. He watched her as she moved about merrily (in the cap which became her so), and gave back chaff for chaff in the crowded Christmassy bar. She had only one sin: she was without beauty. But she had all the heart-breaking desires, and you could see them there, in her charming face, as she laughingly and maternally answered – a creature eternally maternal, eternally fruitless – the insincere compliments of the men.

Ella uses her intelligence more than most, but she is 'for ever seeking little reassurances and excuses for optimism'. As a means of overcoming her sorrowful intuitions she is determined to see the best in everyone – even her horrifying suitor Mr Ernest Eccles. It is her fate to have one of the most dreadful admirers in English literature. As a besieging lover with all the propaganda of youth, the fifty-two-year-old Mr Eccles is a sinister as well as an idiotic man. He presents himself as a romantic figure but appears in Ella's eyes merely as an old man with 'something put by' which could buy her comfort and stability in life.

Money seems more likely than love to change Ella's life, and she is pressured by her circumstances to think of men as Jenny has regarded them – 'appendages, curiously willing providers, attendants, flatterers of an indolent mood, footers of bills and payers of "bus fares"'. She is horrified to find herself calculating that if she inherits money from the death of her stepfather – a bully who carries over-tones of Bernard Hamilton – she will evade marriage to Mr Eccles, which would be a living death. 'I can't stand cruelty,' says Jenny. But everyone is destined to be cruel to someone in these novels: Jenny irresponsibly torments Bob; Bob unwittingly wounds Ella; Ella hurts Mr Eccles, who in turn ill-treats her whenever he gets the chance.

The fact that all this should not depress the reader is a tribute to the power of Patrick Hamilton's storytelling and the exhilaration of his humour. In the earlier pages there are signs of immaturity – some passages of over-deliberation, moments of facetiousness, and an anxious reliance on what J.B. Priestley called Komic Kapitals. But as the book progresses, wonderfully comic scenes proliferate. Mr Eccles, in particular, is a character of Dickensian proportions – Mr Eccles who lives so intensely through his new hat that 'it cost him sharp torture even to put it on his head, where he could not see it', who when looking for his visiting card is 'not unlike a parrot diving into its feathers', who creates a 'private cloakroom for his innumer-able accessories whenever he sits down', who polishes his dignity on a lurching bus 'by peering and looking back in a critical way out of the window, rather as though London was being partially managed by him, and he had to see that the buildings were in their right places'. But though Mr Eccles hardly ever fails to utter the most subtle drivel, he is no one-dimensional character. Touchy, crippled by shyness, desperately lonely and absurd, he too has his dreams of redemption. We feel compassion for anyone who meets him, but are also made to feel compassion for the man himself. He is used to give retrospective detachment to *The Midnight Bell*, for his wooing of Ella is another version of Bob's pursuit of Jenny, and it provokes a similar reaction: 'We all have to take these risks.'

Patrick Hamilton treats the pub as a theatre, describing its exits and entrances, laying down its decor and stage directions ('On your right was the bar itself, in all its bottly glitter, and on your left was a row of tables . . .'), taking us 'behind-scenes just before the show' and up to the attic rooms where Bob and Ella pass their 'endless procession of solitary nights after senseless working days'. Performing against the lurid illumination of the saloon bar, his cast of ordinary habitués is magnified into a troupe of crazed misfits, and the conventions of English life reveal themselves as dramatically foolish.

Patrick Hamilton is an expert guide to English social distinctions, with all their snobbish mimicry and fortified non-communication. He describes wonderfully well how the hyphenated upper classes, yelling at their dogs, splashing in their baths like captured seals, and writing their aloof letters in the third person (like broadcasters recounting an athletic event), remain so mysterious to the lesser breeds. Taking us out of the pub into the swarming streets of London, he gives us a social map of this malignant city as it was in the harsh commercial era of the 1920s and the early 1930s. His Marxism became a method of distinguishing between the avoidable and the unavoidable suffering of people, and, insofar as literature can change social conditions, such a vivid facsimile in fiction may have helped to do so.

The reading public loved the compulsive storytelling of this ambitious novel; while critics and other writers increasingly valued his powers of sociological observation. 'He wrote more sense about England and what was going on in England in the 1930s than anybody else,' commented Doris Lessing. 'You can go into any pub and see it going on.' Here were the defeated classes of the Depression: the homeless, the ostracised, the needy, recreated with loving detail. His characters are ordinary and uneducated people, tormented by their fantasies and tormenting others: 'real people made plain for us', as J.B. Priestley called them. It is not a faultless novel: sometimes the narrative is too wordy, sometimes too mannered. But these are living faults that shadow living characters and are produced by Patrick Hamilton's desire to convey simple people in situations that are beyond them: the sailor-turned-waiter with ambitions to be a writer, the fly-by-night young girl trapped into prostitution, the plain barmaid courted by the monster bore – a relationship developed in *The Slaves of Solitude* between the thirty-nine-year-old Miss Roach and the malevolent Mr Thwaites. They are all observed with humour and tenderness, below which runs a disturbing subtext of fear and revenge. 'There was not even any hope for Miss Roach that Mr Thwaites would ever die.' It is this menacing subtext that rises to the surface and drives the plots of Patrick Hamilton's stage plays.

His first play, *Rope*, was staged in London in 1929, when he was twenty-five. 'I have done exactly what Noël Coward did with *The Vortex*. I am known, established, pursued,' he wrote. 'The world is truly at my feet.' His gratuitous murder story scandalised and delighted audiences even more than Coward's family drama of adultery and drug addiction. It was to be played in theatres round the world for the rest of his life, was adapted for radio and television, and made into a famous experimental film by Alfred Hitchcock. The title had been taken from Nietzsche's *Thus Spake Zarathustra* ('Man is a rope, fastened between animal and Superman – a rope over an abyss'), and the event-plot was derived from a *cause célèbre* in the United States involving two brilliant young students, Nathan Leopold and Richard Loeb, who become obsessed with Nietzsche's theory of the Superman and attempt an immaculate, motiveless murder. Patrick Hamilton himself rather unconvincingly denied that he had founded his play on this case. 'I am not interested in crime,' he said. Though he was pleased by the play's success, he wanted somehow to distance himself from it. 'It bears no relation to the rest of my writing,' he wrote. He called it 'a sheer thriller', and technically this is true.

As Sean French writes in his biography of Patrick Hamilton, *Rope* is a 'supremely effective dramatic machine'. By placing a wooden chest containing the murdered boy centre-stage and inviting his father to eat supper off it, Hamilton 'found an authentic addition to the repertoire of horror'. But by denying all knowledge of the Leopold–Loeb trial, he conceals the fascination he shared with them for Nietzsche, whose superior thought, he believed, was strong enough to free him from the force field of his father's megalomania. There is a mention of Carlyle, but none of Nietzsche in the play, and

Patrick Hamilton represents its savage homo-erotic theme as being merely a piece of the stage business. 'I have gone all-out to write a horror play and make your flesh creep,' he wrote. 'If I have succeeded you will leave the theatre braced and re-created, which is what you go to the theatre for.' But it was 'not intended to be a highbrow play', and so, he added, 'delving into morbid psychologies and so forth' was quite beside the point.

There is a similar exploitation of villainy, a piling on of agony, in his equally successful and much-filmed melodrama *Gaslight*. Here the psychopathic husband brings his wife to the house where he has murdered her predecessor and tries by a variety of devilish stage tricks to push her into madness. Almost all his plays, from the ingenious revenge thriller for radio, *Money With Menaces*, to the gothic stage tragedy of imprisonment and murder *The Duke in Darkness*, show a sadistic relish for applied cruelty which seems at odds with the embracing sympathy and humour of the novels – though terror and the prospect of revenge are never far below the surface of his multi-layered fiction.

These two faces of Patrick Hamilton are subtly brought together in his celebrated novel *Hangover Square* (1941), a Dr Jekyll and Mr Hyde story originally subtitled *The Man with Two Minds*, in which the ungainly, weak-willed George Harvey Bone, lovelorn and innocuous, is intermittently transformed by a snapping sensation in his head, a schizophrenic *click!*, into a predestined killer. The parallel world that this heavy-drinking man enters is colourless, submerged, semi-silent, the world of an automaton, remote from other people except his intended victim, the tantalising Netta Longdon, whom he loves.

As he grew older, Patrick Hamilton's novels became darker. *The Slaves of Solitude* is the most sombre of all. Though there is no sound of gunfire in the book, no sight of blood or spectacle of killing, it is, he tells us, a war novel. Though the only bombshells are verbal bombshells, the grey deprivation of life is as much a part of the war as soldiering. 'The earth was muffled from the stars; the river and the pretty eighteenth-century bridge was muffled from the people; the people were muffled from each other. This was war late in 1943.' The dim black-out, 'like moonlight gone bad', in which these people live mirrors the blackness of the author's spirit.

This blackness seems to have been largely caused by his inability to escape from the acute anxieties of childhood. They had been extraordinarily stimulated by the extravagant unpredictability of his father: his sudden violent tempers, alternating with moods of embarrassing affection, his bouts of drunkenness, his extreme social snobbery and ancestral myth-making all contributing to the dread of his presence in their comfortable home. Whatever Patrick did in later life seemed like a distorted echo of Bernard. When he idiosyncratically took up Marxism to purge his parents' social pretensions and obtain a secure, predictable scientific faith, was he not parodying Bernard's eccentric fascism? When he found a father-figure in Stalin was he not reproducing his father's discovery of Mussolini?

His sexual life too seems to have faltered under the imposing, impotent shadow of his parents. He believed himself to be unattractive to women and may have suspected that he was a repressed homosexual. In any event, he had difficulty in achieving sexual fulfilment with women (scholars have diagnosed premature ejaculation). He idealised glamorous actresses and played sadomasochistic games of bondage with a series of prostitutes. Nevertheless, he married twice, tried to keep both wives content by drifting back and forth between them, and made all three of them unhappy.

Patrick Hamilton's triumph was to turn these disasters of his life into marvellous opportunities for his novels. The near-fatal road accident in the wasteland of Earl's Court (where he was to set *Hangover Square*) had left him with a damaged arm and scarred face. But though this exacerbated his morbid self-consciousness, he turned it to advantage on the page by adapting it into a play for radio called *To the Public Danger*.

He was already a heavy drinker before his accident. By the time he began writing *The Slaves of Solitude* he had become an alcoholic, drinking three bottles of whisky a day. Drink slowed his work and he made most progress on this book during periods of relative abstemiousness, writing in bed all day before going out to drink in the evenings. He was living partly in London, where he had an apartment at the Albany near Piccadilly Circus, and in Henley, where he set his novel, 'a mere village right off the map' which he named Thames Lockdon.

He offers us an ironic self-portrait in *The Slaves of Solitude* as the mysterious Mr Prest, 'the black-sheep of the boarding-house', who, with his beery voice and face of an ex-pugilist, floats through each day with 'an air of having been battered silly by life, of submissiveness to events, of gentleness, of willingness to please, of dog-like gloom and absentmindedness'. Though looked down on by the other members of the boarding-house as being almost an alien ('funny', 'strange', 'odd', 'queer'), he regards all of them with 'the supreme, leisured, and assured contempt of a cultivated man for Philistines . . . indeed, as a sort of zoo, containing easily recognised types of freak animals, into which an ironical fate had brought him'.

The exception is Miss Roach, the shy, modest, decent, over-sensitive, thirty-nine-year-old spinster and daughter of a dentist from whose viewpoint the story is mostly told. She, who had been nicknamed 'Old Cockroach', has an affinity with the man whose name is so nearly 'pest'. But, within the stupefying atmosphere of the boarding-house, she does not recognise this and 'often wondered what exact motive Mr Prest had in being alive – if, and by what means, this seemingly empty, utterly idle and silent man justified his existence'.

But Mr Prest, like Patrick Hamilton himself, divides his life between Thames Lockdon and London, where he can be found at various bars, 'sipping his beer and hoping for the best'. On unfortunate days he stands alone, embarrassed, self-conscious, obsessed by the fear of being 'out of it' and 'not wanted'. But then come lucky days when he joins the crowd and, 'in his old element, now completely elated rather than dejected by his own yesterdays', talks on an equal footing with famous men of the theatre. For Mr Prest has a secret. As 'Archie Prest', he once topped the bills in pantomimes. Near the end of the novel, when, due to the wartime shortage of actors, he is starring in a production at Wimbledon of *Babes in the Wood*, he is miraculously transformed from 'a forlorn, silent man in the corner ... that idler and hanger-about in bars' into 'a wicked but absurd uncle ... preposterously dressed in green'. In this wonderfully comic and surreal scene, partly a fantastical rewriting of a sad late performance he had witnessed by the great old musical comedian George Robey, Patrick Hamilton gives us the opposite of that deadly transformation experienced by George Harvey Bone in *Hangover Square*. This is the ecstatic transformation his characters search for in pubs; which Patrick Hamilton himself, changing his name to Henderson, had looked for when he briefly went on the stage himself in what he called his 'nerve-wracking, ill-adjusted, wretched early youth'; and which, in muted form, he finally achieved in his best novels. Seeing Mr Prest's elderly pugilistic face, so madly painted, as he stands bombarded by the frantic yells of delight from the children, Miss Roach observes 'an extraordinary look of purification about the man – a suggestion of reciprocal purification – as if he had just at that moment with his humour purified the excited children, and they, all as one, had purified him'.

> Somehow his triumph seemed to be Miss Roach's triumph as well, and her heart was lifted up with pleasure ... Looking at him, she had a strong desire to cry ... the elderly comedian ... was pulling it off tremendously in spite of age and long retirement, astonishing everyone, even himself ... And, observing the purification of Mr Prest, Miss Roach herself felt purified.

This too, in its fashion, is the achievement of Patrick Hamilton in *The Slaves of Solitude*. Mr Prest and Miss Roach are the only characters in the novel to escape from the horror and despondence of the Rosamund Tea Rooms at Thames Lockdon and find the possibilities of a fuller life in London. To do this, like characters in Wagner's *Ring*, they must go through the circle of fire laid down by the Blitz, the flying bombs and enemy rockets. They must confront the 'crouching monster' that is London, with its polluted breath that exudes across the first page of the novel. For Thames Lockdon, its name blacked out 'for reasons of security', where the cemetery 'spoke greenly and gracefully of death and antiquity, the Park spoke leaflessly and

hideously of life-in-death, or death-in-life, amidst immature munic-
ipal surroundings', was Patrick Hamilton's purgatory: 'a place to pass
through' with its 'semi-tottering parade of death in life'.

Heaven appears to lie in the country beyond, where Miss Roach
sometimes walks at weekends. It is a place that dominates and sub-
merges 'all things pertaining to men and towns' and brings her spirit
moments of consolation and refreshment. But in the paradox of
war these fields and hills have become a mirage, irrelevant to life,
while Thames Lockdon itself, which people believed had been
'heaven' before the war, was now the very pit of hell.

Patrick Hamilton makes the Rosamund Tea Rooms a palace in
this hell ('this dead-and-alive house, of this dead-and-alive street, of
this dead-and-alive little town'). I myself lived not far away from
Henley during the war and afterwards, and I recognise the authenticity of this guest house, its torpor and apathy. But Patrick
Hamilton makes it hideously and hilariously surreal. Like London,
it is a monster, giving out its repertoire of 'silent noises', its uncanny
gurgling and throbbing sounds from unlocated water-pipes, its
shrieks and bumps and expectorations. It is full of the rage and
prejudice and unhappiness that existed in himself, that exists in all
of us. It contains everything he had acquired from his parents, and
that we acquire from ours. We see aspects of his father in the loqua-
cious and malevolent Mr Thwaites, that archaic 'trampler through
the emotions of others', who carries a mental age of twelve into 'the
bloom of his carefree and powerful dotage'; and also in Lieutenant
Pike, the Lucifer who brings a light that blinds rather than illumi-
nates, and whose inconsequence and unpredictability heighten Miss
Roach's anxieties. And we see the influence of his mother in the
false friend, Vicki Kugelmann, so sinister and ambiguous, who
promises to 'lighten things up' but adds to the awful darkness of the
place.

From these furies Miss Roach finally escapes to her publishing life
in London, as Patrick Hamilton himself escaped into his writing.
The Slaves of Solitude is a powerfully redemptive novel. We are
spared nothing: and nothing is sentimentalised. The condition of
England is subtly blended with the author's own condition, and we

are led from this black hole of boredom, with its thunderous atmosphere of recrimination and insecurity, by a humour that is not merely defensive, but that in its magical fusion of fact and fantasy becomes an illumination of reality.

1987/1999

THE POLYGLOTS

William Gerhardie was twenty-nine when *The Polyglots* was first published in 1925. Like his first novel, *Futility*, it draws largely on personal experiences. The son of a successful British industrialist living in St Petersburg, and his Yorkshire wife, Gerhardie had been considered the dunce of the family and was sent to England in his late teens to be trained for what was loosely called 'a commercial career' – that is, to acquire some financial acumen or, in default, marry a rich bride. But he detested commerce and dreamed only of the dramatic triumphs with which he hoped to take the London theatres by storm. To improve his English style he was studying Wilde: and an elegant cane, long locks and a languid expression were parts of his literary make-up at this time.

During the war he was posted to the staff of the British military attaché at Petrograd and, arriving there with an enormous sword bought second-hand in the Charing Cross Road ('*le sabre de mon père* – a long clumsy thing in a leather scabbard' that makes a momentary appearance in Uncle Lucy's funeral procession in *The Polyglots*), he was welcomed as an old campaigner. The Russian Revolution (which ruined his father, who owed his life to having been mistaken for the British socialist Keir Hardie) sent Gerhardie back to England. But in 1918 he set out again, and after crossing America and Japan reached Vladivostok, where the British Military Mission had established itself. After two years in Siberia, mostly in the company of generals, he left the army with an OBE and two foreign decorations, sailing home by way of Singapore, Colombo and Port Said – a journey that forms the closing chapters of *The Polyglots.*

The Polyglots is the narrative of a high-spirited egocentric young officer who comes across a Belgian family, rich in eccentrics, to whom he is related and with whom he lives while on a military mission to the Far East. There are obvious parallels here with Gerhardie's own life. His impressions of the First and Second Revolution in Petrograd, and the Allied intervention in Russia of 1918–20, of the whole business of interfering on an international scale in other people's affairs, are recorded here and in *Futility.* He draws, too, upon his own family. His Aunt Mary is the prototype for the extraordinary Aunt Teresa; his Uncle Willie was the model for Uncle Lucy, that unfortunate gentleman who hangs himself in his sister's knickers; while the beautiful nincompoop Sylvia is based on a girl Gerhardie met in Westbourne Grove. Gerhardie makes them not comic Russian stereotypes but universal characters, each in his or her own way a corrective to the other. They are ourselves and the people we meet every day. 'There, but for the grace of God, goes H.G. Wells,' remarked H.G. Wells of that amorous knight of the bedchamber Uncle Emmanuel.

On returning to England, Gerhardie went to Worcester College, Oxford. Though he was responsive to the beauty of Oxford, his opinion of academic life was not high and is probably reflected in the Johnsonian statement of the narrator in this novel: 'There are as many fools at a university as elsewhere . . . but their folly, I admit, has a certain stamp – the stamp of university training, if you like. It is trained folly.'

On leaving Oxford, Gerhardie wrote much of *The Polyglots* at Innsbruck. He completed it under difficult conditions while his father was dying. His mother would read out pages from the manuscript to the old man 'to kill time', and for the most part he listened

uncomplainingly and without comment, though occasionally pro-
nouncing some passage to be 'instructive'. But when she came to the
sea-burial of Natàsha, she began to cry, and this bothered him.
'Don't cry,' he urged. 'It's not real. Willie has invented it.'

The narrator in *The Polyglots* has, by the end of the novel, decided
to write the novel we are reading. 'I have already written the title
page,' he announces in answer to his Aunt Teresa's query as to what
they are going to do for money. 'Is it going to sell well?' she demands;
and the narrator notes, 'I was silent.'

On *The Polyglots* were pinned the family's hopes of remaking the
family fortune, but Gerhardie's father died a few months before
publication. The book did make Gerhardie's name as a novelist; but
as to fortune, he later calculated that, contrary to expectation, it
had brought him 'something equivalent, in terms of royalties, to
nothing'.

In later years Gerhardie was to adopt as his colophon the amper-
sand. None of his novels display with more skill and vitality than
The Polyglots the peculiar inclusiveness of his philosophy, and no
happier narrator ever adopted the first person singular. Captain
Georges Hamlet Alexander Diabologh is a young man with literary
aspirations. He labours intermittently at a work whose title, *Record
of the Stages in the Evolution of an Attitude,* suggests the theme ('the
central thing round which the world revolved') of *The Polyglots*.
Our attitude to life, Gerhardie implies, is the same as our attitude to
fiction which is born of our experience of life. When Sylvia, on
board the *Rhinoceros* as it moves through the Red Sea, wants to
know what will happen when they get back to Europe, the narrator
replies that he has noticed with regret 'the same morbid and
unhealthy appetite in the readers of novels'. Gerhardie was to make
a similar point through his story 'In the Wood' (1926). The readers
of this story cannot be certain whether Lieutenant Barahmeiev will
make love to the landlord's wife. We do not know whether he is
what he seems to be, an empty bluffer, or whether she is deceitful.
We can read it several ways. The story carries within it another
miniature story in the lieutenant's recollection of his inconclusive
first love affair. In his audience's response to this story we may hear

a parody of the obtuse critic's reaction to Gerhardie's own work, a warning of how not to read him.

The Lieutenant ceased.

'Well?' we said. 'Go on.'

'That's all,' said the Lieutenant.

'But what happened afterwards?' asked Vera Solomonovna.

'Nothing happened.'

'But *how*?' she said in a tone as though she had been wronged.

'Well, that's all there is to tell.'

'But – it's no proper story even.'

'I can't help that,' he answered, almost angrily. 'This is what happened, and this is where it ended. I can't falsify the facts to suit your taste. We don't, my dear Vera Solomonovna, live our lives to provide plots for stories.'

So the story stands: its readers must evolve.

Our emotions in relation to time past, present and future are seen in *The Polyglots* to guide our method of making the most of life – which itself, in ironic counterpoint, keeps interrupting the philosophical discussions which chart the evolution of the characters' attitude to it. After listening to Wagner, the narrator reflects that music understands what words and thoughts cannot analyse. Inanimate nature behaves as if we were not here and life exists irrespective of our reasoning about it. Therefore life is wiser than reason which, being only the partial discovery of life, is merely inquisitive. By the same token Gerhardie believed that no intellectual credo was demanded of the novelist whose stereoscopic vision saw through everyday happenings to a world of dreams, mystery and immortality. Here the comic and the tragic are not alternative or successive attitudes but deeply intermingled, so that every event – Uncle Lucy's suicide, Sylvia's unexpected wedding night, the Russian Revolution itself with its odd consequences on this miscellany of unwilling refugees moving ever westwards – contains both sadness and humour.

It is in the orchestration of contradictory moods and attitudes that *The Polyglots* excels. Though it owes something to Chekhov (about whom Gerhardie wrote a brilliant little book while at Oxford), the tone is original and unmistakable: 'personal, light and glancing, often lyrical but always self-deflating', as Walter Allen described it. Believing that the invention of psychologically convincing characters and artful well-balanced plots was a mistaken ambition for a novelist in that it cut across the grain of his natural material and ignored the plots that already exist in life, Gerhardie introduces his people and lets them, as it were, carry the event-plot along for him. In *Futility* and *The Polyglots* he brought something new to fiction. The characters, or at least the social personalities they have developed, are suggested very simply by recurring patterns of words: Uncle Emmanuel's '*Que voulez-vous?*' '*C'est la vie*' and '*Courage! Courage!*'; Gustave's cough and adjustment of his Adam's apple; Georges Diabologh's repeated admission, unintelligible to the others, that 'I'm good-looking . . . You think I'm conceited? I think not'; Sylvia's quotations from the *Daily Mail*; the 'stinks' of Major Beastly, the insensitive man with the sensitive skin; the dark smile of Captain Negodyaev, which conceals his view of life; and overseeing them all the indomitable, hypochondriac Aunt Teresa, who can stand anything except disagreement and whose presidential attitude to everyone successfully moves her family and its dependants round the world in the midst of 'the greatest war the world has ever seen'. As Georges Diabologh comments: 'All is in the Hands of God – and Aunt Teresa.'

Living alongside this helpless, agglutinated mass of humanity as it trails back and forth across Gerhardie's pages are the children. They are handled with extraordinary dexterity and in a manner for which it is difficult to find a parallel in other novels. They are observed with passion yet without sentimentality, accurately yet with the dimension of pathos in that they are surrounded by a ludicrous world into which they must grow up. Except Natàsha. Her burial at sea is an anguish of the heart, an involvement in grief chronicled with rigorous detachment. We see the yellow moustache of her father ceaselessly twitching; the curiosity of the passengers on the upper deck; the captain's awareness of his gala uniform and the ship's inflexible routine; the obsolete Russian tricolour covering the child's body; the surgeon puffing at his cigarette; everywhere the atmosphere of unreality surrounding the blunt fact of death that must be faced and may not be understood, Natàsha having gone unharmed through two revolutions, five sieges, two seasons of famine and pestilence to die in plenty and quietude on the tropical ocean.

It was a cloudless morning of extreme heat and stuffiness and damp, and the decks were crowded, noisy and indifferent, and I thought that suffering and death should be in the wind and cold of winter, in the slough and drowsiness of autumn, but not in summer – oh, not in summer . . . The sea went out in large ripples. The gulls flew screaming and wheeling above them . . . The ship had been brought to as near standstill as possible; barely perceptibly she slid along on the deep, deep, flapping sea. The plank was on ropes, like a swing: a seaman on each side – Uncle Tom and a young one. Below loomed the Indian Ocean, stretching out its white paws of froth – like a big cat . . . The mother was held up by her husband and Berthe. She looked pale, pasty, she looked awful. Swiftly the flag was pulled off. Then they swung it – once our way, once to the sea. Natàsha slid off, and describing a curve in the air splashed into the water. A few seconds – and she disappeared beneath the foam . . . the liner, stealthily, relentlessly, like life itself, went on.

Gerhardie's writing at its best is simple but suggests a widening circle of possibilities. He used increasingly the delaying phrase or clause within a sentence, measuring the length of procrastination while declaring the power of time regained. It is this tension that helps to hold in equilibrium the incongruities of life as he presents them to us. 'To maintain a position is to maintain a false position,' he writes. In *The Polyglots* the search for an attitude excludes no attitude. Gerhardie's achievement, as in an artistic conjuring trick, is convincingly to maintain what is intellectually the untenable position.

Beneath the compulsory conviviality of wartime party-going runs a current of melancholy, and this, together with many farcical episodes and philosophical speculations, is interwoven with a number of powerful anti-war passages. 'No one wanted the war,' he writes: 'no one with the exception of a score of imbeciles who had made it ...' The eccentrics who surround the narrator are, we see, no madder than those who run the world and make its wars. There is a strong parallel here, as Anthony Powell has pointed out, between *The Polyglots* and *The Enormous Room*, e.e. cummings' account of being incarcerated for 'careless talk' by the French authorities, which was published in 1922.

Anthony Powell called *The Polyglots* 'a classic', adding that he put off reading it for several years because so many people had recommended it. This was a trick of the English character that Gerhardie never really understood. With *The Polyglots* he came to town. It was taken up by Arnold Bennett and H.G. Wells, Evelyn Waugh and Graham Greene, who was leaving Oxford when the novel appeared, and who wrote that 'to those of my generation he [Gerhardie] was the most important new novelist to appear in our young life'.

As the narrator in *The Polyglots* remarks: 'Oxford is best in retrospect.' In which case, as he later concluded, it was much like life anywhere.

1983

A MONTH IN THE COUNTRY

One morning, early in the 1970s, I received a letter together with an apparently blood-soaked card. My correspondent described himself as a family butcher from Kettering. His letter read:

> Although you may not have heard of the Ellerbeck Literary Award you will be pleased to hear that you have won it. The Prize is awarded at infrequent intervals and you are only its third recipient. The circumstances are that Mr Carr who makes a living by writing is one of my customers and pays me in part with unsold works, known I understand as Remainders. These I give to better customers in lieu of my customary picture-calendars. Mrs Ellerbeck who goes to the WEA [Workers' Educational Association] class and is not averse to a bit of literature suggested some years ago that I award one of these copies as an Encouragement to another member of the Literary World, this to be known as the Ellerbeck Prize.
>
> We decide who it is to be from the most graphic and telling picture of the cultural world outside Kettering that we read during the month that Mr Carr delivers his books and we settle with him. Sometimes it is a complete book that Mrs Ellerbeck

has been reading and sometimes it is only a few lines. In your case it is only a few lines but I hope some day that this will encourage you to write a book about it.

I came across these lines in some newspapers that Mr Timpsons saves us for outer wrappings. It describes you wrestling in the dark beside a wheelbarrow of sodden volumes and cleverly inserting your signature in a book a dissatisfied customer was attempting to return to you. As a tradesman this has happened to me and I can appreciate your courage and skill.

I have removed the dust jacket for two reasons. As I store them in with my carcasses they have a slight taint and also I am told that without the jacket it will be harder to sell.

Mrs Ellerbeck and myself intend to look for more of your writings whenever Mr Timpsons brings his newspapers. Meanwhile good luck to you.

Yours truly

George Ellerbeck

My prize (a non-transferable Meat Token for 1lb of Best Steak) was accompanied by a novel which turned out to be a satire on the teaching profession. The whole package was a rather baffling business, but after the initial shock, I assumed the air of Sherlock Holmes and set about solving the mystery.

Three months earlier I had been invited by the London *Times* to write a comprehensive manifesto celebrating International Book Year. Contrary to my intentions, and against my better instincts, the article developed into a rich inventory of literary humiliations. If literature was thriving, as I bravely attempted to argue, then it was obviously doing so on its deathbed. It was for this work, I recognised, whose bleak comedy must have appealed to my correspondent, that I had been awarded my prize.

The book I had been sent was J.L. Carr's *The Harpole Report*. I picked it up and began reading. Two points were soon clear to me. Although it was narrated as a series of official letters, the novel appeared to be partly autobiographical. What also became clear from its wry, humorous style was that the author and my strange correspondent were one and the same person. Therefore, in my best Sherlock Holmes manner, I concluded that my benefactor was J.L. Carr. Elementary, my dear Watson.

Readers of *A Month in the Country* will immediately recognise the Ellerbeck family. In its pages Mrs Ellerbeck presides over 'a splendid repertory of North Riding dishes' and sees to it that the new arrival at Oxgodby, the war-damaged Tom Birkin, never goes hungry. Her big, fourteen-year-old daughter Kathy, 'a very organising girl' with blue eyes and freckles, is soon coming to the village church where Tom Birkin is uncovering a large mediaeval wall painting, and plays gramophone records to him. Sometimes she brings her wide-eyed younger brother Edgar. Head of the family is the impeccable stationmaster and formidably moustached lay preacher at the chapel, George Ellerbeck. 'My father was a butcher, Mr Birkin,' he modestly reveals over Sunday lunch.

A Month in the Country was published seven or eight years after I received my unexpected prize and the book's publication was the occasion of my only meeting with J.L. Carr. It was a fleeting encounter in unusually grand surroundings. His novel had been short-listed for the Booker Prize and we came across each other, both in our dinner jackets and clasping a glass of champagne, before the dinner started. I wish we could have met in easier circumstances. His humorous face was contorted in mild agony, for he was, I judged, an intensely private man. We exchanged a few polite words, stood around awkwardly and agreed that the Ellerbeck Prize, though not so interesting to bank managers, was a more singular honour than the Booker Prize. Then we were herded to our separate tables. I never saw him again. But I was amused to read in his last novel, a self-published satire on the book business called *Harpole & Foxberrow: General Publishers* (1992) that one of his characters, Mrs Fazackerly, bookseller of Stotfield Magna, having developed the habit of stroking her books in winter, recommends as best for this kind of attention 'one of Mr Holroyd's good solid biographies'.

J.L. Carr's career was relentlessly unconventional. Though he was known as Jim and appears as James on one of his novels, he was actually Joseph Lloyd Carr, born in the North Riding of Yorkshire in 1912. His father was a railwayman and Methodist preacher like George Ellerbeck – indeed the Carr family appears to have had much in common with the Ellerbecks. But J.L. Carr released few details of his life to the public. On the American edition of *A Month in the Country*, his biographical note simply reads: 'J.L. Carr lives in England.'

Having twice failed his eleven-plus examination, which would have qualified him for free grammar school entry, he was sent as a paying pupil to Castleford Secondary School (which the sculptor Henry Moore had attended), then went to the Goldsmiths' Teaching Training College, after which he taught in a school in Birmingham. For one improbable year he travelled to the United States and, on an exchange system, taught children on the Great Plains of South Dakota – an episode that eventually led to his novel *The Battle of Pollocks Crossing* (1985), an eccentric offshoot of David Lodge's *Changing Places*. During the war, he joined the Royal Air Force and served in Sierra Leone, using some of his experiences in his novel *A Season in Sinji* (1967), where he opposes the madness of warfare with the intricate sanity of cricket (a game that, in the opinion of Bernard Shaw, had given the otherwise atheistic English nation a sense of eternity).

Towards the end of the war Carr married the daughter of an Essex farmer. They had a son and in 1951 moved to Kettering in Northamptonshire, where he became a legendary headmaster. His initiatives, which enrich *The Harpole Report*, were famously unorthodox. He would ask the children to put their names and addresses in bottles, then collectively launch them into the fast-flowing river; or organise an arithmetic race in which contestants, running along the course, were obliged to stop at various blackboards set out across the field and solve equations. It was not beyond him to march his pupils along the tree-lined streets of Kettering reciting A.E. Housman's 'Loveliest of trees, the cherry now ...' or hold school assembly near the railway line, or suddenly announce the school play (in which everyone participated) two days before its performance. He would take the children to local churches to hunt for historical clues, and to a quarry so that they might search for fossils. His worst punishment was to sit a pupil near a blackboard with his crime chalked on it and beneath the school puppet, Bondybunda. Unsurprisingly, he was the bane of the local educational authority, though he was loved by the children and came to be respected by their parents. It was a shock for all of them when in 1967, at the age of fifty-five, he suddenly retired to write novels.

He had already published one novel, a contrapuntal revenge melodrama called *A Day in Summer* (1964) somewhat reminiscent of Patrick Hamilton's retributive thrillers, and had saved £1,600 to buy time for writing. But this was a difficult period. In 1968 his wife was diagnosed as having lung cancer and, though this inter-mittently went into remission, it was to kill her fifteen years later – after which Carr added to the 1991 edition of *A Month in the Country* the poignant epigraph by the Irish poet Herbert Trench.

> *She comes not when Noon is on the roses—*
> *Too Bright is Day.*
> *She comes not to the Soul till it reposes*
> *From work and play.*
> *But when Night is on the hills, and the great Voices*
> *Roll in from sea*
> *By starlight and by candlelight and dreamlight*
> *She comes to me.*

In his charming, but not-quite-definitive, twenty-eight-page pamphlet *The Life and Times of J.L. Carr*, Byron Rogers writes that by 1969 Carr had only £200 left, but rescued himself by printing and selling county maps which were illumined with his teasing wit, arcane knowledge and artistic talent. In his spare time he had taken up landscape painting, sculpture and the recording of church archi-tecture in various mediums ranging from pen and wash to acrylic, varnish 'and occasionally finger' on hardboard.

Using the back room of his home in Kettering as well as a garden shed, and employing a filing system consisting of shoe boxes, he created an unusual publishing empire based, he explained, 'entirely on logic'. His publications measured five inches by three-and-a-half, which enabled him to dispatch them in standard-sized envelopes at minimum postage. These 'mind-enlarging micro-tomelets' as *The Times Literary Supplement* called them, consisted of sixteen tiny pages which, he claimed, was just within the public's reading span. He began with a selection of poets, the very first being John Clare, one of whose descendants he had identified as his milkman at Kettering. To these miniature poetry books he then added a bizarre collection of tiny biographical dictionaries of eponymists, usurpers, royal consorts, frontiersmen and others. Readers came to love his wonderful mixture of fact and fantasy, his succinct and opinionated style (Nell Gwynn is a 'ravishing fruiterer'; Henry VIII an 'axe-happy, ulcerated, impotent monster') combined with his prolix titles, such as *Prelates, Parsons, Vergers, Wardens, Sidesmen & Preachers, Sunday School Teachers, Hermits, Ecclesiastical Flower-Arrangers, Fifth Monarchy Men and False Prophets*. So successful was this publishing venture that, when approaching eighty, he decided to publish his own last two novels.

He had taken to writing books for children and continued writing novels that were generally well reviewed but never good sellers. The *London Magazine* called his fourth novel, the extreme football fantasy *How Steeple Sinderby Wanderers Won the FA Cup* (1975) 'simply the best football-based work of fiction'. But, like his other books, it did not flatter people or bow to contemporary fashion. Instead, with derisive gaiety, it delivered in the words of polymath author Benny Green 'some murderous blows at the fatheads who populate professional football'.

Then, in 1980, he published a masterpiece, *A Month in the Country*. In all his other novels, the quirkiness of his talent, like Tom Birkin's facial twitching and stammering, distract his storytelling with dangling footnotes and inconsequential parentheses. But in this novel his various interests and passions seem magically harmonised and we are held, as the summer heat enfolds us, suspended between shadows from the past and premonitions of the future. It is a timeless book recreating a propitious season, another world, a

place of healing. The narrative proceeds rather like Birkin's explo-
ration of his mediaeval wall picture, inching patiently along,
following a hand or face, aiming at something that looks right. 'I was
engrossed in my work. It was tremendously exciting ... I wasn't sure
what I was uncovering.'

Initially, as he tells us in his foreword, Carr believed he was writing an easy-going idyll along the lines of Thomas Hardy's *Under the
Greenwood Tree*. There are superficial similarities: both novels are
rooted in English village life and have plots that revolve round the
village church. Hardy mourns the passing of the old order marked
by the supplanting of the choir by a new church organ. But Carr,
combining ancient and modern, gives a hilarious welcome to the
new chapel organ while, in the church, he reclaims the past as Birkin
finally reveals the fourteenth-century painting (Birkin's affection
for the hopelessly out-of-date stove refers amusingly to Hardy's
novel). Both novelists compensate for a dark pessimism with their
faith in the fundamental decency of the ordinary villagers. But
Hardy, for once contriving a cheery ending, has his heroine, the
flighty Fancy Day, reject the parson and marry the man she loves.
Carr weaves a more imaginative and ambiguous ending: 'I have
sometimes wondered if it was a dream.'

As Tom Birkin teases the wall painting back from its years of
darkness, he feels a sense of kinship with its creator. 'I had lived
with a very great artist, my secret sharer of the long hours I'd
laboured in the half-light above the arch.' It is a feeling which, with
its echo of Conrad, he vividly communicates to his readers so that
they feel a similar affinity with the novelist. *A Month in the Country*
is a novel of resurrection. The nameless mediaeval artist had died
'on the job', but his work, its colour gradually spreading over the
wall, is brought back to life. And Birkin, falling asleep on a tomb
slab, is woken by the appearance of Alice Keach. 'I should have
lifted an arm and taken her shoulder, turned her face and kissed
her. It was that kind of day,' he remembers long afterwards. 'And I
did nothing and said nothing.' It is a scene that recalls John
Donne's early love for Ann More about which he wrote in 'The
Ecstasy':

And whilst our souls negotiate there,
We like sepulchral statues lay;
All day the same our postures were,
And we said nothing, all the day.

A Month in the Country won the Guardian Prize, was reprinted many times, and, in 1987, made into a film scripted by Simon Gray with Kenneth Branagh, Colin Firth and Natasha Richardson in the leading roles. All this popularity and success made no noticeable difference to J.L. Carr's way of life. He was an outsider, a man of integrity, who wrote from his sense of privacy.

He died in 1994 and his funeral service in Kettering parish church was, in the words of Byron Rogers, 'like the passing of a spymaster'. He had such disparate interests that there seemed many J.L. Carrs, and since he compartmentalised his friendships, few of his friends knew each other. 'What I remember most about his funeral service was the fidgeting . . . as the mourners kept squinting sideways to speculate about their neighbours,' Byron Rogers wrote. 'Then, at the very last minute, there was a clatter of high heels and a very young, very beautiful woman came in, dressed in fashionable black. She came alone and at the end was gone, just as abruptly, into the March afternoon.' No one knew her or could find out who she was – an ex-pupil, mistress, cricketer, flower-arranger, Sunday School teacher . . . But readers of *A Month in the Country* may feel that she had stepped out of its pages.

2000

A PASSAGE TO INDIA

O f all early twentieth-century novelists, the figure of E.M. Forster appears the most deliberately unexciting. He was born on New Year's Day 1879, the only surviving child of Alice Clara (nicknamed Lily) and her husband Edward Morgan Llewellyn Forster, an architect, who died of consumption shortly before his son's second birthday. Lily, who came from a robust family of artists with the curious-sounding name Whichelo, had not at first regarded her husband's illness very seriously and to her grief was added the extra guilt of knowing that the Forsters half-blamed her for the tragedy. She never remarried but, as if in expiation, seems to have thrown all her love and an exaggerated sense of protection round her son. Morbidly anxious over his health, she let it be known that (despite a constitution that proved unusually sound) he was delicate and needed genteel doses of sea air at places such as Bournemouth. She 'coddled him obsessively', Forster's biographer P.N. Furbank writes: 'All through his childhood he was never allowed out if there were the slightest threat of rain, and in the mildest wind he had to be swathed in warm coats and mufflers. He imbibed the anxiety himself, and right up to middle age he thought of himself as extremely frail and likely at any time to develop consumption.'

Besides his mother, there was an attentive team of maiden aunts to superintend his upbringing by giving him dolls, and dressing him up in lace collars and Little Lord Fauntleroy suits. Priggish and precocious, he was referred to as the 'Important One' and allowed to develop extravagant tantrums of fury. 'I wish he was more manly and that he did not cry quite so easily,' his mother complained to one of the aunts. At the centre of his life was a love affair with his mother whom, he believed, he would marry once he grew up. After she had explained to him that 'boys can't marry their mothers', Forster replied that he would never go to any wedding 'in case I should be married and I don't want it'. This love, which he wished to last for ever, illumined his childhood but stretched shadows across his adult life. 'He sucks his dummy – you know, those child's comforters – long after his age,' D.H. Lawrence wrote of him in 1915. 'But there is something very real in him, if he will not cause it to die. He is *much* more than his dummy-sucking, clever little habits allow him to be.'

For most of his childhood, with its sewing parties and the strange excitement of garden boys employed by his mother, Forster had been settled in 'Rooksnest' at Stevenage, which he later described in *Howards End*. But in 1893 his mother moved to an unattractive house called 'Dryhurst' so that he could become a day boy at Tonbridge School. Forster's experiences at private and public schools were predictably miserable. He felt homesick and unpopular. Tonbridge, which is bitterly remembered as Sawston School in his favourite novel *The Longest Journey*, was populated by little gentlemen with 'well-developed bodies, fairly developed minds and undeveloped hearts'. The atmosphere of buffeting games and bullying unkindness was enshrined in the school's Kiplingesque anthem,

> *Here shall Tonbridge flourish, here shall manhood be,*
> *Serving God and country, ruling land and sea ...*

The vivacious spoiled darling of 'Rooksnest' was quickly identified at Tonbridge as a cissy, and in self-defence he developed into a demure, elusive figure, shoulders rounded, eyes cast down, tentative,

demanding to be overlooked. The worst trick that school played on
him, he later said, was 'to pretend that it was the world in miniature.
For it hindered me from discovering how lovely and delightful and
kind the world can be.'

The first perception of this kindness and delight came to him at
King's College, Cambridge, where he went in 1897 as a classical
exhibitioner. Here he was particularly influenced by two dons:
Nathaniel Wedd, 'a cynical, aggressive, Mephistophelean character
who affected red ties and blasphemy' and who encouraged him to
write; and Goldsworthy Lowes Dickinson, a rather sentimental
Hellenist philosopher and misogamist, who strengthened Forster's
confidence in resisting Tonbridge standards by teaching him to value
truth over victory. He was soon elected to a secret society known as
the Apostles among whom he was to meet several members of the
future Bloomsbury Group – Maynard Keynes, Lytton Strachey,
Leonard Woolf – all of them under the spell of the philosopher G.E.
Moore and devoted to the principle that personal relationships and
aesthetic sensibility were more important factors in life than the
worldly religion of success. 'Body and spirit, reason and emotion,
work and play, architecture and scenery, laughter and seriousness,
life and art – these pairs which are elsewhere contrasted were there
fused into one,' Forster wrote of Cambridge. 'People and books reinforced one another, intelligence joined hands with affection,
speculation became a passion, and discussion was made profound
by love.'

It was this tissue of connections forming a comprehensive unity
that Forster explored in his novels. At Cambridge, in Italy and
Greece, and then most eloquently in India, he looked for an atmosphere as different as possible from the barbaric climate of school.
But the personality into which school life had subdued him
remained. His unobtrusiveness was startling. He reminded Leonard
Woolf of 'a poor old woman'. His cautiousness became legendary.
Katherine Mansfield objected that he 'never gets any further than
warming the teapot'; and T.E. Lawrence observed that he 'rolled
thunderstorms in teacups, most lightly, beautifully'. His dull exterior
imposed on many people, even some of his friends. 'He's a mediocre

man – and knows it or suspects it, which is worse,' Lytton Strachey decided. 'He will come to no good, and in the meantime he's treated rudely by waiters and is not really admired even by middle-class dowagers.'

'*Méfiez-vous des hommes pittoresques*' warned Nietzsche – a lesson that applies perfectly to Forster, whose hesitant appearance aroused few expectations. Behind the buttoned-up manner, pedantic speech, he was tougher and more lively than his critics allowed. Even at Cambridge, Keynes spied him out as the 'elusive colt of a dark horse'. It is true that his mother continued to deal with him like a child, paying his bills, choosing his clothes, though this was increasingly her need rather than his; and it was also true that he had been so circumscribed by English suburban life that not until the age of thirty did he understand how copulation took place. Yet here was the novelist from whom as robust a literary personality as Norman Mailer admitted he had learned most; who in 1910, at the age of thirty-one, emerged as a celebrity whose fame was to become international fourteen years later with the publication of *A Passage to India*.

A Passage to India is dedicated 'To Syed Ross Masood and to the seventeen years of our friendship'. In the novel, the relationship between Fielding and Aziz recalls something of this special friendship. With Masood, a charming and princely-looking Muslim, Forster fell in love deeply but silently, since unlike himself Masood was not homosexual. When, years later, he did suddenly reveal his love, Masood replied laconically: 'I know.' These feelings for Masood were more intense than his devotion to his mother and utterly different from anything else he had felt before. He became more open in expressing emotions, experiencing a few homosexual affairs that made him feel 'a grown-up man'. His debt to Masood, he wrote, was 'incalculable'. Without him *A Passage to India* would never have been written.

He woke me up out of my suburban and academic life, showed me new horizons and a new civilisation, and helped me towards the understanding of a continent. Until I met him, India was a vague jumble of rajahs, sahibs, babus and elephants, and I was

not interested in such a jumble; who could be? He made everything real and exciting as soon as he began to talk.

Though he had met Masood in 1906, it was not for another six
years that, having assembled sheaves of introductions and prepared
himself with visits to the zoo and some riding lessons from Leonard
Woolf, he set off with Goldsworthy Lowes Dickinson for India. For
over five months he travelled widely, feeling at moments that 'one
could easily "lapse" into an oriental'. India helped to distance him
from his adolescence, gave him greater maturity, purged his style of
its Stevenage primness. For him, no less than for Kipling, it was a salvation. It was in the creation of a cleansing boys' world, with none of
the 'impurities' of Forster's life, that Kipling could imagine himself
performing all the military and athletic deeds that poor eyesight
and health had denied him. His conceit and bumptiousness were the
means by which he survived the shock of his childhood in England
away from his parents, a shock that restricted his capacity for loving
and replaced it with resentment. For all Forster's apprehensive
manner, it was Kipling who was the more timid, his animal wariness
and instinct for self-protection cutting him off from emotional intimacy with people. From his loneliness he distracted himself with the
contemplation of vivid outdoor excitements that could not bruise
his feelings. His books turn the world inside out, making it a battlefield where a nameless enemy is exposed and vanquished.

Forster's world is less imaginative than Kipling's and more exact.
On this first visit to India he met as many Anglo-Indians (at whose
clubs he was miserable) as Indians themselves, with whom he
'almost always felt happy'. Although these months were carefree and
exciting, there were also darker aspects that were to become more
prominent when he returned there in 1921. 'I had English friends in
the civil service and I could pass from one camp to another with
results that were interesting but painful,' he wrote.

The English had been trained in a fine tradition of paternal
government. Times were changing and they found it difficult
to change. Some of them accept the new situation with a good

grace, most of them with a bad one, and the manners of their womenfolk could be ghastly. Looking back on that first visit of mine to India, I realise that mixed up with the pleasure and fun was much pain. The sense of racial tension, of incompatibility, never left me. It was not a tourist's outing, and the impression it left was deep.

Forster had great difficulty in writing *A Passage to India*. His standards were high, but he lacked ambition; and with the success of *Howards End* in 1910, some of his creative vitality appears to have leaked away. He had started a new novel called *Arctic Summer* before going abroad. India, he predicted, 'will either kill or cure it – if it doesn't kill me'. Forster survived, the novel was aborted and he contemplated writing a travelogue based on the diaries he had kept. But in the summer of 1913 he began translating his Indian experiences into a new novel. By the autumn, however, he had switched to *Maurice*, the homosexual novel that was to be posthumously published in 1971, and though he seems to have returned from time to time to *A Passage to India*, he could not see his way through it. 'Shall never complete another novel,' he noted in his diary at the end of 1914.

Forster's fear of literary sterility seems to have been one of the factors that brought on the sterility he feared. Before resuming *A Passage to India* after the war, he burned (as a symbol of this sterility) a number of indecent stories he had written and which, he decided, had 'clogged' his imagination. He believed that he had stopped creating rather than become uncreative. 'I have never felt I'm used up,' he explained to Forest Reid. 'It's rather that the scraps of imagination and observation in me won't coalesce as they used to.' During periods of depression he was convinced that he had lost the ability to write. 'I am dried up,' he claimed. 'Not in my emotions but in their expression.' Yet in the reflection of Mrs Moore's collapse after her expedition to the Marabar Caves, we can see that Forster's apprehensions may have had a deeper focus, threatening the drying-up of all interest in life, and making him believe he had 'got tired of people and personal relationships'. In Mrs Moore's departure from

India and death at sea, he found a method of putting these fears of uncreativity to creative use; and by returning to India in 1921 he revivified his emotional involvement with people, and resurrected his novel.

Forster's second visit to India lasted nine months, most of which he rather improbably spent as private secretary to the Maharajah of Devas – a period he describes in *The Hill of Devi*. His duties on behalf of this small, bright, sympathetic Indian (ostensibly those of a courtier) ranged from superintending the Maharajah's mail, motor cars, tennis courts and 'electric house' generators to lassoing cows and pulling them off the palace gardens. Although he travelled less widely than on his first visit, he immersed himself far more deeply in the rich confusion of Indian life, recording as the 'strangest and strongest Indian experience ever granted me' the nine-day festival commemorating the birth of Krishna, which emphasised the union with God through human love – on which he built the last section of his novel. He saw Masood again, 'as companionable as ever', but observed that, because of political changes in the country, the British had made 'a hasty and ungraceful change of position'. Partly because it is not primarily a political novel, this late-flowering liberal reform did not alter Forster's picture of the British in *A Passage to India* who remain irretrievably pre-First World War. But in several other aspects the novel did change. At the end of his first visit he had been accused of having 'a wrong idea of Indians' through seeing them as too foolishly sentimental. After his second visit he felt less in love with them. 'When I began the book I thought of it as a little bridge of sympathy between East and West,' he wrote to Masood, 'but this conception has had to go, my sense of truth forbids anything so comfortable. I think that most Indians, like most English people, are shits, and I am not interested whether they sympathise with one another or not. Not interested as an artist.'

In this new mood the book became less romantic, more sombre. The ludicrous bridge party in Chapter 5 is almost a parody of his original concept of the novel. His skilful interweaving of theme and story emphasises the disunity of Indians and the British: 'Perhaps it is futile for men to initiate their own unity,' he writes, 'they do but

widen the gulfs between them by the attempt.' This disunity is kept
actively at work by the poison of nationality, and by the spirit of the
Indian earth 'which tries to keep men in compartments'. From both
of these there evolves an elaborate pattern of misunderstanding.
Forster plots the arid tidiness of the British army of occupation
with its 'roads named after victorious generals and intersecting at
right angles' with the infinite fissures of the Indian soil 'riven into
sects and clans which radiate and join, and change their names
according to the aspect from which they are approached'. To attempt
any reconciliation between such differences is by ordinary standards, Aziz concludes, 'a foolish experiment'. Yet in the festival of
Krishna, Forster provides an *extraordinary* method of synthesis – 'a
nightingale between two worlds of dust'. The theme of all Forster's
works is in the shorthand of his epigraph to *Howards End*: 'Only
connect . . .' In *A Passage to India* the formula he suggests for this
connection between Will and Imagination is more subtle, though
less explicit, than elsewhere in his writing. In the final paragraph of
the novel, the forces of the physical world (the horses) and the religious world (the temple) combine to prevent this connection. Yet
Forster implies that there is a more sophisticated way of combining
actuality and reality, prose and poetry; that there is a different
rhythm of friendship moving with those horses as they swerve apart
and finding in the chorus of a hundred voices that answer 'No, not
yet,' 'No, not there,' a harmonious refrain to our call for the Friend
'who never comes yet is not entirely disproved'. This is no longer the
Bloomsbury view of personal relationships, having the extra dimension of mysticism that Bloomsbury, in its reaction against
nineteenth-century religiosity, generally distrusted. But as Forster
wrote in a letter to Malcolm Darling:

> I have acquired a feeling that people must go away from each
> other (spiritually) every now and then, and improve them-
> selves if the relationship is to develop or even endure. *A
> Passage to India* describes such a going away – preparatory to
> the next advance, which I am not capable of describing. It
> seems to me that individuals progress alternately by loneliness

and intimacy, and that legend of the multiplied Krishna . . . serves as a symbol of a state where the two might be combined. The King's [i.e. Bloomsbury] view over-simplified people: that I think was its defect.

On Forster's return to England it seemed as if this second visit to India had failed to restore his creative power. But he was encouraged to go on with the novel by Leonard Woolf and helped by J.R. Ackerley who, with his entertaining letters from India, where he was secretary to the Maharajah of Chhatarpur, extended his Indian experiences at second hand. The chief influences on the final chapters came from his reading of Proust, which 'tempts me to emphasise the atmosphere, and so to produce a meditation rather than a drama'; and from his reading of T.E. Lawrence's *Seven Pillars of Wisdom*, which reinforced his faith in the co-existence of strength and sensitivity. 'It is exactly what I want,' he told Siegfried Sassoon. 'It moves me so deeply that I nearly cry, but my emotion is not entangled with any affection for the author . . . it is disinterested and so durable.'

A Passage to India was published in June 1924 and scored an immediate critical success. 'He has quite lost the touch of preciousness, of exaggerated care for nature and the relationships of human beings, that may faintly irritate some readers of his earlier books,' wrote Rose Macaulay in the *Daily News*. 'The imagination [is] at once richer, less fantastic, and more restrained . . . it is, I think, the best and most interesting book he has written.' Many other reviewers saw it as Forster's most mature and accomplished work. 'The difference between *A Passage to India* and the former novels,' Leonard Woolf wrote in the *Nation and Athenaeum*, 'is that now Mr Forster knows exactly how to use the elements of his genius.' But as L.P. Hartley observed in the *Spectator*, it is 'a disturbing, uncomfortable book'. It might be true that, as *The Times Literary Supplement* reviewer explained, 'not the least distinctive quality of Mr Forster is his fairness', but since he was using this distinctive fairness to demonstrate that 'most Indians, like most English people, are shits' he was assured of accusations of unfairness from both sides. He defended himself vigorously against these charges. To what extent, he asked, was 'blue-book accuracy' desirable in a novel? 'The facts might be right, but the accent would remain, and how on earth is one to do away with one's accent?' Perhaps, he added, we would one day get the 'perfect, the unaccented book'. But in another mood, he criticised his novel for being too fairminded. 'Isn't fair-minded-ness dreary!' he wrote to Goldsworthy Lowes Dickinson. 'A rare achievement, and a valuable one you will tell me, but how sterile in one's own soul . . . Where is truth? It makes me so sad that I could not give the beloved a better show. One's deepest emotions count for so little as soon as one tries to describe external life honestly, or even readably. Scarcely anyone has seen that I hoped Aziz would be charming.' It is by this refusal to exploit easy sympathy or senti-mentality, by this uncomfortable truthfulness, that the book succeeds in telling us something 'about the search of the human race for a more lasting home', as Forster expressed it; 'about the uni-verse as embodied in the Indian earth and the Indian sky, about the horror lurking in the Marabar Caves and the release symbolised by the birth of Krishna.'

The one episode that has perplexed and elaborately misled critics is this 'horror lurking in the Marabar Caves'. Generations of students and professors have kept themselves busy digging for what Forster *really meant* by this symbolism of the caves. Other readers, such as Roger Fry ('O Lord! I wish he weren't a mystic'), have simply objected to the unsolved riddle. In his first draft, Forster actually made 'someone' follow Adela Quested into the caves and attempt to assault her. Later he changed this version and contrived '*a particular trick I felt justified in trying because my theme was India*', he told Goldsworthy Lowes Dickinson. 'It sprang straight from my subject matter. I wouldn't have attempted it in other countries, which though they contain mysteries and muddles, manage to draw rings round them. Without the trick I doubt whether I could have got the spiritual reverberation going. I call it "trick": but "voluntary surren-der to infection" expresses my state.'

D.H. Lawrence, who thought the book good, didn't 'care about Bou-oum', but in fact Forster was simply using an accurate tran-scription of the echo from the caves in the Barabar Hills which were his model for the Marabar Caves. He deliberately leaves the episode unexplained – 'it is *either* a man, *or* the supernatural, *or* an illusion' he wrote – to represent the unexplainable mystery of India.

A Passage to India was a commercial as well as a critical success, selling almost 17,000 copies in Britain by the end of 1924 and over 54,000 in America. Forster enjoyed his prosperity and fame, though noting in his diary: 'Too much good luck, and too late. I cannot live up to it.' He was never to write another novel. The achievement of his previous novels, however, and the growing reputation of this book, supported by some distinguished non-fiction writing, was to ensure that the cissy of Tonbridge, the mediocre man who could never bring the tea to the boil, developed into someone recognisable in J.R. Ackerley's description of him as 'this great man with his modesty, his courteous manners, and the perennial liveliness of his youthful spirit'.

1983

ALL WRONG ON THE NIGHT

Over the two years I lived in Ireland I saw more theatre than during my previous ten years in England. Even at the time this struck me as strange. After all, compared with London, there was little being staged that I craved to see. I would read the British newspapers, find out what I was missing, then go off to something else. It was, I now think, partly the ease of parking the car, partly the poor television, that prompted me to go out quite so much. The Gate, the Gaiety, the Peacock and Abbey: they were all so simple to reach. You drove a few yards, stopped and walked in. An extra luxury was the absence of complicated machinery (as at the National Theatre in London) for booking tickets. The telephones lines seemed always open, the prices inexpensive, and even when there were no seats available there were still *some* seats: they would obligingly smuggle you in. If you happened to have no money on you, you might barter something else for a ticket: some groceries, perhaps, or a few articles of clothing.

I preferred the Abbey to the Gate. At the Gate (where I saw by far the best production I have ever seen of *The Doctor's Dilemma* and almost the worst *Major Barbara*) it was advisable to take a hip-flask and a couple of rugs. Even the coffee during the interval was biting.

By contrast, the Abbey was far more spacious, with two bars and a quickening selection of Irish portraits along the walls and up the staircase: W.B. Yeats with his smoky hair and the grandmotherly Lady Gregory; and that myopic pair Lennox Robinson and Sean O'Casey were among the names decipherable to English eyes. Other personalities, such as Mícheál Ó hAoda, chairman of the directors, offered difficulties.

To English eyes Ireland itself is theatre: the north tragedy; the south comedy. Historians will tell you that during the 1970s the country was divided between the promise of financial prosperity from Europe and the threat of disaster from Ulster. Twenty-five years before, after a performance of *The Plough and the Stars*, the Abbey had gone up in flames. 'It was as if God had struck a match and set the whole thing alight,' Sean O'Casey was reported as saying in *The Irish Times*. After fifteen years of exile at the Queen's Theatre (which subsequently collapsed under the strain) the new Abbey had risen in the summer of 1966 on its old site. The foundation stone had been laid by Eamon de Valera. Those who see the importance of the theatre as being, in the strictest sense, political, like to treat the drama as sociological barometer. There was the occasional good play, such as Brian Friel's *Volunteers*, that dwelt on Ulster; but nothing (praise be to God) I spotted that took its inspiration from the European Common Market, no VAT-inspired drama. The tradition of the Abbey Theatre seemed firmly set in pantomime – which may itself reflect something political. Almost everything, I came to realise, can be raised to this pitch of pantomime if you are sufficiently serious about it and can tie a bit of carnival, with flags, ribbons and balloons, to the last act. I had never before appreciated the comic potential of so many regular classics, *King Lear*, *Othello*, *Tamburlaine*, *The Duchess of Malfi* and the rest. Mr Crummles's *Romeo and Juliet* would have found a natural home at the Abbey.

Because Eire is not quite real to the English, what they do when they get there doesn't seem to count: at least not count against them. After all, what one does on stage isn't *real*. It must have been this unreality that accounted for visitors behaving so curiously out of character when they came to stay with me. I don't mean that they behaved badly: just surprisingly. The most formidable puritan, blinkered by the Protestant work ethic, would relax in that sultry Catholic atmosphere and look around; and those whom, out of shyness, I would have hesitated to ask to lunch in England, I boldly beckoned to Ireland for a long weekend. Some visitors I had never seen before in my life, but were friends or enemies of friends or enemies and invited themselves; others who would not have crossed the street to speak to me in London readily crossed the Irish Sea once they realised I was safely exiled. It was delightful but, so I confirmed when eventually I returned to England, misleading.

One of the entertainments I could always offer my guests was an evening at the Abbey. It became for them a piece of theatre within the theatre of their visit: as if we were all Pirandello characters. One evening of this sort was spectacular. Earlier that week, on the telephone, I had been speaking to a woman in London about something connected with work. I knew her only slightly but, in the pause before ringing off, asked (as one may in Ireland) whether she would like to pop over to Dublin next weekend. She sounded extremely surprised at my invitation: I was equally surprised by her acceptance. We were surprised – but were we joking? 'Every jest is an earnest in the womb of time.' In this case the womb of time amounted to two or three days. She telephoned me later that evening, in the tone of someone calling another's bluff, to advise me as to the times of aeroplanes. I countered this by advising her that *The Plough and the Stars* (I think it was *The Plough and the Stars*, though it might have been *Purple Dust* or *Cock-a-Doodle Dandy*) was on at the Abbey the evening of her arrival. Should I get two tickets? She answered, rather flatly, that I should. All right, I said. The jest was in earnest for both of us.

But there was to be a trick planted in all this earnestness. Forty-eight hours later the ground staff at the airport announced that they were working to rule and that flights would be erratically delayed. Again my visitor telephoned, this time from Heathrow. It was Friday afternoon and she was stranded. God alone knew when she would be taking off and He wasn't telling. Apparently what He was doing was to give both of us a chance of acting on second thoughts. The voice at the other end of the line sounded cross. 'I'm sorry,' I said inadequately.

'It's a terrible mess here,' she insisted. I said it must be and asked if I should cancel the theatre tickets – meaning this as a code for cancelling the weekend. But she seemed to understand it literally, sighed with exasperation, and took the initiative. No, I must certainly not cancel anything. I should go to the Abbey by myself. After she landed she would take a taxi to the theatre and join me, possibly during one of the intervals, probably at the end of the performance, or even later at my house: at any rate, she thought, some time. I began to congratulate her on her generalship under difficult circumstances, but the pips made my words ridiculous and, with some relief on both sides, we were cut off.

I went out to the shops, came back, had a bath, drove to the Abbey. The foyer was crammed with Americans who had been jostling round Europe: now it was Friday and Dublin. I pushed through them and above a thousand twanging voices handed in one of my tickets with what sounded to my ears rather an Irish explanation of the circumstances. Whether it was the noise of the crowd or my own verbal convolutions I don't think the girl there understood much. The gong began to sound and I shuffled in with the Americans and found my seat. A few minutes passed then, as the curtain rose, someone moved across and sat down in the seat next to me. I looked: it was no one I knew – a girl with rather elaborate hair and determined eyes. She leaned over to me and whispered a request to borrow my programme. I knew immediately what had happened. Here was one reason why there were always seats available at the Abbey. You asked, they gave. All my elaborate explanations about the ticket, so politely received, had signified nothing. I sat there hardly noticing Sean O'Casey's play which seemed a pale thing compared to the drama that might erupt if my visitor arrived in the interval. She could hardly, even by Abbey standards, sit on my knee. Perhaps I could tell her it was an awful production and we could go straight home.

As I turned over the possibilities I became aware that the girl next to me was, if not actually picking me up, at least making up to me. She was positively alone, it seemed, and at the interval stood up and said to me: 'Let's go and have a drink.' There was no question of refusing. I walked behind her, concealing myself as best I could behind her coiffure and peeping out to see if my weekend guest had turned up. Fortunately there was no sign of her and for safety I suggested moving to the upper bar. We passed Yeats and Lady Gregory, looking severe and aloof; Lennox Robinson and O'Casey with their eyes closed in dismay. Most of the interval I spent fighting for drink. 'Who's the girl?' someone I knew asked me. I smiled enigmatically. As I got the drinks the gong began sounding again and we had only time to swallow them down and hurry back.

No wonder I cannot now be certain whether it was *The Plough and the Stars, Purple Dust* or *Cock-a-Doodle Dandy*. I was exclusively involved with my own predicament. What would happen in the next interval? Also: how extraordinary this all was. It could never have happened in London – and it seemed highly unlikely in Dublin. What was worse, now that I had had the chance to look at her, the girl next to me appeared glowingly attractive. If only I knew her. There were brains, I decided, under that hair; and an excellent sense of taste and judgement behind those magnificently determined eyes. Should I ask for her telephone number? What should I do?

I was attending less and less to Sean O'Casey. The comings and goings on stage seemed misted over in my mind and it was only gradually I realised that the mist was not of my imagination. The volume of coughing and spluttering from the audience rose as the characters on the stage became slowly obscured by smoke. The girl took my arm and I looked bravely perplexed. I knew that waves of white smoke often rolled across the boards of pantomime, but this was black and soon engulfed the whole auditorium. What was happening? Whatever it was, the main drama appeared to be located in the stalls and circle, and I had the impression once or twice of the actors stopping to watch us with interest as (like drowning men and women) we struggled to loosen our ties, remove jackets and shoes. The coughing and spluttering changed to a sort of lowing, with momentary squeals: sounds one might hear in an abattoir. And it was getting hotter. Long before the second interval, the audience began to stampede. Elderly Americans hurdled gamely over the backs of the seats, husbands attached desperately to their wives. They fell over themselves to get out. It was Vietnam. In the thickening smoke some of them lost their way, arrived on the stage and became, like Stoppardian creatures, fatally involved in Sean O'Casey's plot, which was still courageously proceeding.

By the time the next interval came there was almost no one in the theatre left to enjoy it except my new girlfriend and myself. Dressed as if for the beach, our eyes streaming, we struggled into the street holding on to each other. A few yards away some fire engines were pumping water into a building. Behind them stood a convoy of charabancs into which the Americans were pouring. There seemed to be the general impression among them that they had landed up in Belfast by mistake and were being dive-bombed by the IRA. Among the few people, mostly Dubliners, who remained in the theatre there was knowledgeable talk of what had happened all those years before at *The Plough and the Stars*. Was God, we wondered, at His matchbox again? I wandered out and spoke to one of the firemen. It seemed that there had been a trifling accidental fire, the smoke from which had blown directly through the Abbey's ventilating system. It was almost completely out now and there was nothing to fear.

There was a long interval with no fighting for drinks. My companion and I talked excitedly about it all, looked down on nostalgically by Yeats and Lady Gregory, Lennox Robinson and Sean O'Casey. Mícheál Ó hAoda was nowhere to be seen.

I had forgotten all about my impending visitor. At least there would be a seat for her if she arrived. The smoke had largely cleared by the time we went back in for the last act. We were almost the only people there, like royalty who had commanded a private performance. We moved to the very best seats, adjusted our clothing, saw the rest of the play huddled shoulder to shoulder. The actors occasionally threw us bewildered looks, but the show went on, the flags, ribbons and balloons, then the final curtain fell. We clapped frantically, the actors smiled, bowed to us and, like Russians, applauded us back. It was over.

We walked out together hand in hand. I looked round. No one was waiting. After such an experience should I offer the girl supper – explaining that it might develop into a supper-*à-trois*? There was a moment of awkwardness. I opened my mouth to speak, but she spoke first. 'I'll get my suitcase from the booking office. Where have you parked the car?' My mouth remained open ...

We drove home. Though she had a good sense of humour I could never reveal my failure to recognise her through three acts and two dramatic intervals. It was a good lesson too for my vanity that had imagined advances being made to me by strangers. She had come to see Ireland rather than myself. I was her chaperone in case she fell in love with the place. Over the weekend we laughed a lot over that evening at the Abbey. But I had one secret laugh in which she could never join.

1982

AMONG THE AMERICANS

In foreign lands it is the obvious that often foxes us. Before my first visit to New York in 1968 I had read a good deal about it, but nothing prepared me for the hellish smoke that rises through holes in the street as if from an inferno below; or for the electric shocks that stung me each time I tried to open a door, switch on a light, tactfully stroke a cat.

I had been dreadfully spoiled on that first visit. At intervals the telephone would sing out, and there was my friendly publisher with his list of friendly questions. What about fitting an extra lunch into my hectic schedule? Could I, in the next ten days or so, manage to sign one copy of my book? How was I weathering the drastic strain? Between these calls I slept, went for walks, saw a few films, wrote letters, slept again. In restaurants I was given drinks looking like heavy water or tropical salads. Each day I was positively required to do nothing. If I murmured something practical about sales or promotion, I was stared at as if I had lapsed into bad taste. It was a time of relentless goodwill, and the world was full of gentlemen who had been told (by whom I cannot imagine) that I was a best-seller.

When people spoke of the 'excitement' of New York, I felt nonplussed. In my three weeks there I clocked up more hours of unmitigated sleep than anywhere else in the world. No wonder I enjoyed the place so much. A gentle security wrapped me round. Had I missed something? Was my experience incomplete?

My best moment came when someone mistook me for Albert Finney. Was I Albert Finney? 'Yes, of course I am,' I answered. 'And I'm reading this splendid book by Michael Holroyd. Buy it.' I would not have come up with such an instantaneous response in England. It sounded good to me. Besides, I did not really feel myself in New York. It was a pleasant release.

The next two visits reinforced this conclusion. New York *is* a sleepy place, and curiously old-fashioned. I struggled to keep awake, for there was research to do and I was on my own.

No publisher likes to see his author at work on a book. The sight is too painful. That Ancient Mariner monologue, those glazed red eyes like cocktail cherries, the white complexion, racked figure, make an awful spectacle. To ask a publisher for practical help at the research stage of a book may be as embarrassing as to volunteer help on publication day. What publishers need, what they crave, is their authors' intoxicating absence. Usually publishers and writers communicate via a literary agent. He is a reader – of contracts. There is nothing agents like more than settling down with a good contract: many of their best jokes are contractual. My own American agent's speciality is copyright. Though otherwise (he tells me) a modest man, he is a self-confessed master of legal intricacies. I used to open his letters with trembling hopes of some film, ice or opera adaptation of my latest article – only to be dashed by his congratulations: 'Loved your copyright line.' More than once he has generously pursued me with cables about this copyright line, and for him, I suspect, it is often my best line.

In the years since my first trip there seems to have been some diminution in the fatiguing excitement of the place. That time I had seen a man fall down in a Manhattan street. The traffic did not stop, but hooted and surged on, islanding him in the middle. In 1975 I saw a similar incident. A woman fell, lights changed to green, the cars moved forward: then, in a quivering herd, they halted a few inches away. There was a pandemonium of impatience – but they stopped. It was International Women's Year.

Perhaps there is a little more reality apparent now – certainly the crime figures have gone up. Many people's working lives are so calm that they need the fantasy of violence. The unnourishing diet of routine and hysteria common to many cities appears in New York to form part of an *Alice Through the Looking-Glass* pattern: the symptoms come first, and reality reluctantly has to follow. On everyone's lips there was the sound of fear. Atrocities were conceived in talk. People huddled in their padlocked apartments, listening for it, whispering about it, waiting for it, willing it. Fire trucks, ambulances, police cars waltzed and bounded through the streets trailing their screams. But over three months' walking along these streets from Greenwich Village, through Central Park, to Harlem at most hours of the night I saw no crime, no fires, no shooting, no rape. What was wrong with me? Americans were not pleased when I told them how peaceful their city was. Most of them wanted the scent of danger, and read about it all the time in their newspapers and books. I do not claim there is no crime. My belief is that much of it has been willed into existence by desperately well-behaved people who would never hurt a fly.

There is a danger in the brief journey followed by the long essay: the danger that one will be enthusiastically misunderstood. Of course, no writer wishes to deny his readers the pleasure of a good misunderstanding. From Dickens to Donleavy there are, in the American context, heady precedents for this. They seem to show that, up to the 1930s, the United States had been aping whatever Europe was doing. But now Europe, especially Britain, tries to copy the United States and does it very badly. Criticism of the United States may be one of the better ways of sparing her this caricature.

When I arrived this last time in New York, I telephoned my publisher and gave my name.

'How do you spell it?' a cigarette voice asked. I explained. '. . . WHY DEE,' echoed the voice, and uttered a long pause.

To myself I have always been moderately well-known. But the further I travel from Yorkshire (where I have never lived), the deeper is the bewilderment provoked by my North Country name. There are optimists who hope for Hollywood or Polaroid; while among literati I have been merged with David Holbrook. On his account I have been so grossly flattered, cut so abruptly dead, that we shall shortly form a charity to which people who get us wrong will be pressed to contribute, half and half. At other times, other places, I have been identified as a pantomime animal, the first part being Richard Holmes, the second Peter Ackroyd – a syllable from each. I perform by catching in mid-air all the compliments thrown to others.

In the United States my identity comes under serious siege. My publisher's pause, pregnant with my non-existence, reminded me of this; and a party at which I had met William Buckley Jr, editor of the *National Review*, positively asserted it. William Buckley had demanded to be introduced to me. After his long handshake, my whole body ached with his committed praise. I felt myself moving to the right. On leaving the party he again sought me out, and I braced myself for further encomiums. 'Well,' he cried, 'keep those novels rolling out and . . .' with just a flicker of hesitation, 'those short stories!'

My non-existence is not principally as a biographer but as a pedestrian. American pedestrians come in two classes: the quick and the dead. The former can be seen in white shorts and T-shirts; they jog, are often bald and coated (like racehorses) with sweat. The second category appears to take care of the rest. In Washington DC almost the only pedestrians seem to be policemen. They are fitted with whistles and sound like a vigorous dawn chorus. I remember, in the desert of southern Illinois, my excitement, like Robinson Crusoe's, at spotting a shoe print in the snow, though it was only my own print from the previous week. At all times, everywhere, the streets are alive with cars that have evolved the independent life of a superior breed. The attitude towards pedestrians varies from place to place. In Austin, Texas, they are so much feared that people keep troupes of dogs to drive them off in case they decide to attack. But any car that happens to nudge one is liable to atrocious penalties, for, as in some game reserve, the authorities are anxious for them not to become extinct. Elsewhere – Beverly Hills, for instance – pedestrians are treated more abruptly and may be picked up on suspicion of walking with intent. Many of the sidewalks along which one hopefully sets out lead nowhere, abandoning one on some island encircled by a growling herd of wheeled monsters. It is this architecture, rather than any lurid romances of the street, that accounts for the diminishing number of actual people.

It was as a self-employed, foreign pedestrian that my extinction became almost complete. On my first day I went into a bank and presented it with all the money I had. It was, I see now, a pornographic scene – the naked notes spilling out from my clothing, lying exposed on the counter for all to see. They glared at me; eyebrows thickened; hands went to revolvers. 'Whose is it?' they asked.

New York is rich. You have only to hear the size of her overdraft to know just how rich. But no one ever carries money: not too much money, anyway. Money is like the body used to be. We are entitled to glimpse an ankle: but I had stripped her bare. I was hustled to a corner where the questioning began.

This questioning was largely a matter of forms, none of which fitted my case. Name: we took a long time over that and it didn't, I felt, improve my chances. Then came the question that, in one way or another, on telephones, at libraries, in hotels, everyone would ask me: 'Whom do you belong to?' Now it's a sad business (though of my own making), but I belong to no one. In the Great Computer, however, there is no slot for pathos. If I didn't belong, I didn't exist. And at that stalemate we languished several days.

Fortunately, I had chosen a bank in the same building as my publisher. My visits to establish my identity upstairs with him were so prolonged that one of my cross-examiners in the bank downstairs assumed that I was employed by him, and entered this information on her forms. I grasped at the indignity with gratitude, and so did the computer. I was given a chequebook with my name handsomely printed on it, and my triumph lasted until I realised that no one would accept these cheques – not even other branches of the same bank. Restaurants, hotels, shops should all hang up the same sign: WE DO NOT TRUST YOU. For that is the truth. They have been cheated and robbed so often, I was told, that now they look on everyone as a crook. So the crook is victorious, for to defeat him we have accepted his standards.

My next experiment was with travellers' cheques. Wherever I went, in whatever hamburgered desert or forest, I would approach one of the palatial banks with these glossy cheques. But they were not so easy to convert back into money as I had believed. Bank officials would at once ask for my EYE DEE (meaning, confusingly, identity card). EYE DEES are miniature placards, embellished with 'mug shots', that are carried in the clothing or worn boastfully on the chest like a battalion of medals. I didn't have one. The problem was: how officially to identify someone who has been recognised as having no official existence? Letters, books, membership cards of the Automobile Association, the New York Public Library, British Museum, London Library, National Book League – all useless. My driving licence was a positive handicap: I was clearly no motorist. At one super-bank even my passport was judged inadequate, since it failed to list my weight, seemed uncertain about the colour of my eyes, presented a photograph (nine years old) of some accomplice and mentioned a 'peculiarity' so microscopic and intimately placed as to be valueless for bank purposes. Yet if I were not to be extinguished, I needed money. After all, this was my own money I was trying to recover.

Using the contents of my briefcase and my most tiresome, pedantic manner, I set out to construct a convincing self-portrait of a blue-eyed biographer. Warming to this task, calling unsuccessfully for a *Who's Who* (when will that book be of use?), adding one ingenious circumstantial detail to the next, I grew so self-immersed as to overlook the lack of corresponding interest from my bank audience. Not liking my work to be dismissed, I accused them of ignoring reality for empty procedure. I had built up a plausible prima facie case. But, as one of the cashiers gently explained: 'We couldn't care less.'

It is a tribute to my desperation that I did cash my travellers' cheques on agreeing to have the transaction filmed for possible use by the police. You may judge how infuriating I had become when (once the money was in my hands) I asked whether I might buy this film for repeat performances at banks all over the country.

What I really needed was a bank card. Without this I could make no flight reservations and was barred from hotels (spending one night under the stars). So, stumbling through a musical dog show playing there that day, I returned to the bank. The building was full of posters and pamphlets soliciting me to take one of these bank cards, but when I tried to do so I found I was not entitled to one. This time my paralysis came from the lack of a social security number. Once again I did not exist.

Scattering the dogs, I fled upstairs. Since it was becoming so difficult to get my money back, and no one could accept my cheques, I had arranged to make air and hotel reservations through my publisher, repaying him with money from downstairs. This system exploded when the publisher's computer failed to 'accept' me. It said I had no 'code'. But if I did not exist, I argued, surely there was a need to invent me; otherwise to whom had my generous advance on royalties been paid? This question proved curiously telling, and a fictional entity, equally myself, was created – a numbered and nameless being (though allowed the courtesy title of Michael Holroyd) which everyone seemed to prefer to the old familiar one. Once this operation had been performed upstairs, I took the idea downstairs, where, following some amused discussion, it was successfully repeated. After nine weeks, upstairs, downstairs, I was reborn.

In the United States everything is made easy. There are no difficulties, only problems. 'What is your problem?' was the question most frequently flung at me. One of my problems is that I belong to a mathematical but not a cultural minority. Had I, for instance, succeeded in being a woman (it has been done), I would have found in New York a special Women's Bank. But there are simply not enough self-employed people to achieve minority status. In the bad old days there had been discrimination against not a minority, but the majority of Americans: the blacks, women, homosexuals, Jews, almost everyone alive and, for all I know, even the dead. The regular 100-per-cent American, whom no one had bothered to penalise, was a pretty pale and purposeless creature. Vitality and humour belonged to the deprived. There was almost no one who had escaped at one time or another some aggressive discrimination, and who now could tell of having weathered it.

Even the police have claimed minority bonuses. This type of segregation helps to conceal the taint of having been part of the majority, and enables each special category justifiably to wave its flag of liberation.

But vitality and humour now seem on the wane. Everything is solemnly categorised, segregated, polished up by fashion. When I went into a bookstore at Harvard to inquire after Shaw's *The Adventures of the Black Girl in Her Search for God*, I was directed to the 'Black Studies' and then the 'Women's Studies' sections where, the book not having recently been remaindered, I did not see it prominently displayed. When I asked, bearing in mind the gender and colour of the author, whether I should try Men's or White Studies, I was suspected of joking – though why one joke should be better than another I don't know.

The adults of America are the machines. They are very fine. If you want anything done, ask a machine. Machines buy and sell, produce, convey, communicate. They keep you alive, or don't. No wonder human beings are almost redundant. To make a secret of their decline has become a national preoccupation. A popular method is for Americans to resemble their machines in much the same way as Englishmen are said to resemble their dogs. It is astonishing what willpower can achieve. Sometimes you can hardly tell them apart. They congregate within windowless constructions, bathed in homogenised lights (some of which can never be switched off), protected from burglars, rapists, muggers, murderers, pedestrians. They are guarded by bulging policemen, fat with revolvers, radios, batons, helmets and other brave impedimenta. No one may speak without signing a form, may enter a building without submitting to a search or go anywhere without waving his EYE DEE like a drowning swimmer.

Once upon a time there were two types of problem: the avoidable and unavoidable. The art of life lay in distinguishing between them. Americans (and I suspect ourselves) excel at the former. Some of the problems you hear being debated could easily be solved between breakfast and lunch: but then – and this is our real predicament – what to do between lunch and tea? On average, Americans watch six vacuum-packed hours' television a day, but that still leaves several hours when they are plainly unplugged from their sets. It is the threat of this emptiness that agitates people so acutely, the time when you switch off from automatic pilot to find your own way. For where are we going? The answer to that may be so bleak that we prefer to obliterate it, lumber the road with phantom rocks and boulders that cannot be got round because, in any real sense, they do not exist. From politics to the plains of Academe, the manufacture of these problems is a bursting industry. It is assisted by newspapers. In the days before Elmer Gantry (in the unconvincing shape of Jimmy Carter) rode again through the country, various Americans were spotted brandishing firearms near President Ford. He was a difficult target, one of the quick. Unaided, he tripped, dodged, lurched, hurtled, staggered, fell from place to place, 'meeting with' the people and spending their money.

It was impossible to tell whether or not he had been hit, poor man, every few hundred yards. No wonder people spoke of his courage. But those ladies who lined up to watch him limp and bluster along, and who waved (like flags) their guns as if to orchestrate his progress were not honestly trying to kill him. Why should they, unless there was no other way of achieving what they wanted? What they wanted was notoriety; a public notoriety to overcome their feeling of inadequacy – that same sense of individual non-existence that threatened me. Some commentators remarked on how fortunate it was that they had missed their lurching target. But they were not aiming for Ford. They aimed at the cover of *Time* and *Newsweek*, at the front page of *The New York Times* and *Washington Post* – and they hit a bull's-eye.

There is space in the United States and lots of weather, lots of food. The space is not all empty and the food not at all good; but the weather is always climacteric. It is reported incessantly on the radio, and its temperature flashed to us from street corners. Weather has become the focus of the best and (together with some westerns) most authentic television programmes. Hurricanes, blizzards, 'line storms', vast snow, severe warnings – there is plenty of live drama staged each evening by satellite. The television companies compete with one another to give you the best weather. They provide not just the information, but the experience. From your room with its neutral climate of air-conditioning or central heat, you may feel the high and low pressure systems, the tropical heat, frigid squalls pass over you in the space of a few seconds. Almost all this is better than British (to say nothing of Irish) weather, and much more accurately prophesied.

The food is described less accurately. Though often reported as 'hearty', it is usually bland. Everyone knows the generosity of American meat, but few have written about those meals that, beginning with coffee, appear to European minds to proceed backwards. It would astonish most Americans to learn that the glass of melting ice and paper napkin that comprises their traditional *hors d'oeuvres* baffles many foreigners. Some people will advise you to 'eat ethnic', but this can be just as difficult as it sounds. In many regions the sandwich is the chief obstacle to eating. Order a steak, roast beef, lamb chops, boeuf stroganoff, some eggs or fish, any class of poultry and you will probably get some salad followed by a sandwich. And if, in desperation, you switch your order to jumbo shrimp cocktail and chocolate peppermint cake, you will still get salad and a sandwich on the same plate as shrimps and cake and melting ice and napkin.

This provokes panic in some travellers. What panics the Americans is wine. Wine is a fearful substance, only to be bought at some places in brown paper. In North Carolina, I was transformed into a leering, shambling, dipsomaniac monster, capable of loping off on a four-mile hunt to track down a brown-paper glass of wine. Elsewhere, in non-dry states, wine is treated with extreme deference. Carried in the bottle as if it were an explosive, it is poured, with agonising slowness, into tiny sherry glasses to be sipped as a cocktail before the sandwiches.

Eating in restaurants, living in expensive one-night motels, brought me up against the extreme politeness of the Americans. American politeness is *so* polite that it has become one of the chief causes of American violence. I had come across a similar paradox in

Ireland, where they do it on the roads. Irish motorists generally drive with extreme caution, seldom exceeding (even for a red light) 15 miles an hour. Their remorselessness stimulates the few others to feats of extreme recklessness. In a similar fashion, American pornography proceeds from the gigantic rest room of American euphemisms. In England, politeness is a weapon, implanting guilt; in Ireland it has become an alibi, the charming explanation for doing nothing. But in the United States, the foreigner is conscious of being bathed in a milky bath of politeness. It is a push-button politeness, supplied in a few plastic formulas – 'Have a nice day', 'You're welcome', 'Enjoy' and so on. This computer-talk, travelling from the airport into the house, has become the language of human beings. And it drives people mad.

But scattered through the United States, often with little knowledge of one another, is a small army of individuals who have resisted this Orwellian outpouring of idiocy, and benefited from the informality and freedom of the country. It is an army because it is composed of people who are fighting for their own standards, and perhaps those of their children, some students, a few friends. Almost by definition, they do not appear on television or on the front page of newspapers. Often they depend for money on people who understand nothing of what they do or represent. They are given little encouragement and must generate their own enthusiasm. But it is to this private army that a writer should seek to belong. This is his or her true minority, comprising not (as is so often believed in England) rivals, but international compatriots.

1978

THE BATTLE FOR PUBLIC
LENDING RIGHT

This year, 1999, marks the twentieth anniversary of the Public
Lending Right Act. For younger writers in Britain the principle
and practice of paying authors for the use of their books in libraries
must seem as natural as the rising of the sun at dawn. But for some of
us old warhorses in the thirty-year campaign to establish this legal
right, the dawn seemed so long in coming that we still feel a tremor of
wonder, a ferment of secret rejoicing, when our payments arrive.

The campaign itself began quietly on 3 February 1951 with a
modest proposal in the trade press for circulating libraries to pay
authors a halfpenny every time their books were lent to a subscriber.
This suggestion was taken up and improved by the writer John
Brophy, who argued that users of public libraries would not object
to paying a penny – 'less than the cost of half a cigarette' – as a royalty to the authors of those books they were borrowing. He called on
the Society of Authors to take up Public Lending Right as a matter
of policy. It did so: and 'Brophy's Penny' became famous during the
1950s as a symbol of public interest in books providing their authors
with a just and reasonable income.

The Society of Authors was extremely active in the 1950s. It
drafted memoranda, lobbied MPs, issued reports, printed articles,

hosted debates, contacted writers abroad, provoked interviews on radio. And the result of all this democratic activity was zero. The Government White Paper 'The Structure of the Public Library Service in England and Wales', published in 1959, successfully avoided any reference to PLR.

It was then that the Society of Authors decided to switch tactics. It brought in a comedian, an entertainer of genius, A.P. Herbert, to lead the campaign. Sometimes he would appear with some poor bewildered publisher as his straight man; at other times he brought in a troupe of recalcitrant librarians and threw custard pies at them. His achievement was to make PLR well known and understood throughout the country. Unfortunately, his performances became so popular that the public, it seemed, never wanted them to end. Despite all the deputations he led to Parliament and the warm welcome he regularly received from MPs, the Public Libraries and Museums Bill of 1964 contained no provision for PLR.

In a farewell performance at the Royal Society of Literature, A.P. Herbert told his audience: 'We have won no medals . . . in Whitehall, in Parliament, we have got nowhere, and I have nothing but frustration to report . . . [We] have been using sweet reason and balanced argument. Personally, I am tired of sweet reason. We are entitled now, I feel, to anger – and, if possible, action.'

But what action could writers take? 'We can't strike,' complained John Fowles; 'we can only be struck.' But then, as the authors' comedian bowed out, the government introduced as the first minister for the arts in Britain a comedian of its own. Her name was Jennie Lee. She was all heart; and for a time it seemed as if we did not need to abandon sweet reason after all. But Jennie Lee's comedy differed from A.P. Herbert's. It dispensed with wit and went all out for pure nonsense. Her amazing strength, which survived five years' battering of PLR education, was ignorance. She was completely sincere. At banquets and festivals, often amid frantic applause, she spoke of her desire to do something for authors. Something or other. Why did we listen to her? We listened because of what she did with the Open University and performing arts. These were genuine achievements. We listened too because we thought her friend Lord Goodman would persuade her to honour her promises and do something sensible. But all she did was to dam up authors' anger with hope. All she did was to waste time.

In the late 1960s I took over the baton from A.P. Herbert and, like many others were to do, ran my lap of the PLR circuit. I began with 2,000 words of invective in *The Times*, born of the collective frustration we all now felt after eighteen years of energetically getting nowhere. I appealed for a drastic change in the libel laws to enable us to express our anger adequately. Though I was accused of being 'venomous' and 'hysterical', my only apprehension a little later on was whether I might have so exhausted my vocabulary on Jennie Lee as to leave nothing appropriate for her successor, Lord Eccles, who took over as arts minister in 1970 after the Conservatives came to power. She was disappointing. He was a disaster.

Lord Eccles began by promising to do 'something' in three months. The next three years were spent by everyone interested in the subject trying to find out what that something was or had been. A letter to *The Times* not long before his retirement at the end of 1973 asked whether anyone knew if Lord Eccles was still alive. There was no answer.

Lord Eccles had been a good minister of education before he became the hideously mistitled 'paymaster general with responsibility for the arts'. What is it about the arts ministry that, under whatever title it goes, has reduced politicians so regularly in the past to buffoons? Could it possibly be that aspiring politicians simply have no time for the arts? In what other Cabinet post can you, with absolute impunity, do the equivalent of describing Jeanne Moreau as a 'distinguished Frenchman'? During my involvement with PLR I dealt with half a dozen arts ministers. As soon as one of them had learned the ropes and was in danger of what politicians call 'going native' (that is, getting genuinely interested in the subject) he was removed, and the arduous process of educating another would begin again. One of them, I remember, on being told at lunch that an omelette had been named after the novelist Arnold Bennett, innocently inquired: 'Is Arnold Bennett here today?' Another, who happened to have the title minister for the arts and libraries, believed after four years in the job that the London Library was part of the British Library. Later on, when my name was put forward as a member of the Arts Council, there was a delay of six months while the minister (he was by then secretary of state for national heritage), thinking it might be better to appoint a woman, tried to summon Angela Carter who, being dead at the time, never answered his letters.

Such gaffes, which become funny over time, are hopelessly depressing at the time. My worst experience over PLR came after I sent the draft of something I proposed publishing in a newspaper to the Department of Education and Science and received a telephone call that night from the minister himself threatening to blight my career if I went ahead. So far as I knew, I didn't have a career: I simply wrote books and, being self-employed, was unblightable. Nevertheless, I was shaken and went to see Lord Goodman next morning with the text. He read it, inserted after the minister's name 'to whom we all owe so very much', and gave it back to me. With that single addition it was then published and the minister telephoned his congratulations.

Lord Goodman was a good friend to authors in their battle for PLR. During the early 1970s, when Maureen Duffy and myself were serving on what was called a 'Technical Investigation Group', he came spectacularly to our rescue. It was the beginning of a new technological era, and the computer experts, lawyers, civil servants, librarians in the group all spoke different languages. It was Maureen's job and mine to acquire the gift of tongues and translate one language into another. It was painful labour and Lord Goodman, attending one of our meetings as president of the National Book League, decided that deliberate obfuscation was being employed to halt our progress. Hope, like a wounded animal, was dying in front of us. So, in the lunch interval, he took Maureen and myself aside and explained that he was going to stage a terrible scene in the afternoon which he calculated would clear the atmosphere and allow us an easier passage. We were half an hour into the afternoon session when he suddenly exploded. Although I was expecting it, I still felt shocked by his apparently spontaneous fury.

Khrushchev himself could not have pulled it off more forcefully. At the end, he got to his feet and strode out of the room. We sat there appalled, dazed, transformed into different people. And it was true that we did make progress afterwards over the debris he had created.

This new energy of anger and determination was what we needed and what we got from the Writers' Action Group that was founded by John Brophy's daughter Brigid Brophy with Maureen Duffy, Francis King and others in 1972. They made PLR contentious, a fighting issue, something radical and exciting. To be with Brigid and Maureen was to live on the barricades. These were dangerous times, for Brigid and Maureen were not afraid, in the interests of the cause, to turn their artillery of abuse on their closest allies if they looked like retreating an inch. Such resolute tactics were needed, they believed, to cleanse the legacy of confusion left by Lord Eccles. For a working party he set up had recommended a system of distributing PLR money based on library purchases that conflicted with the principle of payment for use. Whether it would be better to accept this 'purchase price right' in the interests of achieving quick legislation which might be amended later; or to back the simple stock-sampling system that operated in Denmark; or go for the more complex but equitable loans-sampling method already working in Sweden, divided authors dramatically. Brigid and Maureen ruled out all but the last option because they knew that although the technology could not by the mid-1970s deliver a sophisticated sampling system, it would have advanced sufficiently to do so by the time any new law came into force.

But could we wait that long? So heated was the in-fighting that some authors could not bear to remain in the same room and breathe the same air as others who held different opinions. At one operatic moment, when practically no one was speaking to anyone else, Brigid proposed that a special ballot be held. With an inspired piece of mistyping she wrote that 'a ballet be held' and suddenly, mercifully, our differences were dissolved in laughter.

We soon discovered how to exploit our differences politically. If an arts minister strayed or dawdled, there was Brigid flashing her green fingernails to put him right or hurry him along. And if he behaved well, there was the new chairman of the Society of Authors, Lady Antonia Fraser, to congratulate him. On Antonia's iron diplomacy we all came to depend. So, at the psychological moment, we had come together and learned to smile and smile again in the modern manner.

'No one changes his mind,' explained Norman St John Stevas, 'but ideas evolve.' With him as our evolutionary arts minister we positively careered. It was he who in 1974 first proposed a government bill that would establish PLR as a separate right, rather than an amendment to the Copyright Act five years later. Among the fourteen other countries that now have some form or other of PLR, that legislation is generally regarded as having delivered a Rolls-Royce of systems.

In 1975 I had gone to live abroad. When I returned two years later Brigid and Maureen were still campaigning. I had been involved in PLR for half a dozen years; they fought for over nine years of their writing lives and gave the impression that they were prepared to go on fighting for ninety-nine if necessary. But no one wanted a third generation of Brophys to become engaged in the battle, and it was Brigid and Maureen who finally reached the winning post together early in 1979 when the Public Lending Right Act became law. They are rightly seen as the heroines of the campaign.

But there were others, some now dead, some half-forgotten, who also stood on the barricades and did noble deeds. Victor Bonham-Carter at the Society of Authors, Denis de Freitas from the Performing Rights Society, the political lobbyist and publisher Alastair Service, the lawyer and crime writer Michael Gilbert, the novelist Frederic Raphael, Ernle Money the MP, Michael Foot, and others, many others, reaching back to those pioneers, A.P. Herbert and John Brophy, deserve to have their names recorded as water marks on those Notifications of Payment that are posted to us each year.

1999

NOTES WITHOUT MUSIC

One day, in the winter of 1996–7, I received a telephone call from Jim Parker, the Public Lending Right registrar in Stockton-on-Tees, asking me to allow my name to be put forward as chairman of the PLR Advisory Committee.

I hesitated. As I grow older I become more grudging with my time. Besides, I had recently found myself agreeing to succeed John Mortimer as chairman of the Royal Society of Literature. Nevertheless PLR held a special place in my past. In the 1960s and 1970s I had been one of those who battled for its implementation, and I still believe that PLR is the most important legislation affecting authors to have been passed during my writing career. So when Jim Parker pressed me a little, I agreed.

My predecessor, Philip Ziegler's, three-year term as chairman finished at the end of 1996 – and no one was appointed to take his place for more than seven months. One reason for this extraordinary delay may have been that the position had already been offered to a distinguished novelist and biographer by the dying Conservative government. He accepted: and then had the carpet whipped from under his feet by New Labour.

I knew none of this at the time. Nor did I know who else was being approached in addition to myself. The system of selection was somewhat invidious. After being amiably persuaded on the telephone to say 'yes', you are sent a forbidding Public Appointments Nomination Form on which you must give a 'self-appraisal', spelling out why on earth you believe you are so marvellously well qualified for such appointments. This 'information' is stored in a computer so that, for the rest of your life (and sometimes beyond it), your name can be 'accessed' for an uncomfortable-sounding 'raft of posts'. As the ice age of technological information advances, so personal knowledge recedes. My own view is that those who spill great quantities of professional jargon on to these forms are the very people you don't want.

After a long silence, I was formally offered the chairmanship on 7 August 1997. On the same day Hilary Mantel and Claire Tomalin joined the committee. Then the Department for Culture, Media and Sport (DCMS) went into action. In hardly less than two months, it issued a one-page press release that, being no longer news, gained no attention from the newspapers. So, you could say, no harm had been done.

But harm was about to be done to PLR. Jim Parker, I discovered, could find no way of avoiding a reduction in the rate per loan paid to authors for the borrowing of their books from libraries. Whatever savings he could squeeze out of administrative costs, the central PLR grant from the government was simply insufficient. So this, it appeared, was to be one of the Advisory Committee's most urgent problems. The arts minister, Mark Fisher, when questioned by Clare Francis at a Library Association reception in October, had appeared disconcertingly vague about the crisis. But he promised to attend my first committee meeting the following month. And I prepared myself to confront him.

He came; he saw — and suddenly he was a convert to Public Lending Right. He promptly agreed to several minor changes we recommended, encouraged us to boldly go into Europe in search of reciprocal agreements, and even urged us to 'think the unthinkable' when considering how to develop the scheme. Finally he pledged to find us the extra £18,000 we needed to avoid reducing the rate per loan – a pledge he swiftly honoured. No confrontation had been necessary and I found myself remarking how pleasant it was to be dealing with an arts minister who showed some interest in the arts.

My vituperation against previous arts ministers has never achieved much. It is my praise that appears to have a devastating effect. Not long after our second committee meeting Mark Fisher was suddenly replaced as arts minister by Alan Howarth. It was rumoured that, then aged fifty-two, Mark Fisher was considered by Tony Blair as too old – rather a dismaying consideration for some- one such as myself who was more than nine years older still. As for Alan Howarth, although he was actually four months older than Mark Fisher in calendar terms, he was still considered young in a special political way, having not long before skipped across the floor of the House of Commons from the tottering ranks of the old Conservatives to join young New Labour.

What were we to make of Alan Howarth? I was determined to prove the optimist. He was said to write poetry in private which was, in its very privacy, I argued, a good omen. And surely his job as assistant to Field-Marshal Montgomery on his *History of Warfare* should stand him well in any future battles with the Treasury? But the question remained: would he understand and support Public Lending Right?

To find out I decided to invite him to the Royal Society of Literature (RSL) to speak about his responsibilities for the welfare of contemporary writing. An invitation was sent to him at the DCMS early in September 1998, and then another in October. By November the RSL had still received no reply. We telephoned and left messages and we faxed reminders – all with the same lack of response. Perhaps his staff of civil servants had been cut so drastically that the new 'effi- ciency' had merged into simple incompetence. I was to have this trouble again later and became sure of getting a reply only when, in the manner of a solicitor serving a writ, I would press a letter on to the minister's very person. So I was amused to see that among the official 'aims and objectives' of the DCMS is that of answering letters within eighteen working days – in which case they must work one day a week.

Over Christmas, the RSL took a startling initiative, the result of which may be read in *Hansard* for Wednesday 27 January 1999.

'*Mrs Virginia Bottomley (South West Surrey)*: To ask the Secretary of State for Culture, Media and Sport, what plans he has to meet the Chairman of the Royal Society of Literature.'

Since this written question had been received on 13 January, the DCMS had finally got in touch with me, and so the next sentence read:

'*Alan Howarth*: I will be meeting the Chairman of the Royal Society of Literature on 18 February.'

My meeting with Alan Howarth at the Department for Culture, Media and Sport that February was to brief him as to what subjects we would like to hear him address when he came to speak to us the following month. I pointed out that whereas we heard a good deal about sports from various sports ministers, and much about the media from the secretary of state, Chris Smith, we had picked up almost nothing from the arts minister over six months beyond a few polite words about the Booker Prize and a late gesture in support of the poets abandoned by Oxford University Press.

When arts ministers do tentatively touch on matters of art they mention the performing rather than the composing arts. It is the performing arts that attract the media: literature in contrast gets little coverage – indeed it looks quite naked. It is assumed that whereas the performing arts unfortunately do need a little money, literature can still be produced in its clichéd garret with its well-known candle, and needs nothing. But it was time, I suggested, that the composing arts were promoted at the DCMS and given a higher priority. The performing arts could sometimes get money from business sponsorship because of their advertising potential. Literature, which could seldom do this, needed government support.

Alan Howarth made a note on a piece of paper.

Among the specific points I raised were our concerns over copyright and the new technology, as well as over the closures and restrictions on opening hours of public libraries. We would, I added, like to hear a renewed commitment in favour of introducing American-style tax relief on gifts to the arts. I argued that ever since

MPs had voted themselves off the self-employed register some twenty years ago, self-employed writers who had worked hard all their careers but had erratic incomes have found themselves unable to afford steady pension schemes and are increasingly obliged to ask for charity from the Royal Literary Fund. So we find ourselves supported in old age more via Walt Disney than by our own country. Also, it is difficult for older writers to sell their manuscripts to libraries in Britain because of the government's ever-dwindling budget to the Heritage Memorial Fund. As for the Heritage Lottery Fund, this did not support the acquisition of papers by living writers, preferring to nourish the dead. This was, in the words of Philip Larkin, 'a neglected responsibility' which we had gone on neglecting. So why not, I suggested, stop neglecting it?

Alan Howarth made another note.

My top priority was of course PLR. I 'reminded' Alan Howarth that almost 30,000 authors were now registered for the scheme which was operated with supreme efficiency from Stockton-on-Tees and regarded by the entire writing community as a just reward for the borrowing of books from libraries. It ran so smoothly that it attracted little notice in the media. Yet it was an extraordinary success story, and we should invest in success. The number of book loans sampled had risen from less than seven million in the late 1980s to over fifty million in the late 1990s. But in real terms the government's grant-in-aid had fallen by over 20 per cent. This was judged to be a serious devaluation of the government's commitment.

I was pleased to see that Alan Howarth was taking notes.

The RSL was crowded for Alan Howarth's speech on 25 March. Our president, Roy Jenkins, was there, most of our council and many fellows. Representatives from other literary organisations, from the Poetry Society to the Writers' Guild, had been invited. Alan Howarth had perhaps wisely rejected a proposed title – 'From Haworth to Howarth' – for his address. 'His talk is untitled,' I explained in the introduction, 'giving rise to unlimited expectations. Will he announce a quadrupling of the Public Lending Right Fund? Is he seeking harmonisation with the Republic of Ireland to gain artists and writers tax-free status? Does he intend to introduce literature into the Millennium Dome? There is only one way to find out.' I then handed over the microphone.

Alan Howarth's speech was a sober survey of events rather than an array of intoxicating initiatives. What was good about it was the obvious fact that he had written it himself. Describing the responsibility of government towards literature as 'a delicate matter', he declared: 'We believe that we do have a responsibility, with due tact, to seek support for you . . . I hope that the minister for arts can be a friend in need to writers.' He was encouraging about the Heritage Lottery Fund's policy review which would include a reconsideration of its refusal to buy the archives of living writers, and he pointed to a small increase in the Arts Council of England's funding of literature. He mentioned the National Year of Reading as part of the government's National Literacy Strategy, trawled through some literary prizes, touched on the state of publishing and bookselling, and emphasised the importance of our public library system. On PLR he acknowledged its practical as well as symbolic value:

> It is a way in which the Government, on behalf of the library-using public, can recognise the contribution which our contemporary authors make to the cultural life of the country . . . The Scheme is not standing still. The PLR Advisory Committee was established to advise Ministers and the Registrar and we have asked its members to consider how it might be developed in the future . . . It is a strength of the Scheme that authors' views are heard and taken into account by the Registrar, the Committee and the Department.

In the lively question-and-answer session afterwards, I noticed that the minister was taking plenty of notes.

I had arranged a dinner for Alan Howarth afterwards to which the RSL had invited representatives from the Society of Authors, the Arts Council, the British Council, English PEN and others. Despite his annotated map, as well as a driver and car, Alan Howarth somehow lost his way in the five hundred yards between the RSL and the restaurant. For an hour he wandered round the purlieus of Paddington in the company of the novelist Rachel Billington, president of English PEN, while the rest of us waiting for him drank several bottles of wine. When he did arrive, he was greeted with considerable teasing which he took extremely well. Some of the audience at his speech had thought his manner rather defensive, but now over dinner informality reigned. I did not see his losing the way as symbolic.

I never met Chris Smith during my term as PLR chairman, though I once received from him at my home a pile of Christmas cards for the entire Advisory Committee. Intermittently, too, I would get his 'Dear Michael' letters accompanied by solid DCMS publications 'bearing the Department's new distinctive visual identity'. One of these had confirmed the very modest increase in the three-year funding allocation for PLR between 1999 and 2002. We had been told of this at the end of 1998 and it had come as a sad disappointment following a DCMS 'News Release for the Arts' in the summer of that year headed 'Biggest Ever Increase in Capital Funding'.

Our modest increase still left us over 20 per cent short of inflation. But what now encouraged all of us was the apparent flexibility of this three-year plan that Alan Howarth indicated when urging us to assist him in helping us. What he needed, he said, was a strong written case that he could put with confidence before the Treasury. It would help him, he added, if authors themselves would write letters of support to their MPs.

It was now my turn to take notes.

The PLR Committee is an advisory rather than a campaigning group. It adjudicates borderline eligibility issues and deals with problems that arise between co-authors, editors, illustrators. It monitors three-yearly surveys throughout Britain of authors' views on the operation of the scheme. It advises on maximum and minimum payment thresholds and examines the process of registration as well as methods of calculating payments. It attempts to address future difficulties such as that raised by the extension of posthumous copyright (one day there will be more dead than living authors registered), reviews cost-saving measures, and looks at the feasibility of seeking alternative sources of funding (can we get money, for example, from the Lottery?). Above all, it makes recommendations for the improvement of the scheme. Should it be developed within the European Union or extended to audiobooks and reference works? Can prison, hospital and school libraries be included in this sample?

Our two chief recommendations in the summer of 1999 were that PLR be opened to European Union authors, and that its overall efficiency be maintained by increasing the fund by £1.8 million to take account of inflation.

Besides authors, librarians, booksellers and those with expertise in publishing and intellectual property, there are several assessors on the committee from the Society of Authors, Writers' Guild and the Authors' Licensing and Collecting Society (ALCS). It was to be these organisations, as well as PEN and the RSL, which ran the supporting campaign.

This campaign opened on 30 June with a grand party, sponsored by ALCS, at the RSL headquarters in Hyde Park Gardens to launch a book of essays, *Whose Loan is it Anyway?*, celebrating PLR's twentieth anniversary. The book had a congratulatory foreword by Alan Howarth who, standing between the legendary figure of Maureen Duffy and the still-optimistic figure of myself, assured us that he was 'working with the Registrar and the Advisory Panel to consider how the Scheme can be further developed and improved in the future'.

It is one of the curiosities of our political system that if you write directly to a minister he may not see your letter. But if you write to your local MP mentioning the minister's name, your letter must be forwarded to him and he will reply to your MP, who is obliged to pass this reply on to you. When Jim Parker and I met Alan Howarth on 22 July to examine the developments and improvements recommended by the Advisory Committee, he remarked that both he and Chris Smith had 'received a large number of letters from authors and their MPs in recent weeks in support of an increased PLR fund'. It was true that one or two MPs had thought it was a 'Public Lending Write' and that the DCMS itself, having drafted a form letter of reply with a blank space where the author's name could be filled in, had sometimes not bothered to put any name in the blank space. But I did not see these as worrying symptoms. Whenever Chris Smith rose to speak on culture and the performing arts, there was an author in the audience (notably H.R.F. Keating) to beard him on PLR. All seemed to be going to plan – the plan that Alan Howarth himself had outlined.

At our meeting in July, Alan Howarth felt unable to grapple with the complexities of reducing the postmortem duration from seventy years, or to simplify the annual procedures involving Parliament that take place every time a rate per loan is set. As for the inclusion of reference works and non-book material such as audiobooks, he proposed that the former be reviewed 'at some future time', while the latter could be conveniently passed to the about-to-be established Museums, Libraries and Archives Council. On the subject of Lottery funding, he suggested that this 'would require more thinking'. We were getting through our agenda pretty fast, though not perhaps developing and improving the scheme very dramatically.

There remained our two main recommendations. The registrar reminded the minister that by not extending the scheme into Europe we risked being in breach of the Treaty of Rome, and I pointed out to him that here was a rare opportunity of doing what was legally and morally right at the same time as being affordable insofar as the costs would not lower the rate per loan. There was a pause – then we were asked whether we should not first 'test the water'. But we were prepared for this. Britain had already tested the water with Germany, with which a reciprocal arrangement has existed since the mid-1980s. 'The discussion concluded with "an agreement",' our minutes record, 'that the scheme should be amended to enable authors resident in EU countries to qualify for PLR with effect from 1 July 2000. The first payments would therefore be made under new arrangements in February 2001.'

We then came to the increase in funding. The PLR office having made great efforts to reduce running costs, it seemed reasonable that the DCMS now play its part. PLR was, after all, the most direct financial way available to the government of fulfilling its aim of promoting culture in respect of literature. Alan Howarth accepted this and said he looked forward to studying the registrar's case for extra funding.

The 'Case for Increased Funding' which Jim Parker had prepared at the request of the Advisory Committee was a lucid, well-argued document with annexes showing business growth over the last eleven years, projected growth over three years, and a comparison of the rate per loan calculated on present government figures as against what it would have been had the fund kept pace with inflation (almost a penny per loan higher). It was, as Alan Howarth himself admitted, 'a clear and convincing explanation of why the PLR Advisory Committee is recommending that the PLR fund should be increased'.

This clarity and conviction were to count for nothing. For Alan Howarth's letter of 20 September 1999 explains that the case cannot be considered because 'we, and the other bodies we fund, have to live within the three-year allocation that has been announced'.

My reaction to this was one of anger and dismay. All that work by so many people had been pointless. Alan Howarth appeared to have quite casually and incompetently misdirected us. If we had known, as he now informed us, that 'the Government is undertaking a Spending Review in the course of the next year [2000] for the years 2001–2 to 2003–4', and that the present allocation was unalterable, we would have timed everything differently. I felt like abandoning a sterile committee room, going out into the street, and throwing stones at the DCMS windows.

On 14 October Jim Parker and I again saw Alan Howarth to go over a so-called 'funding agreement', and I voiced my dissatisfaction. The minister replied that he was obliged to draft his letter as he had, and that the 160 or so letters he had received, though many of them were from 'important people', were not enough for him to go to the Treasury with an overwhelming argument. Knowing the difficulties of getting letters through to him, and remembering the number of times I had pointed out the problems of gaining publicity for literature, I regretted that our case had not been judged by its content.

Looking through the PLR annual reviews during the last six years, I saw that recommendations from the Advisory Committee that needed extra money were never acceded to by the government. 'Ministers were not prepared to agree at present to this recommendation on the grounds of costs to the fund.' 'Ministers were unwilling to agree any extension to the Scheme that had funding implications.' And so on year after year. This is the dark side of that 'delicate matter' of arts ministers' never-ending wishes to 'be a friend in need to writers'. This, too, is where the reiterated determination of the DCMS to 'develop and improve' PLR always breaks down. The Society of Authors needs now to redirect its campaign. And members of the Advisory Committee must ask themselves what their advice is worth.

Postscript

The spring and summer of 2000 were filled with political activity: a public presentation of the 'Case for Increased Funding' at the Royal Society of Arts, various newspaper reports and radio programmes, the handing into the DCMS of a petition with almost 5,000 signatures, and a street demonstration, organised by the Society of Authors, press photos of which showed Alan Howarth being amiably mobbed by Beryl Bainbridge, Doris Lessing, Caroline Moorehead, Deborah Moggach and of course Rachel Billington, as well as many other engaging women – and men.

In July came the spending review announcement by the chancellor, Gordon Brown (who had been politely lobbied on PLR by Melvyn Bragg). Chris Smith's department was to be given more money for the arts, though it was widely reported in the newspapers and on television that it would all go to theatres. But the following week, in the House of Commons, Chris Smith revealed that the funding allocation for PLR between 2001 and 2004 would rise from £5.2 million to £7 million and then to £7.2 million. Our case had been met in full – if rather later than we would have liked – and Alan Howarth was warned that he would have to attune his ear to the unusual sound of applause from authors. He faced congratulations on having provoked all those energies needed to complete the obstacle course of bureaucracy, semantics and accountability that leads to the granting of public money.

Alan Howarth and I are excellent friends now. Sometimes we send each other enthusiastic messages, sometimes we are seen in public shaking hands. As an aide to Field-Marshal Montgomery, he is well able to evaluate our strategy of appearing to be newsworthily at odds as having made our alliance all the more effective. But more important is the fact that 5,000 authors will soon be receiving PLR payments for the first time. There will also be more money for those already qualifying for payments. Altogether 22,000 authors will be paid from the central fund.

And the future? Since the principle of linking the PLR fund to inflation has been established, my successor, Clare Francis, should be able to recommend improvements to the scheme without bringing into play again such a costly, laborious and tautological exercise in persuasion. We shall see. But she will not be dealing with Alan Howarth. For whatever reason, he was removed from office at the next election.

2000/1

A DARK-ADAPTED EYE

When the bank manager sent me a new bank card, he explained that I must have been waving the old one near a television: that would account for the power having gone out of it. I mentioned this in some amazement to a friend, but she merely added that 'because of radiation' I had better keep eight feet away from any colour set myself or the power would go out of me too. After this I began to feel differently about television.

Television is friendly, one of the necessities of life, a periscope that can show us, as we huddle below, all the world's wonders. It is our passport to go anywhere, our encyclopaedia to know everything. Yet its friendliness is deceptive. We are free to travel everywhere so long as we don't move, to find out anything without a thought. Television has begun to impregnate us with an illusion of freedom.

Freedom was a word used very persuasively by Peter Jay in his keynote address on the future of television at last year's [1981] Edinburgh Festival. As head of the company recently awarded the breakfast-time franchise by the IBA, he has come to see himself as a potential successor to the great seventeenth-, eighteenth- and nineteenth-century heroes of free speech.

'Those who care passionately for freedom in communication and publishing,' he said, 'whether print, electronic or simply oral, need now to gird themselves for a prolonged struggle against old habits and vested interests to ensure that new freedoms, which new technology will make possible, are translated into real freedom for both producers and consumers.'

The telly Utopia for which Mr Jay was girding us depended upon the concept of 'freedom of opportunity'. Into his embodiment of this principle he breathed promiscuous life. 'Individuals who wish to make their own programmes will be free to do so,' he declared. 'Theoretically, there could be as many programmes as there are viewers.'

Dazzled by the romance of machinery, he imagined new freedoms of fibre-optic technology that could create a magic grid connecting every home in Britain and producing an eternal revolution of multitudinous programmes. It was a blinding rather than an illuminating vision, and reminded me of a perpetually lit library where I had once worked in the United States. You could switch the lights there from 'bright' to 'brighter'; and then to 'brightest': but you could not switch them off. These lights turned night into day, burning away all traces of privacy and acting (it was explained to me) as a wonderful deterrent to burglars.

What Peter Jay appeared to be attacking was censorship. But it is on another freedom, 'freedom of information', that television – and particularly breakfast television – chiefly preens itself. Mr Jay was especially effective at ridiculing politicians, busybodies and self-appointed cultural and moral nannies who, in the belief that television had 'mystical, hypnotic and unique powers', were opposed to newcomers with new ideas entering the business. Many new ideas, it seems, are pumped into television: few, to all appearances, emerge. The black box, like a black hole, is a devouring machine.

That Peter Jay is not alone is shown by a recent article in the *Listener* by the former head of current affairs at the BBC, John Gau.

Mr Gau's vigorous case on behalf of breakfast television had the unconsciously ironic effect of putting the opposition's point of view more convincingly than many opponents could have managed.

'People want to find out what has been happening while they have slept,' he explained. 'They are keen to know what the day may have in store for them.' He obviously detected nothing humorous in such statements and nothing questionable in such an extreme notion of vicarious living. It was essential to develop this 'important strand of programming' along American lines.

In the United States, where I have recently been waking up to morning television, there is a wide choice of early programmes – sport, yoga, religion, perhaps a soap opera in Spanish and at least three or four versions of the news. The great majority of Americans watch the 'less demanding' programmes and this has provided a useful recipe for the 'popular mix' we would have to offer in Britain. Mr Gau's romanticism was more domestic than Mr Jay's mechanical embrace, and ended on a memorable note of fireside poetry:

> 'Life indoors,' wrote Nathaniel Hawthorne, 'has few pleasanter prospects than a neatly arranged and well-provisioned breakfast table.' He might have been talking of breakfast television. Information, properly packaged, and served up at regular times – that is what people need as they get ready to go off to work, or school, or even the Job Centre. As they prepare for the day, common sense suggests that they want to know first how the world is and what lies ahead.

The remorseless sentimentality of such a vision ignores the fact that as a medium for information television is inferior to radio. Like travel, television may narrow the mind. Shakespeare did not need to go to Denmark to write *Hamlet*. Experience derives from what we feel, not simply what we see – which may become a substitute for feeling.

Television has made us extraordinarily well-informed on subjects we know nothing about. This is why we are said to 'consume' programmes. Pictures often determine the selection of news on television and current-affairs programmes that give us the illusion of understanding. But if we really wanted more information we would hand more money to radio. 'The total British television budget for some 22,000 hours annually is over £700 million, shared between BBC and ITV,' Aubrey Singer, the BBC's managing director of radio, has calculated. 'The total radio budget is about £180 million, for some 300,000 hours of broadcasting annually, shared between BBC and ILR.' The more television news we are persuaded to see at the expense of radio the less actual information we are likely to receive.

There is far less pressure on radio than on television to sell space and create 'newsworthy' programmes round that space. Radio, which is poorly supported by the press compared with TV, was conceived in a more decorous age. In the old Savoy Hill days there would on occasions be no news. Big Ben would strike nine; the announcer would come to the microphone and inform the waiting public that nothing important had come to his notice that evening. He would then play a little encouraging music. It was unsophisticated, but unpretentious. Today there *has* to be news and tomorrow there will have to be *more* news – even if it is the same news. With concepts such as 'radiovision', radio is being tempted to imitate television. If nothing much has happened, the media must create something or collaborate with those who want to be 'in the news'.

The argument, put forward in several books by Richard Clutterbuck, that violent men use the media to win an audience for their theatre of the street, seems largely to have been resisted – and with good reason. For if you accept such reasoning it may lead naturally to intolerably bureaucratic controls. Nevertheless, everyone acknowledges that news programmes can be stage-managed. What is bad news for the human being in the street is often good news for television, for the individual is always outnumbered by the audience and it is the requirement of spectators rather than participants that wins currency. It is not that we, the viewers, support the bad guys against the good. Nor is it that television, in any obvious sense, is a Great Persuader. It is merely a blank cheque. Whatever we see tends to endorse our prejudices, helps to grow a cuticle of insensitivity, pays us dividends in virtuous indignation. We need a new Orwell to expose this illness within the dictatorship of democracy.

One method by which television has changed the meaning of words is by suggesting that they do not matter much. The epithet 'meaningful' (once a philosophical term) has now to be added to any combination of words that may actually mean something. In the beginning was the Word: in the end it is the image that counts. Talk is reduced to 'chat' and a meaningless stream of electronic gestures from well-photographed faces: 'You know what I mean' – which may only mean: 'You know what I look like.'

The most effective literary censorship in the world is the habit of not reading. Many writers have come to feel that, however well they may write, they can affect nothing. In the nineteenth century people believed that literature acted as a moral force. We smile now at that simple belief, but have reluctantly come to accept the idea that spectators of television violence may be induced to act violently themselves.

This is not imitation without motive. Most of us must find ways of overcoming our lack of self-esteem. We join groups of similarly afflicted people – family groups, class groups, team groups, national groups – that assuage our lack of self-esteem by inflicting defeat on other groups in class, civil and political warfare and in the ritual of war enacted on the sports field. The leaders of these groups are 'stars'. They are largely created by television, which has become the chief vehicle for a love-hate obsession with 'personalities' that, T.S. Eliot prophesied, might lead to our cultural breakdown in the twentieth century. We put them up, put up with them, pull them down. It's fun.

Actors impersonate politicians these days less frequently than politicians play-act. They dare not miss any photo-opportunity. For to be well-known to oneself is not enough. We are nonentities until recognised by others, until we are popular. It is how they see us that gives us our identities, our agenda. 'I will become the most famous teenager in the world,' claimed Marcus Sargent who, having been rejected by various groups, let off some blank shots on television near the Queen. 'I want to be somebody. I wanted to be famous.' He was rocketed from obscurity into the news for a day. Then he vanished like a ghost in the machine.

Punctuating the roundabout of news and current affairs there will still be, in John Gau's phrase, 'the occasional cultural spot'. Too

often it is a black spot: the convenience talk to accompany convenience food. Whatever moments of excellence it achieves, television is
a natural enemy of the other arts and has almost overwhelmed
them. It has taught us to be impatient. We almost want the pictures
in our galleries to *move*, at least to do something more than hang
idly on the wall; we want our theatres to fill accustomed slots with
television characters; we do not really want a cinema industry
because, as Sam Goldwyn once said, people cannot be bothered to
'go out and pay money to see bad films when they can stay at home
and see bad television for nothing'.

The difference between television and literature is fundamental. It
seems to me that the incident of my bank card can legitimately be
used as a symbol of the mental bankruptcy even futuristic, interactive
television could generate. My argument does not depend on the
alleged poor quality of programmes: it does not depend upon the
discrepancy between a technology that is far above my understanding
sending out programmes the content of which is occasionally below
my comprehension. After all, there are bad books, bad pictures, bad
music – that does not invalidate all literature and art. The case
against television versus literature rests on the very process itself.
When we read a book we participate with the author and join what
the novelist Henry Green called 'an intimacy between strangers'.
The reader collaborates with the author to *make* literature. He reads
at his own pace, quick or slow, returning to previous pages at will to
make specific connections within the text, and controlling to some
degree what is read. The words are provided by the author but most
of the images are evoked by the reader, and to some extent the
sounds too. For it is an imaginative process, this reading, something
requiring active participation. Such an investment of emotional,
intellectual and imaginative energy is not always easy, but it is stimulating and it does pay dividends. So a good book becomes a
meeting between the imagination of writer and reader: it is a joint
effort.

Now consider, by contrast, the act of viewing television. We
switch on and receive identical pictures and sounds succeeding one
another at an identical pace. Of course we have our different tastes,

but essentially we are receivers rather than active participants. It is a different process and allows us far less flexibility. We are, in a sense, dictated to by television. Everything is supplied instantly. So much is done for us that we may be in danger of becoming inert, like my bank card. We are spectators at the scene, and a society that has too many spectators and too few participants becomes a dissatisfied and eventually an aggressive society.

We watch for much the same reason that we drink – to be rid of ourselves; to switch life on to automatic pilot. We use televisions as we use Valium – to keep ourselves quiet, to keep our children quiet.

Perhaps this is the place for me to make a confession. I watch television. I watch it frequently, and can switch it on, and myself off, as easily as anyone – more easily, I suspect, than most. I think of myself as 'the common viewer' in much the same way as Dr Johnson spoke of 'the common reader'. And I rejoice to concur with him or her. It is true that I prefer programmes that I prefer – but I will watch anything rather than nothing. This may seem eccentric, but it makes me part of the majority. I understand the temptation to attack anyone who criticises television, using the words killjoy, Luddite, élitist. I don't want anyone to ration television or take it away. Is it not friendly to old people, tired parents, tireless children? Doesn't the Open University support literature and all the arts?

Because I watch and see what happens to myself while watching, I believe I know the danger. It is not violence or obscenity that offends me. Quite the contrary. I rather like violence – it soothes me; and any normal dialogue needs obscenities. It is the overwhelming triviality that offends me. This triviality, which seems so harmless, is a weed that, manured with plenty of money, spreads everywhere. It will choke everything if we don't retaliate. It is creating a barren place.

But are we really not better informed, and does television not make us, as we claimed for literature in the nineteenth century, a more enlightened and understanding people? Television certainly flatters us in this way – but is it true? The amount I watch should have made me one of the most enlightened and understanding people in the country – yet I doubt if my opponents will concede this. 'Where is the knowledge we have lost in information?' asked T.S. Eliot in his poem 'The Rock'. What we have lost is the knowledge of our ignorance. Television is better at shocking us than teaching us. Everything comes rather easily – then goes easily. We can only sit and stare. We are not tolerant, we are indifferent.

My argument, therefore, is that television over-simplifies in a way that is alien to literature. When you make a programme, you often have to fit the words to an already-made picture. The picture has priority. Most television people are not interested in words. For essentially television is not a verbal medium or a literary discipline. Why should it be? That is why so many programme-makers are frightened that viewers will be bored by what they call 'talking heads'.

The argument I have heard most often advanced to prove that television is the friend of literature goes back to *The Forsyte Saga*. The long and successful television series added immensely to the sale of Galsworthy's novels. He never had it so good – posthumously speaking. And what happened to Galsworthy has also happened to other novelists – Arnold Bennett, Henry James, Dickens, Jane Austen and Paul Scott. No need to stop there either. Television has likewise benefited Arthur Hailey, Howard Spring, Nevil Shute, Catherine Cookson and others. It is quite random in its favours. But as an argument demonstrating the kinship of television and the novel, this is threadbare. No one disputes that a publisher can exploit the sales for some months of a single title. But this hardly shows television inculcating the habit of reading, especially since, as Richard Hoggart has written, there is no evidence that more copies sold is more copies read. What it does show us more than anything else is the pathetic financial reliance of literature on television. One of the most extreme sights in the book world was that of an actor who had por-trayed Christ on television sitting in a bookshop, signing copies of the Bible. Books and television are competitors for our time. There is only so much time: time is money; and television is a 'licence to print money' – and to devour time.

Pulled into the force field of television, books and the theatre rotate like dying worlds without the energy to establish independent life. They have come to rely on television for money: and money, which should provide freedom of action, has imprisoned them.

The proposition that television is the enemy of literature is not dented by the fact that good programmes may take their source material from literature, or that one or two books sell well because of television adaptations. The proposition does not require any wholesale condemnation of television. It depends upon the habit of viewing being inimical to the habit of reading, and even threatening to take its place among children. Even if the television serial actually fulfils something of the social role of the long Victorian novel, that does not make it a friend but a replacement. There can be little doubt that the power of the word has retreated from the time when Shelley could describe poets as the 'unacknowledged legislators' of our land, and that some of this power has been transformed from the page to the screen. The prevalence of television is not in question, but what are its aims? The aim of literature, according to Matthew Arnold, is 'to see the object in itself as it really is'. The general aim of television is to cover the object or event with a film, which implies a different level of involvement, no less interesting in its way, but collective rather than individualistic in the making, and in its final product not complementary to the novel, poetry or written history.

For a long time the written word held a monopoly. That monopoly has now been broken and with a vengeance. Television, as an enemy, is a challenge. Recently the writers of this country held a mass rally to oppose the implementation of VAT on our printed literature, our books. Nowhere in *The Times* was this reported. Instead, on the front page, was the news that *Dallas* was to be shown by Thames Television instead of the BBC. In other papers the VAT rally was reported by means of a picture that took up more space than the written information underneath it. And that, in a sense, was good, because we pay more attention to pictures now and find it more difficult to respond to the written word.

Television belongs to the present. Its single eye is fixed on matters of the moment. It speaks, sometimes, with extraordinary instantaneous effect: but it is less good as a vehicle for the communication of thought. The country is still dependent for its ideas on what it reads – whether the country knows it or not. On its ideas rests its future. There will always be a tension between present and future: and that fundamentally is the tension that exists between our television and literature.

1982

Endpiece

ILLNESS IN ENGLAND

A year ago, while walking along the street with my wife, I cracked what I thought to be a harmless joke and was suddenly halted by a searing pain in my back. The remaining couple of hundred yards took a lifetime to complete, and I spent the most painful night of my life trying to find some position that was not wholly intolerable.

I belong to a generation that does not call out doctors – not at night, anyway. Next morning, my wife asked the GP to visit me. It would not take long, she reassured him. So he came, decided that I had slipped a disc in a rather funny place, and gave me some painkillers. Before hurrying off, he quoted Voltaire at me: 'Doctors entertain the patient,' he said, 'while nature performs a cure.' I wasn't sure how entertaining this was. I had to stay in bed, be patient, do nothing – all accomplishments within my powers.

The crisis came, as it always does, at the weekend. I was endeavouring to reach the bathroom for a call of nature – that very nature that was supposed to perform a cure – when I fell and, with another awful crack, snapped my knee. This was no joking matter. A locum arrived, gave me an injection, and remarked that, if he were me, he would get into hospital. If I had been him I might have managed it quite easily. But I was immobile and up three flights of stairs on a Sunday.

In theory, I could have entered a hospital as a National Health patient for what is called 'free' treatment – 'free at the point of delivery', which means that you've paid for it in advance. But there would have to be proper delays before a 'strategic plan' could be devised and I could be 'targeted' towards a bed. I was in a lot of pain, but my condition was not dangerous. So I went by stretcher and ambulance into a private hospital.

I hadn't been in a hospital for forty years. Things had changed. Then I had been a patient, now I was a client, a consumer of health facilities. Everyone was very nice and there were different nurses each day. What controlled everything was the central technology. Unfortunately, I'm not very good with technology. It must have been this incompatibility that resulted in my having the wrong portion of my body scanned and, on another occasion, receiving green tablets instead of red ones.

I particularly liked my surgeon because he had read one of my books. He told me that the trouble with my back had been due to my knee. He therefore planned to cure my back with an operation on my knee. This was fortunate because he was a knee specialist. I tried not to think of *The Doctor's Dilemma*.

After ten days of tests and preparations, I was told that my operation was imminent, and the following day the nurse wheeled me off to the theatre. 'Time for your operation, Mr Miller,' she said cheerfully as we went down in the lift. I sensed there was something wrong here, and mentioned that my name was not Miller. She laughed. 'No getting out of your operation like that,' she replied. I did eventually persuade her and was taken back. I never found out what Mr Miller's operation was.

Mine, however, was a complete success. My surgeon announced this the next day and confirmed it a month later when I called on him in his consulting room. It was true that I couldn't walk – or only very painfully with a stick – but technically, it was a beautiful job. I like to think that my stick added a special authority to my last meetings at the Arts Council that year. And I imagine that my Byronic limp added a peculiar fascination to my appearance on the film set of *Carrington*, adapted by Christopher Hampton from my biography of Lytton Strachey – certainly both Jonathan Pryce and Emma Thompson looked alarmed.

But I am weary of this limping now. Not that I lack advice on how to make a total recovery from my successful operation. Everyone, it appears, uses a physiotherapist or osteopath or chiropractor, an expert in Chinese needles or the Alexander technique. David Lodge, in his novel *Therapy*, even suggests that a religious conversion can assist a recalcitrant knee.

What seems certain is that I must now finally quell those dreams of the clamouring telephone and an urgent summons to open the batting for England at Lord's. When I hear the call 'Next please,' I will know the game is really up.

I did actually get quite an important call – a penultimate call, I suppose it was. A nurse brought me the telephone and I murmured 'Yes?' weakly into it.

'Is that Mr Holroyd?' It was a young man's voice.

'What's left of him.'

'Pardon?'

I relented. 'Yes it is. I am Mr Holroyd.'

'Thank God for that. It's been a devil of a job reaching you.'

I apologised and asked what he wanted.

'A couple of facts about your schooling, if you don't mind.'

'Really? What for?'

'Your obituary.'

I paused. 'Who are you?'

He named a name – and a newspaper – and with mingled feelings I gave him the facts as I remembered them.

'Is that all?' I asked tentatively.

'Yes. I think that completes it, thank you.'

For the time being.